Judicial Approach to the Interpretation of the
Constitutions in
Nigeria, Australia, Canada and India

Malthouse Law Books

Abdulrazaq, M T, *Revenue Law and Practice in Nigeria*
Adah, C E, *The Nigerian Law of Evidence*
Akande, I. O., Local government law and policy in Nigeria: cases and materials
Asuzu, C., *Fair Hearing in Nigeria*
Bambale, Y Y, *Crimes and Punishments under Islamic Law*
Bambale, Y. Y., *An Outline of Islamic Jurisprudence*
Bambale, Y. Y., *Islamic Law Relating to Property and Commercial Transactions*
Beredugo, A.J., *Nigerian legal system: an introductory text*
Emiri, F, & Deinduomo, G., *Law, Oil and Development Challenges in Nigeria*
Emiri, F. & Deinduomo, G., *Law and Petroleum Industry in Nigeria*
Emiri, F., *The Law of Restitution in Nigeria*
Emiri, F., *Law and Medical Ethics in Nigeria*
Emiri, F., *Equity and Trusts Law in Nigeria*
Fogam, P, *Law of Contract*
Goldface-Irokalibe, I.J., *The Law of Banking in Nigeria*
Gurin, A. M., *An Introduction to Islamic Family Law*
Igweike, K, *Nigerian Commercial Law: Agency*
Igweike, K, *Nigerian Commercial Law: Contract*
Igweike, K, *Nigerian Commercial Law: Hire Purchase*
Ikoni, U.D., *An Introduction to Nigerian Environmental Law*
Ladan, M.T., *Introduction to Jurisprudence: classical and Islamic*
Maidoh, D.C., Oho, F. *et al., Judicial Administration and Other Legal Issues in Nigeria*
Mowoe, Kehinde, *Constitutional Law in Nigeria*
Nkum, K.J., *Nigerian legal system: contemporary developments and challenges*
Okoh, Sheriff E. E. *Succession under Islamic Law*
Olong, Adefi *M., Administrative Law in Nigeria: an introduction*
Olong, Adefi M., *The Nigerian Legal System: an introduction*
Omorogbe, Yinka, *Oil and Gas Law in Nigeria*
Omotesho, Aboaba, *The Law of Tort in Nigeria: Selected Themes*
Sagay, I, *Law of Succession and Inheritance*
Sagay, I, *Nigerian Family Law: Principles, Cases, Statutes and Commentaries*
Utuama, A A, *Nigerian Law of Real Property*
Utuama, A A, *The Law of Trusts and their Uses in Nigeria*
Utuama, A. A., *Planning Law in Nigeria*
Uvieghara E E, *Labour Law in Nigeria*
Uvieghara E E, *Sale of Goods (& Hire Purchase) Law in Nigeria*
Yalaju, J.G., *Media law in Nigeria*

Judicial Approach to the Interpretation of the
Constitutions in
Nigeria, Australia, Canada and India

By

Hakeem Olasunkanmi Ijaiya, PhD
Faculty of Law, University of Ilorin, Ilorin, Nigeria

m a l t h o u s e [λϼ]

Malthouse Press Limited
Lagos, Benin, Ibadan, Jos,Port-Harcourt, Zaria

Published and manufactured in Nigeria by

Malthouse Press Limited
43 Onitana Street, Off Stadium Hotel Road,
Off Western Avenue, Lagos Mainland
E-mail: malthouse_press@yahoo.com
malthouselagos@gmail.com
Website: malthouselagos.com
Tel: +234 802 600 3203

Dedication

To the memory of
Alhaji Mustapha Kajogbola Ijaiya My Father, a Nigerian patriot

Acknowledgements

This book could not have been written and published without the invaluable help and encouragement received from Emeritus Professor D.A. Ijalaye, Professor Ademola Popoola and Dr. A.A. Idowu of the Obafemi Awolowo University, Ile-Ife, Nigeria and the unflinching support and intellectual motivation from Professor Raheem Adebayo Lawal, former Deputy Vice-Chancellor (Academics), University of Ilorin, Nigeria.

Preface

The study examined the judicial interpretation of the constitutions in selected Commonwealth jurisdictions. It also undertook a survey of the theories of constitutional interpretation and adjudication, examined the rules applied by the courts in the interpretation of the provisions of the constitutions, and determined the extent to which the existing approaches to the interpretation of the constitution have hindered the development of constitutional jurisprudence in some selected Commonwealth countries.

The study relied on primary and secondary sources of information. The primary sources include the Constitution of Australia, Canada, India and Nigeria, Statutes and subsidiary legislation, judicial decisions, international conventions and treaties. The secondary sources of information include books, journals, monographs, conference proceedings, newspapers, magazines, internet materials. The information obtained from these sources was subject to content and contextual analysis.

The study found that statutes and constitutions are often expressed in English language and some words are prone to distortions thereby requiring the need for the courts to discover the intention of the legislators when interpreting such statutes and constitutions. The study further revealed that the theories and rules of interpretation currently adopted by the courts are conflicting. The study found that this is partly due to vagueness and also that in many cases, where a rule appears to support a particular interpretation, there is another rule, often of equal status, which can be invoked in favour of an interpretation which could lead to different result.

The study concluded that the existing approaches of constitutional interpretation are inefficient and inadequate to enable the courts to effectively discover the intention of the legislators; therefore the courts must be allowed to examine all relevant parliamentary documents and debates.

Abbreviations and Acronyms

AC	Appeal Cases
AC	Appeal Cases
AG	Attorney-General
AGF	Attorney-General of the Federation
ALL NLR	All Nigeria Law Report
Ch.D	Chancery Division
DPP	Director of Public Prosecution.
FCA	Federal Court of Appeal
FWLR	Federation Weekly Law Report
IGP	Inspector General of Police
JCA	Judge Court of Appeal
JSC	Justice of the Supreme Court.
KB	King Bench
NCLR	North Central Law Report
NLR	Nigerian Law Report
NMLR	Nigerian Monthly Law Report
NWLR	Nigerian Weekly Law Report
QB	Queen's Bench
SC	Supreme Court
SCNJ	Supreme Court of Nigeria Judgment.
US	United States
WLR	Weekly Law Report

Table of Cases

Arcadia *v.* Ohio Power Co. 498 US 76
Archbishop Olubunmi Okogie & Ors *v.* A.G. Lagos State (1981) 1 NCL R 218
Ariori *v.* Muraimo Elemo (1983) 1SC 13
Ashburg Railway Carriage & Iron Co. *v.* Riche (1975) LRHL 653
Attorney-General *v.* Moagi (1981) AC 578
Attorney-General *v.* Seccombe (1991) 2KB.6
Attorney-General, Abia State & Ors *v.* Attorney-General, Federation (2002) SCNJ
    158
Attorney-General (cth); Ex Pel Mc Kinsley *v.* Commonwealth (1975) 135 CLRI
Attorney-General Bendel State *v.* Attorney-General Federation (1981) 10 SC I
Attorney-General Federation *v.* All Nigerian Peoples Party (2003) FWLR (pt. 167)
    839
Attorney-General, Federation *v.* Alhaji Atiku Abubakar (2004) 7 NWLR (pt. 871)
    63
Attorney-General (V.C) *v.* Commonwealth (1935) 52 CLR 533
Attorney-General of Gambia *v.* Momodu Jobe (1984) AC 689
Attorney-General of Ondo State *v.* Attorney-General of the Federation (1983) 2
    SCNL R 269
Attorney-General (NSW) *v.* Brewery Employees Union of New South Wales
    (1908) 6 CLR 469
Attorney-General *v.* De Keyser's Royal Hotel (1920) AC 508
Attorney -General *v.* Prince Ernest Augustus of Hanoter (1957) AC 436.
Attorney-General Lagos State *v.* Attorney-General of the Federation & Ors (2003)
    6 SCNJI.
Atuyeye *v.* Ashamu (1987) SC 58
Augua Eyo Okon *v.* The State (1988) I ALL NLR 173
Australia Capital Television Pty Ltd. *v.* Commonwealth (1992) 177 CLR
Awe *v.* Alabi (1970) 2 ALL NLR 16.
Awolowo *v.* Federal Minister of Internal Affairs (1962) 11R177.
Awolowo *v.* Sarki (1966) 1 NLR 178.
Awolowo *v.* Shagari (2001) FWLR (pt. 73) 53
Aya *v.* Henshaw (1972) 5 SC 87
Baginda *v.* Dato Ombi Syed Alwi bin syed Idrus (1981)l MLJ 29
Balewa *v.* Doherty (1963) I WLR 949
Balogun *v.* Salami (1963) I ALL NLR129.
Bank of Toronto *v.* Lambe (1887) 12 App. Cas 575
Bank of New South Wales *v.* Commonwealth (1948) 76 CLR
Baxter *v.* Commissioner of Taxation (NSW) (1907) 4CLR 1087
Beck *v.* Smith 50 ER 724
Belfast Corporation *v.* O.D. Cars Ltd 1960 AC 490
Bello & Ors *v.* A.G. Oyo State (1985) 5NWLR (pt. 45) 828
Bello *v.* Diocesan Synod of Lagos (1973) ALL NLR 176.
Bhim Singh *v.* State of Jammu and Kashimir (1985) 4 SCC 677

Black Clawson Int. Ltd. *v.* Papiewerke Waldtrof (1975) AC 591

Halton v. Cove (1830) 1B & Ad 538
Henty v. Wrey (1982) 12 Ch.D 332
Heydon's Case (1984) 3 Cal. Rep. 78
Hibbs v. Winn 542 US 88, 133 (2004)
Hinds v. The Queen (1977) AC 195
Hobbs v. C.G. Robertson Ltd. (1970) IWLR 980
Hon. Justice E.O. Araka v. Justice Don. Egbue (2003) 7 SCNJ 14.
Hoechst Pharmaceuticals Ltd. v. State of Bihar (1983) 4 SCC 45
Hunter v. Southern (1984) 2 SCR 145
Hyde v. Hyde (1866) LRIP & D 130.
IBWA v. Imamo (Nig.) Ltd. (1988) pt. 3 NWLR (pt. 85)124
I.C.S. (Nig.) Ltd. v. Balton V.V. (2003) 8 NWLR (pt. 822) 223
Idehen v. Idehen (1991) 7 SCNJ 222.
Ifezue v. Mbadugba (1984) I ALL NLR 256.
Income Tax Commissioner v. Pemsel (1891) AC 531.
Isagbe v. Alagbe (1981) 2 NCLR 1424.
Ishola v. Ajiboye (1994) 6 NWLR (pt. 352)
J.P. Unnikrishnan v. State of Andhra Pradesh (1993)1 SCC 645
James v. Commonwealth of Australia (1936) AC 614
James G. Oruba v. National Electoral Commission & Ors (1989) 2 NEPLR 24.
Jammal Steel Structures Ltd v. African Continental Bank Ltd. (1973) I ALL NLR 208
Joseph Osemwegie Idehen & Ors v. George Otutu Idehen & Ors (1991) 7 SCNJ 196.
KP Varghese v. Income Tax Officer, Ernakulan & Anor. (1981) 4 SCC 173
K.C. Gajapati Navain Deo v. State of Orissa AIR 1953 SC 375
Kalu v. Odili (1992) 5 NWLR (pt. 240) 130
Kammins v. Zenith Investment Ltd (1971) AC 830
Kayode Ajulo v. The President of the Senate, Speaker of The House of Representatives and Attorney-General Of the Federation Suit No. FHC/ABJ/CS/28/10
Keshavananda Bharati v. State of Kerala (1973) A.I.R (SC) 1461
Keshrji Ravij & Co. & Others v. Commissioner of Income Tax (1990) 2
Kihoto Hollon v. Zachillnu (1992) Supp (2) SCC 651
Kolawole v. Albelto (1989) 1 NWLR 382
Koowarta v. Bjelke – Peterson (1982) 158 CLR 168
Kotoye v. Saraki (1994) 7-8 SCNJ 524.
Krucblak v. Krucblak (1958) 2 Q.B. 32
Lange . v Australian Broadcasting Corporation (1997) 189 CLR 520
Lauvi v. Renad (1892) 3 Ch. D. 403
Law Society of Upper v. Skapinker, Supreme Court of Canada (1984) LSCR 357
Lawal v. G.B. Olivant (1972) 3 SC 124.
Less v. Summer gill (1811) 17 Ves. Jun 508 ER 197
Lemboye v. Ogunsiji (1990) 6 NWLR (pt. 155) 210
Likiw v. Samuels (1963) 2 ALL ER 879

Sarasvati v. The Queen (1990) 172 CLR 1
Salomon v. Commissioner of Customs & Exercise (1967) 2 QB 116
Salomon v. Salome (1897) AGP 22
Samuel Montagn & Co. Ltd. v. Swiss Air Transport Co. Ltd. (1966) 2 QB 306
Satwant Singh Sawhney v. Ass. Passport Officer,
Government of India AIR 1967 SC 1836
Saumur v. The City of Quebec (1953) 1 SCR 299
Savannah Bank v. Ajilo (1987) NWLR (pt. 57) 421
Senator Adesanya v. The President of the Federal
Republic of Nigeria (2001) FWLR (pt. 46) 859
Stock v. Frank Jones (Tipton) (1978) 1 WLR 231
Shagwati Charon Shulka v. Provincial Government
S.P. and Berar (1947) AIR 1
Shannon Real Properties Ltd. v. De St. Michael (1924) AC 185
Sheffield v. Radcliff (1616) Hob 334
Strick land v. Rocla Concrete Pipes Ltd (1971) 124 CLR 468
State (Ryan) v. Lennon (1935) I.R. 170
Smith v. United States 513 US 115
Smiley v. Citibank (South Dakota) 517 US 735
Succex Parage Case (1844) 11 CL & F. 85
Sue v. Hill (1999) 73 ALJR 1016
Societe United Docks & Others v. Government of Mauritius (1985) AC 585
Solicitor-General Western Nigeria v. Adebanjo (1971) 1 ALL NLR 198
State v. Makwanyane (1995) 3 SA 391
State v. Queensland Bar Association (1989) 168 CLR 461
State v. Zuma (1995) 2 SA 642
State of Tamil Nadu v. Kodaikanal Motor Union (P) Ltd(1986) 3 SOC 91
State of Gujarat v. Shantilal Mangaldas AIR (1969) SC 634
Supreme Court Advocates –on-Record Assn. v. UOI (1993) 4 SCC 441
Tarka v. DPP (1961) I ALL NLR
Tax v. Commonwealth (1904) 1 CLR 329
The Berge v. Gelerie d'Art du Petit Champlain (2002) SCR 336
The Chong Poh v. Public Prosecutor (1979) 1 MLJ 50
Teriola v. Williams (1982) INCLR 263
Texaco Panama Incorporation v. Shell Petroleum Development Corporation of
    Nigeria Ltd (2002) 2 SCNJ 102.
Tinubu v. IMB Securities Plc (2001) FWLR (pt. 77) 1003
Tonge v. Wilkinson (1957) CLY 3054
Trap v. Dulles (1985) US 86
Tribune v. IMB Securities (2001) 8 NWLR (pt. 740) 192
Tukur v. Government of Gongola State (1989) 4 NWLR (pt. 117) 517
Tva v. Hill 43 US 153 (1979)
UTC (Nig) Ltd. v. Pamotel (1989) 3 SCJN 79
Udoh v. OHMB (1993) 7NWLR (pt. 304) 139
Udoh v. Okudo (1979) 6-7 SC 32

Table of Statutes

Nigeria
Constitution of Nigeria, 1960
Constitution of Nigeria, 1963
Constitution of Nigeria 1979
Constitution of Nigeria, 1999
Constitution (Suspension and Modification Amendment) Degree, 1985
Constitution (Amendment No. 2) Decree 1976
Chiefs (Appointment and Depositions) Law, Laws of Kwara State, 1994
Child and Young Persons Act, 1993
Criminal Code of Western Nigeria
Criminal Code, Laws of the Federation and Lagos, 1958
Criminal Code, Laws of the Federation, 2004
Criminal Justice (Miscellaneous Provisions) Act, 1966
Criminal Procedure (Amendment) Act, 1966
Criminal Procedure Ordinance
Custom and Excise Act, 1952
Drugs (Price Control) Order, 1979
Electoral Act, 2002
Electoral Decree, 1977
Evidence Act, Laws of the Federation, 1958
Federal Military Government (Supremacy and Enforcement Power) Decree, 1984
Interpretation Law (Lagos Laws) 1973
Interpretation Law (NN Laws) 1963
Interpretation Law (WRN Laws) 1959
Land Acquisition Bill 1992
Land Use Act, 1978 Laws of the Federation 1990
Laws of the Federation and Lagos, 1958
Laws of the Federation, 2004
Magistrates' Court (Lagos) Ordinance
Official Secret Act, 1911
Oil in Navigation Waters Act, 1955
Petroleum Profits Tax Acts, 1959
Press (Emergency Powers) Act, 1931
Registration of Titles Act, Laws of the Federation and Lagos, 1958
Rent Control (Lagos) Amendment Act, 1965

Wills Act, Bendel State

Australia
Australia Constitution Act 1900
Australia Interpretation Act 1901
Australian Acts, 1986
British North America Act, 1867
Broadcasting & Television Bill 1992
Business Licence (Amendment) Bill, 1992
Commonwealth of Australian Constitution Act, 1900
Constitution of Australia (19)

Canada
Constitution of Canada 1867
Canadian Charter of Rights and Freedoms 1982
Commonwealth Conciliation and Arbitration Act, 1904
Constitutional Act, 1867
Constitution Act, 1967
Constitution Act, 1982
Constitution (Fifty – Second Amendment) Act 1985
Copy Right Act; Canada 1985
Act of Union 1707
Act of Settlement 1701

India
Constitution of India 1950

United Kingdom
Association Legislation, Government of Wales Act, 1998
English Bill of Rights 1628
English Law Report Commission, 1969
English Naturalization Act, 1870
English Official Secrets Act, 1911
English Sunday Observance Act, 1677
Family Law Act 1975
Government of Wales Act 1998
Hire Purchase (Amendment) Decree, 1970
Human Rights Act 1998
Income Tax Act, 1961
Inland Revenue Act, 1889
Interpretation Act, 1964
Magna Carta 1215
Privy Council (Limitation of Appeals) Act, 1968
Racial Discrimination Act 1975
Royal Marriage Act, 1772

Table of Contents

3. Judicial Approach to the Interpretation of the Constitutions in Australia, Canada and India - 87

Chapter 1

Introduction

The Constitution

A constitution refers to a country's supreme law, which contains the guiding principles according to which that country is governed. A constitution is a text which outlines the powers of parliament, the executive, judiciary and other national institutions.[1] A constitution is an instrument of government under which laws are made and is not a mere Act or law. The construction which the court will give to a constitutional provision must be such that will serve the interest of the Constitution and best carry out its object and purposes and give effect to the intention of the framers. A constitution is an autobiography of a nation. The Constitution is the supreme law of the land. It creates and organises the States and government. It sets parameters and limits the operations of organs of government, actions of people and institutions.

Section 1(3) of the Constitution of the Federal Republic of Nigeria, 1999 provides:

> If any other law is inconsistent with the provisions of this Constitution, this Constitution shall prevail, and that other law shall to the extent of the inconsistency be void.[2]

The Constitution creates an independent judiciary as one of the Constitutional safeguards, with a mandate to interpret, protect and apply the Constitution and all other laws.

A Constitution is the legislation or compact which establishes the State itself. It paints in broad strokes on a large canvas the institutions of that State; allocating powers, defining relationships between such institutions and the people within the

---

[1] A written Constitution is defined in *Unity Dow* v. *The Court of Appeal*, (1991) 6 as "the legislation or compact which establishes the state itself. It paints in broad strokes on a large canvass the institutions of the State; allocating powers, defining relationships between such institutions and the people within the jurisdiction of the State, and the people themselves. A constitution often provides for the protection of the rights and serves as opportunities for defining the relationship between the domestic law of a State and its treaty obligations.

[2] The Laws of the Federation 2004 cap C 23.

jurisdiction of that State, and between the people themselves. A Constitution provides for the protection of the rights and freedoms of the people, which rights and freedoms have thus to be respected in all future State action. The existence and powers of the institutions of State, therefore, depend on its terms. The rights and freedoms, where given by it, also depend on it. No institution can claim to be above the Constitution; no person can make any such claim. The Constitution contains not only the design and disposition of the powers of the State which is being established but embodies the hopes and aspirations of the people. It is a document of immense dimensions, portraying, as it does, the vision of the people's future.[3]

A Constitution cannot be amended by the Legislature like other legislation. Also, a Constitution cannot be considered on the same footing like other statutes or legislation. As Lord Wright put it when dealing with the Australian case of *James* v. *Commonwealth of Australia*:

> ....it is true that a Constitution must not be construed in any narrow and pedantic sense. The words used are necessarily general, and their full import and true meaning can often only be appreciated when considered, as the years go on, in relation to the vicissitudes of fact which from time to time emerge. It is not that the meaning of the words changes, but the changing circumstances illustrate and illuminate the full import of that meaning.[4]

On the proper approach to the interpretation of the Constitution, the Interpretation Act provide thus:

> Every enactment shall be deemed remedied and for the public good and shall receive such fair and liberal construction as will best attain its object according to its true intent and spirit.[5]

The Interpretation Act advocated a liberal approach to the interpretation of the Constitution. However it has been suggested that the Constitution being an important document when compared with ordinary legislation should not be construed in a narrow and pedantic sense. As Lord Wright in James v. Commonwealth of Australia puts it:

---

[3] Emerton R. and Bymes Women's human rights: Leading international and national cases. Routledge – Cavendish, Taylor and Francis group. www.Tramigo.net. 27/8/2009
[4] (1936) A.C 578 at 614.
[5] Laws of the Federation 2004, cap. 1 section 26.

It is true that a Constitution must not be construed in any narrow and pedantic sense. The words used are necessarily general, and their full import and true meaning can often only be appreciated when considered, as the years go on, in relation to the vicissitudes of fact which from time to time emerge. It is not that the meaning of the words changed, but the changing circumstances illustrate and illuminate the full import of that meaning.[6]

In interpreting the Constitution previous authorities on the related issue could be a guide. Thus the courts in some cases adopted this approach in interpreting the provisions of the Constitution. In *Attorney General* v. *Moagi*, Kentridge JA said:

...a Constitution such as the Constitution of Botswana, embodying fundamental rights, should as far as its language permits be given a broad construction. Constitutional rights conferred without express limitation should not be cut down by reading implicit restrictions into them, so as to bring them into line with the common law.[7]

In *Petrus and Another* v. *The State*[8] Aguda T. A. when reviewing the courts' approach to constitutional construction said:

It was once thought that there should be no difference in approach to constitutional construction from other statutory interpretation. Given the British system of government and the British judicial set up, that was understandable, it being remembered that whatever statutes that might have the look of constitutional enactment in Britain, such statutes are nevertheless mere statutes like any others and can be amended or repealed at the will of Parliament. But the position where there is a written Constitution is different.[9]

The view of Aguda T.A is supported by Higgins J of the Australian High Court in *Attorney General for New South Wales* v. *Brewery Employees Union of New South Wales* thus:

...although we interpret the words of the Constitution on the same principles of interpretation as we apply to any ordinary law, these very

---

[6] (1936) AC 578.
[7] 1981 BLR 1. at p. 32.
[8] (1985) LRC (Const.) 699 at 719; (1984) BLR 14 at p. 34.
[9] Ibid.

principles of interpretation compel us to take into account the nature and scope of the Act that we are interpreting – to remember that it is a Constitution, a mechanism under which law are to be made and not a mere Act which declares what law is to be.[10]

Decided cases around the world have given valuable guidance on the proper approach to the courts in the task of constitutional interpretation.[11] The courts must begin its task of constitutional interpretation by carefully considering the language used in the Constitution. But it does not treat the language of the Constitution as if it were found in a will or a deed or a charter party. A generous and purposive interpretation is to be given to constitutional provisions protecting human rights. The courts have no licence to read its own predilections and moral values into the Constitution, but it is required to consider the substance of the fundamental right at issue and ensure contemporary protection of that right in the light of evolving standards of decency that mark the progress of a maturing society. In carrying out its task of constitutional interpretation the court is not concerned to evaluate and give effect to public opinion, for reasons given by Chaskalson P in *State* v. *Makwanyane* thus:

> Public opinion may have some relevance to the enquiry, but in itself, it is no substitute for the duty vested in the courts to interpret the Constitution and to uphold its provisions without fear or favour. If public opinion were to be decisive there would be no need for constitutional adjudication. The protection of rights could then be left to Parliament, which has a mandate from the public, and is answerable to the public for the way its mandate is exercised, but this would be a return to parliamentary sovereignty, and a retreat from the new legal order established by the 1993 Constitution. By the same taken the issue of the constitutionality of capital punishment cannot be preferred to a referendum, in which a majority view would prevail over the wishes of any minority. The very reason for establishing the new legal order, and for vesting the power of judicial review of all legislation in the courts, was to protect the rights of minorities and others who cannot protect their rights adequately through the democratic process. Those who are entitled to claim this protection include the social outcasts and marginalised people of our society.[12]

---

[10] (1908) 6 CLR 469 at pp. 611-612. See also *Nafiu Rabiu* v. *State* (1981) 2 NCLR 293 at p. 326.

[11] *Weems* v. *United State* (1909) 217 US 349 at p. 373, *Trop* v. *Dulles* (1958) US 86 at pp. 100-101; *Minister of Home Affairs* v. *Fisher* (1980) AC 319 at p. 328, *Union of Campement Site Owners and Lessees* v. *Government of Mauritius* (1984) MR 100 at 107; *Attorney-General of Gambia* v. *Momodou Jobe* (1984) AC 689 at pp. 700-701, R v. Big M Drug Mart Ltd (1985) 1 SCR 295 at 331, *State* v. *Zuma* 1995 (2) SA 642, *State* v. *Makwanyane* (1995) 3 SA 391, *Matadeen* v. *Pointu* (1999) 1 AC 98 at 108.

[12] (1995) 3 SA 391.

The Constitution should be interpreted broadly, liberally and purposively so as to enable it to continue to play "a creative and dynamic role in the expression and the achievement of the ideals and aspirations of a nation, in the articulation of the values bonding its people, and in disciplining its governments".[13] In the Privy Council, Lord Wilberforce called for a generous interpretation avoiding what he described as "the austerity of tabulated legislation.[14] In Australia, Dixon CJ reminded that a Constitution "should be construed with all the generality which the use admit".[15] In Botswana, Aguda JA stressed that the courts must not allow a Constitution to be "a lifeless museum piece" but must continue to breathe life into it from time to time when there is opportunity to do so. He said:

> The overriding principle must be an adherence to the general picture presented to the Constitution into which each individual provision must fit in order to maintain in essential details the picture which the framers could have painted had they been faced with circumstances of today. To hold otherwise would be to stultify the living constitution in its growth. It seems to me that a stultification of the constitution must be prevented if this is possible without doing extreme violence to the language of the constitution. I conceive it that the primary duty of the judges is to make the constitution grow and develop in order to meet the just demands and aspirations of an ever developing society which is part of the wider and larger human society governed by some acceptable concepts of human dignity.[16]

Basically, a Constitution being the supreme law of a State or Federation, must be interpreted differently from an ordinary statute. The Privy Council in *Hinds* v. *The Queen* said:

> To seek to apply to constitutional instruments, the Canons of construction applicable to ordinary legislation in the field of substantive criminal or civil law would... be misleading.[17]

---

[13] *Government of the Republic of Namibia* v. *Culture,* 2000, Supreme Court of Namibia (1993) 3 LRC 175.

[14] *Minister of Home Affair* v. *Fisher,* Privy Council on appeal from the Supreme Court of Bermuda (1980) AC 319, at pp. 328-9.

[15] *R. V. The Public Vehicle Licensing Appeal Tribunal of the State of Tasmania,* ex.parte Australian national Airways Pty Ltd. High Court of Australia (1964) 113 Commonwealth Law Reports 207, at 225, See also Re President is Reference of the Constitution of Vanuatu and the Broadcasting and Television Bill 1992, the Business Licence (Amendment) Bill 1992, and the Land Acquisition Bill 1992, Supreme Court of Vanuatu (1993) 1 LR C 141, per d'Imecourt CJ at 159, Re Minimum Penalties Legislation, Supreme Court of Papau New Guinea (1984) PNGLR 314, per Bredmeyer J at 334.

[16] *Dow.* v. *Attorney General, Supreme Court of Botswana* (1992) LRC (Const.) 623 at 668.

[17] (1976) 1 ALL ER 353 see also Liyanage v. Regina (1966) 1 All ER 650.

In *Minister of Home Affairs* v. *Fisher*[18] the Privy Council was faced with interpreting the fundamental rights provisions of the Bermuda Constitution. It concluded by saying that these provisions call for a generous interpretation avoiding the austerity of tabulated legalism, suitable to give to individuals the full measure of the fundamental rights and freedom.[19]

Similarly *in Dewan Undangan Negeri Kelantan & Anor.* v. *Nordin bin Salleh & Anor.*, the court of Putrajaya said thus:

> Secondly, as the Judicial Committee of the Privy Council held in Minister of Home Affairs v. Fisher at p. 329, a constitution should be construed with less rigidity and more generosity than other statutes and as sui juris, calling for principles of interpretation of its own, suitable to its character but no forgetting that respect must be paid to the language which has been used in this context[20]

It is also worth recalling what Barwick CJ said when speaking for the High Court of Australia in *Attorney General of the Commonwealth, Ex relatione Mc Kinley* v. *Commonwealth of Australia* said:

> The only true guide and the only course which can produce stability in constitutional law is to read the language of the constitution itself, no doubt generously and not pedantically, but as a whole and to find its meaning by legal reasoning.[21]

Bindra[22] speaks of two theories of interpretation of the Constitution namely, the mechanical and organic theories. It stated that the organic method is to be preferred. He said "the organic method requires us to see the present social conditions and interpret the Constitution in a manner so as to resolve the present difficulties".

One other important guide in the interpretation of the Constitution is as follows:

> The Constitution must be considered as a whole, and so as to give effect, as far as possible, to all its provisions. It is an established canon of constitutional construction that no one provision of the Constitution is to be separated from all the others, and considered alone, but that all the

---

[18] (1979) 3 ALL ER 21.
[19] Ibid., see also *Teh Chong Poh* v. *Public Prosecutor* (1979) 1 MLJ 50.
[20] (1992) 2 CLJ 1125, (1992) 1 CLJ (Rep) 72.
[21] Cited in *Dewan Undangan Ngeri Kelantan & Anor* v. *Nordin bin Salleh & Anor.* Ibid. p. 17.
[22] Bindra's Interpretation of Statutes, (10th ed.) at p. 1295.

provisions bearing upon a particular subject are to be brought into view and to be so interpreted as to effectuate the great purpose of the instrument. An elementary rule of construction is that, if possible, effect must be given to every part and every word of a Constitution and that unless there is some clear reason to the contrary, no portion of the fundamental law should be treated as superfluous.[23]

The difficult task of interpreting constitutional guarantees of fundamental rights and freedoms, of giving life to them and of determining whether a statute or other State action breaches those rights, is entrusted in most democratic countries (in the Commonwealth and elsewhere) to an independent judiciary.

In approaching this task, the Privy Council and other Commonwealth Courts have often applied the generous approach to constitutional interpretation articulated by Lord Wilberforce *in Minister of Home Affairs* v. *Fisher.*[24] In that case Lord Wilberforce stated that the way to construe a Constitution on the Westminster model is to treat it:

> as sui generis, calling for principles of interpretation of its own, suitable to its character...without necessary acceptance of all presumptions that are relevant to legislation of private law.[25]

Construing the fundamental rights and freedoms guaranteed by the Bermuda Constitution, Lord Wilberforce observed thus:

> This constitutional instrument has certain special characteristics, (1) It is, particularly in Chapter 1, drafted in a broad and ample style which lays down principles of width and generality (2) Chapter 1 is headed "Protection of Fundamental Rights and Freedoms of the individual" It is known that this chapter, as similar portions of other constitutional instruments drafted in the post-colonial period, starting with the Constitution of Nigeria, and including the constitutions of most Caribbean territories, was greatly influenced by the European Convention for the Protection of Fundamental Rights and Freedoms. That convention was...in turn influenced by the Universal Declaration of Human Rights 1948. These antecedents, and the form of Chapter 1 itself, call for a generous interpretation suitable to give to individuals the full measure of the fundamental rights and freedoms referred to.[26]

---

[23] See *Danaharta Urus Sdn Bhd* v. *Kekatong Sdn Bhd* (2004) 1 CLJ 701.
[24] (1980) A.C 319, 329 (PC)
[25] Ibid.
[26] Ibid.

This statement was repeated and approved by the Privy Council in *Ong Ah Chuan* v. *Public Prosecutor*[27] as a relevant principle of construction of the fundamental rights provisions in the Constitution of the Republic of Singapore.

Most recently, this principle was again reaffirmed by the Privy Council in construing the Constitutions in the Gambia, and the Mauritius. In *Attorney-General of the Gambia* v. *Momodou Jobe*,[28] Lord Diplock said:

> A Constitution and in particular that part of it which protects and entrenches fundamental rights and freedoms to which all persons in that state are to be entitled, is to be given a generous and purposive construction.

In Societe United Docks and Others v. Government of Mauritius[29] Lord Templeman, delivering the judgment of the Privy Council said that the same broad interpretation should be given to the Constitution of Mauritius.

This approach to the interpretation of constitutional guarantees of fundamental rights and freedoms has also been adopted elsewhere in the Commonwealth. For example, in *Dato Menterii Othman bin Baginda* v. *Dato Ombi Syed Alwi bin Syed Idrus*[30] Raja Azian Shah Ag Lp of the Federal Court of Malaysia, cited Lord Wilberforce's statement with approval as the correct approach in construing the Malaysian Constitution. He observed thus:

> A Constitution, being a living piece of legislation, its provisions must be construed broadly and not in a pedantic way.[31]

It is also widely recognised that the judgments of constitutional courts in common law jurisdictions, such as United States Supreme Court, the Indian Supreme Court, the Privy Council and other constitutional courts are of strong persuasive authority in cases involving the interpretation of constitutional guarantees of fundamental rights. The Supreme Court of India, in particular, has drawn freely on the rulings of the British Courts, and on those of the United States and Canada as precedents of high persuasive authority in such cases. In *Ong Ah Chuan case*, the Privy Council indicated that it was not appropriate to have regard to U.S decisions to construe fundamental rights in Constitutions on the Westminster model. However, the Privy Council has not subsequently

---

[27] (1981) AC 648.
[28] (1984) AC 689, 700.
[29] (1985) AC 585, 605.
[30] (1981) 1 MLJ 29 at p. 32B.
[31] Ibid.

followed that restrictive approach; nor is it a correct approach in view of the universality of the underlying concepts and values.

Judicial activism and judicial passivity are competing theories of judicial attitude to the interpretation of the Construction. Based on the declaratory theory of the judicial function, the latter assigns a passive role to the courts, namely to declare what the law is (*jus dicere*) but not to make it (Jus dare), in strict accord with the doctrine of separation of powers.

Judicial possivists interpret the law literally, i.e. they seek to ascertain the purport of the law (sentential legis) through the sole medium of the words used (*litera legis*). They assume that the legislature had said what it meant and meant what is said. The maxim is "*ita scriptum est*" (it is so written).

Judicial activism is constitutive in theory, liberal in conception and teleological in essence. It assumes that every legislation has a purpose; that a Constitution is a social charter of a dynamic society based on certain ideological or philosophical presuppositions. In interpreting the Constitution, it seeks to ascertain these underlying principles and give effect to them. Giving effect to the ultimate goal of the Constitution is the essence of its interpretive effort.

Nigeria has inherited the common law tradition which disclaims judicial activism or creativity. The most radical rejection of judicial activism in the common law system is the speech of Lord Jowitt (Lord Chancellor from 1945-1951) at the Seventh Legal Convention of the Law Council of Australia (1951) where he pleaded, *inter alia*:

> ...please do not get yourself into the frame of mind of entrusting to the judges the working out of a whole new set of principles which does accord with the requirements of modern conditions. Leave that to the legislature, and leave us to confine ourselves to trying to find out what the law is.[32]

The traditional Commonwealth jurisprudence is influenced by the doctrine of parliamentary supremacy and attitudes of judicial restraint. The initial period of applying the human rights provisions of the new Commonwealth nations, judicial attitudes were greatly restricted by common law notions and techniques. First, great reliance was placed on the traditional principles of statutory interpretation. Second, there was also a tendency to regard the new Bill of Rights as mere codifications of the common law as expressing no more than the rights which had always existed. Third, there was a reluctant to quash executive

---

[32] (1951) Aust. L.J. 296. It is ironic that this observation was made in conjunction with the decision of the *English Court of Appeal in Candler v. Crane Christmas & Co.* (1951) 2 K.B. 164.

decisions or legislative measures on the ground of inconsistency with human rights principles unless they could be categorised as irrational.[33]

There had however been earlier recognition of the true nature of constitutional instruments. In a Canadian case, *Edwards* v. *Attorney General,*[34] Lord Sankey in delivering the opinion of the Privy Council described the constituent statute of the Dominion as a "living tree capable of growth and expansion within its natural limit" and added:

> The object of the Act was to grant a Constitution to Canada. Their Lordships do not conceive it to be the duty of this Board-it is certainty not their desire to cut down the provisions of the Act by a narrow and technical construction, but rather to give it a large and liberal interpretation.[35]

In *Hinds* v. *The Queen*[36] Lord Diplock, in delivering the majority opinion of the Privy Council, stated:

> A written constitution, like any other written instrument affecting legal rights or obligations, fall to be construed in the light of its subject-matter and of the surrounding circumstances with reference to which it was made; (but he added) to seek to apply to constitutional instruments the canons of construction applicable to ordinary legislation in the field of substantive criminal or civil law would, in their Lordships' view, be misleading.[37]

For most of the Commonwealth the true seminal change enacted from Lord Wilberforces' opinion delivered in 1979 in *Minister of Home Affairs* v. *Fisher*[38] and which concerned with the Constitution of Bermuda was stated by His Lordship as follows:

> It can be seen that this instrument has certain special characteristics
>
> (1) It is, particularly in Chapter 1, drafted in a broad and ample style which lays down principles of width and generality.
>
> (2) Chapter 1 is headed "Protection of Fundamental Rights and Freedoms of the individual"[39]

---

[33] Barnett O.J. International Human Rights Norms and their Domestic Application: Judicial Methods and Mechanism. Re vista 11DH vol. 29.
[34] (1930) A.C. 126 (136).
[35] Ibid.
[36] (1977) A.C. 195.
[37] Ibid.
[38] (1980) A.C. 319 (328).
[39] Ibid.

It is known that this chapter, has similar portions of other constitutional instruments drafted in the post-colonial period, starting with the Constitution of Nigeria (and including the Constitutions of most Caribbean territories), was greatly influenced by the European Convention for the Protection of Human Rights and Fundamental Freedoms.[40]

Similarly, in the Indian case of *Peoples Union for Democratic Rights* v. *Union of India*[41] Bhagwati J. said:

> The Constitution-makers have given us one of the most remarkable documents in history for ushering in a new socio-economic order, and the Constitution that they have forged for us had a social purpose and a mission and therefore every word or phrase in the Constitution must be interpreted in a manner which would advance the socio-economic objectives of the Constitution.[42]

The above historical and philosophical justification favour liberal approach to the interpretation of the Constitution.

The problems of Interpretation
The general problems of interpretation are drafting and communication.

Drafting
In the process of drafting a statute, the draftman often used words that are ambiguous and cause confusion to the court while interpreting the statute. As Salmond L.J. pointed out *in Cannaught Fur* v. *Cramas Properties Ltd*:

> The draftsman has however, adopted a most slovenly mode of expression; he has used a form of words which is highly ambiguous – so ambiguous that the minds of all the judges who have considered this case, not least my own, have fluctuated again and again during the course of the argument. I can only sympathize with the parties to this litigation, and echo the wish once expressed in similar circumstances by Scrutton L.J., namely, that if it were possible to order the costs here and below to be paid

---

[40] (1953) (Cmd 8969). That Convention was signed and ratified by the United Kingdom and applied to dependent territories, including Bermuda. It was in turn influenced by the United Nations' Universal Declaration of Human Rights 1948. These antecedents, and the form of Chapter 1 itself, call for a generous interpretation avoiding what has been called "the austerity of tabulated legalism", suitable to give to individuals the full measures of the fundamental rights and freedoms referred to.
[41] AIR 1982 SC 1473 (1490).
[42] Ibid.

out of the pocket of the draftsman who created this maze in which we now find ourselves.[43]

In the *Guardian* v. *The Federal Government*,[44] Pats Acholonu JCA in determining the issue whether the Federal High Court had Jurisdiction to entertain the suit, referred to Section 1 (2) (b) (1) of the Decree 12 of 1994 and Decree 107 of 1993. He stated that the draftsmen who framed the legislation were:

> Consumed with their frame of mind to manufacture a law that is so awesome in its content and fidelity that would be accorded to it but by the decree of terror it generates carelessness of the menacing consequences of such laws.[45].

Badaiki[46] noted that the draftsmen may not foresee the various aspects of that which they proceed to put into legal language. The law does not penalize draftsmen no matter how perfunctory they are in drafting statutes; rather, it provides principles to unravel the meaning of statutes.[47]

Communication
Words used in the statute may have different meanings, it may have intended, ordinary, syntactical or normative meaning thereby creating difficulties to the court while interpreting them.

According to Badaiki:

> A lot of impediments beset easy interpretation of statutes. There is difficulty of communication. It is difficult to find unequivocal languages by which to convey the intention of the legislature. Words have no particular meaning except in a context[48]. Words may have intended, ordinary or comprehended meanings. Or they may have even syntactical or normative

---

[43] (1965) NWLR p. 46 at p. 54. See also Badaiki A.D. Interpretation of Statutes, Tiken Publishers, pp. 1-10.

[44] (1995) 5 NWLR (pt. 398) p. 703. See also Badaiki ibi pp.1 -10.

[45] Badaiki Ibid.

[46] Badaiki Ibid.The learned Trial Magistrate made the remark in Okumagba v. Egbe (1965) ALLNLR (pt. 395) p. 418. In *Seaford Court Estate Ltd.* v. *Asher* (1945) 2 K. B. 461 at p. 498 Denning M. R. said "whenever a statute comes up for consideration it must be remembered that it is not within human powers to foresee the manifold set of facts which may arise; and that, even if it were, it is not possible to provide for them in terms free from all ambiguity".

[47] Badaiki Ibid. pp. 1 – 10.

[48] Obilade, A. O. *The Nigerian Legal System*. Spectrum Law Publishing Ibadan (1990) p. 83. See also Badaiki A.D. Ibid. pp. 1-10.

meanings[49]. In dealing with complex subject matter, the draftsman may find it difficult to convey precisely what he has in mind.

Badaiki also observed thus:

...legislature or draftsman may not foresee all contingencies which may occur in future so as to state them in statutes in clear and express words on any given matter. Statutes may thereby contain vague words[50]. Even when words in a statute are clear, giving effect to the clear meaning could result in absurdity. There may be a mistake in terms of using a wrong word in a statute and a court faces the predicament as to the necessary correction it can effect where it can only ascertain the intention of the legislature if only the mistake is corrected. A statute may contain a lacuna, a gap and a court is not expected to fill gaps for to do so would mean that the court has usurped the function of the legislature.[51]

In *Seaford Court Estate Ltd* v. *Asher,* Lord Denning M.R said:

Whenever a statute comes up for consideration it must be remembered that it is not within human powers to foresee the manifold set of facts which may arise and even if it were, it is not possible to provide for them in terms free from all ambiguity. The English Language is not an instrument of mathematical precision.[52]

Other Problems of Interpretation

The rules of statutory interpretation, although individually reasonably clear, are often difficult to apply, particularly where they appear to conflict with one another and when their hierarchy of importance is not clearly established. The difficulty which faces the courts may be enhanced by present limitations on the means, other than reference to the actual text of the statute, for ascertaining the intention of the legislature. These difficulties are especially noticeable where English courts are called upon to interpret legislation implementing international conventions.

---

[49] Glanville, Language and the Law (1945) 61LQR71, 179, 293, 383; (1946) 62 LQR 381. See also Badaiki A.D. Ibid. pp. 1-10.

[50] *Ifezue* v. *Mbadugba* (1984) 1 SCNLR p. 427, *Kalu* v. *Odili* (1992) 5 NWLR (pt. 240) 130. See also Badaiki A.D. Ibid. pp. 1-10.

[51] Badaiki Ibid. p. 6.

[52] (1945) 2 K. B. 461 at 498; see also Badaiki. Ibid., *Nafiu Rabiu* v. *State* (1990) 9 – 11 SC 130; (1983) 2 NCLR 293.

The rules of interpretation especially the common rules of interpretation i.e. literal rule, golden rule and the mischief rule are less satisfactory, when they, are used to justify the meaning given to a provision. The ultimate function of a court in the interpretation process is not simply to decide whether it is bound to follow a literal interpretation on the one hand or to adopt on the other an interpretation reached in the light of the golden or mischief rules. It is rather to decide the meaning of the provision, taking into account, among other matter, the light which the actual language used, and the broader aspects of legislative policy arrived at by the golden and mischief rules, throw on that meaning.

To place undue emphasis on the literal meaning of the words of a provision is to assume an unattainable perfection in draftsmanship; it presupposes that the draftsmen can always choose words to describe the situation intended to be covered by the provision which will leave no room for a difference of opinion as to their meaning. Such an approach ignores the limitations of language, which is not infrequently demonstrated even at the level of the House of Lords when Law Lords differ as to the "plain meaning" of words.[53] Furthermore, the literal approach affords no solution to cases where, for example, a statute prescribes certain consequences which are to attach to a house, "unfit for habitation", and the question before the court is whether a particular house, with the window of one of its two bedrooms with a defective sash cord, is so unfit.[54] This is not a question which could even be solved by looking at the words alone; in such a case[55] the legislator in effect leaves to the court a limited creative role (even if the court fulfils it in the language of interpretation) within the limits set by the general policy of the statute to be discovered from the context of the statute as a whole and certain other contextual considerations outside the statute.

The golden rule sets a purely negative standard by reference to absurdity, inconsistency or inconvenience, but provides no clear means to test the existence of these characteristics or to measure their quality or extent. When a court decides that a particular construction is absurd, it implies, although often tacitly, that the construction is absurd because it is irreconcilable with the general policy of the legislature.[56]

The mischief rule as expressed in *Heydon's case*[57] describes a somewhat more satisfactory approach to the interpretation of statutes. But, apart from the archaism of its language, it reflects a very different constitutional balance between the Executive, Parliament and the Public. The *Heydron's case* is also somewhat

---

[53] See e.g., *London and North-Eastern Railway Co.* v. *Berriman* (1946) A.C. 278.
[54] A problem which faced the House of Lords in *Summers* v. *Salford Corporation* (1943) AC 283.
[55] Other examples are provided by the frequent cases in which the courts have had to decide whether an accident arose "out of and in the course of employment"
[56] (1984) 3 Co. Rep. 7a.
[57] (1984) 3 Co. Rep. 7a.

outdated in its approach, because it assumes that statute is subsidiary or supplemental to the common law, where as in modern condition many statutes mark a fresh point of departure rather than a mere addition to, and qualification of, common law principles. Furthermore, the mischief rule was enunciated before the rules excluding certain material, which might bear on the mischief and "true reason of the remedy", had been developed. If a court has inadequate means of discovering the policy behind a statute, a mere exhortation to consider that policy may not be very effective. It may be for these reasons that attempts in some Commonwealth countries to give statutory effect in modern language to the principles underlying *Heydon's case* do not appear to have had any significant effect in practice on the interpretation of statutes.

If defects in drafting complicate the rules of interpretation, it is also true that unsatisfactory rules of interpretation may lead the draftsman to an over-refinement in drafting at the cost of the general intelligibility of the law. Moreover, there are practical limits to the improvements which can be effected in drafting. Account must be taken of the inherent frailty of language, the difficulty of foreseeing and providing for all contingencies, the imperfections which must result in some degree from the pressures under which modern legislation has so often to be produced and the difficulties of expressing the finely balanced compromised of competing interests which the draftsman is sometimes called upon to formulate. Difficulties may also arise when words are inserted into a Bill in the course of its discussion in Parliament without sufficient regard to its overall structure, as originally planned.

Most problems often arose as a result of limitless time in drafting statutes. As Sir Frank Kitto said:

> Alas for parliamentary counsel, there are not be time for a further draft. And the attention span of those giving instructions may be limited, at least in the amount of time that the policy makers are able to invest in a particular project.[58]

Addressing this problem, Scrutton, L.J. in Bowe v. Russell said:

> I regret that I cannot order costs to be paid by the draughtsmen of the Rent Restrictions Acts, and the members of the Legislature who passed them, and are responsible for the obscurity of the Acts... [59]

---

[58] Sir Frank Kitto Why Write Judgments? (1992) 66 ALJ 787
[59] (1928) 2KB 117 at 130.

Another problem of interpretation is the application of the law to the fact of the case. As Dawson J puts it in *Davis Securities Pty Ltd.* v. *Commonwealth Bank of Australia*:

Facts tends to be black or white but the law very often is not.[60]
Diplock, L.J remarked that:

...the law is nearly almost obscure in those fields in which the judges say, the principle is plain, but the difficulty lies in its application to particular facts.[61]

Judges sometimes get snaky when faced with apparently contradictory statutory commands. There is a tendency to blame the drafter, because it is assumed that the difficulty would have been removed had it been perceived before the legislation was enacted. It is certainly a step along the way to solving a problem to know that it exists, but many policies and legal principles are ambiguous and contradictory in their nature. Even the canons of statutory interpretation have been said to be incompatible one with the other. [62]

The above situation sometimes put the court in a difficult situation. For instance it would be intolerable for a court to tell a litigant that he or she is caught in a cross-fire of conflicting statutory demands. The problem for judges is that they take up the strain of reconciling conflict between statute and common law and between statute and statute. Judges do not have the option of saying "it is too hard" or "No answer to your problem is available" or "The matter is remitted to Parliament to have a second attempt at explaining itself.[63]

Thus, the bedrock principle that the law is a coherent unity, forces the court to come up with answers and drives the court into searching for a sometimes non-existent intention. Judges need to recognise that their experience of legislation is bound to be jaundiced. [64]

The language of the Legislature is another problem to statutory interpretation. *In Nolan* v. *Clifford* the court when considering the interpretation of a section of the Crimes Act 1900 (NSW) said:

---

[60] (1992) 175 CLR 353 at pp. 40 2-3.
[61] *Ilkiw* v. *Samuels* (1963) 2 ALL ER 879 at 889.
[62] Karl Llewellyn, Remarks on the Theory of Appellate Decision and the Rules or Canons about how statutes are to be construed (1950) 3 Vanderbilt Law Review 395.
[63] Mason K The view from the other side – Judicial Experiences of Legislation (2005) http://www.lawlink.nsw.gov.au/lawlink/SupremeCourt/11 sc.nsf/pages/SCO mason.
[64] See Justice Keith Mason, The Unity of the Law (1998) 4TJR 1.

We have been asked to refer to the brevier, the note of the consolidating commissioner, to find out what he meant. I do no think this reference is of any value, because we are not to consider what the commissioner thought, but what Parliament has said, and what it meant by what he has said.[65]

Most statutes are designed to take the law outside the judicial comfort zone (i.e. the realm of the common law). This causes many judges to get their hackles up, often unreasonably. History is littered with prolonged unwarranted battles by judges reluctant to understand or accept ground-breaking legislation. In the process of resisting change to the familiar wisdom of the common law, judges may feel like hitting out at the messenger rather than the message. Many statutes transport judges into a universe of discourse in which they have no familiarity at all.

On the issue of updating of laws, it is a common problem with interpretation that the legislature rarely goes back and updates their laws. As Solove D.J puts it:

One of the problems with interpretation above is that legislatures rarely go back and update their laws. They pass laws, the courts encounter ambiguities and difficulties and unexpected cases. Yet only sometimes do legislatures go back and fix the laws to address these problems. Often, the legislature just makes the law and walk away. I have a casebook, and it is a chore constantly updating it. But I feel an obligation to keep it up to date. It is too bad that legislatures feel no similar obligation with respect to the laws they pass. [66]

There seems to be a fundamental problem, if the legislatures are not diligent about following up over the way their laws are being interpreted. In most cases, the legislature fails to follow up old laws because, it is hard work; revising laws can be difficult political battles; there are many other pressing issues on the table; or it just isn't on the current legislature's radar screen unless there's an egregious or highly-publicized case involving the law. [67]

In the words of Calabresi, G.

Courts should actively fix and update laws. Interpretation is one common way that courts already do this. It allows courts some leeway in ensuring that laws are interpreted reasonably and justly. If the legislature doesn't like the result, it can change the law. Most likely it won't as I've pointed out

[65] (1904) 1CLR 429.
[66]Solove   D.J.   Statutory   Interpretation   and   Legislature   Unresponsiveness,   (2007) http://www.concurringopinion.com/archives/2007/12/statutory.inter.html.(1982).
[67] Ibid.

above. But at least interpretation will let laws be a bit more flexible and responsive to the unique situations they might be applied to. That said, the ideal solution is to figure out the way to encourage legislatures to keep their laws in better shape. But is there a solution to this problem? Any ideas? In the absence of an effective solution, does this problem justify interpretation?[68]

The origin of most problems of Statutory Interpretation is Language. As Lord Simon of Glaisdale said:

> Words and phrases of the English languages have an extraordinary range of meanings. This has been a rich resource in English poetry (which makes truthful use of the resources, overtones and ambiguities), but it has a concomitant disadvantage in English law which seeks unambiguous precision, with the aim that every citizen shall know, as exactly as possible, where he stands under the law. [69]

As the late poet Laureate, Ted Hughes observed:

> A word is its own little solar system of meaning. [70]

Lord Simon of Glarisdale has referred to the need for an interpreter to tune in to the linguistic register of the drafters when he said:

> Statutory languages like all language is capable of an almost infinite gradation of "register" i.e. will be used at the semantic level appropriate to the subject matter and to the audience addressed (the man in the street, lawyers, merchant, etc). It is the duty of a court of construction to tune in to such register and so to interpret the statutory language as to give it the primary meaning which is appropriate in that register (unless it is clear that some other meaning must be given in order to carry out the statutory purpose or to avoid injustice, anomaly, absurdity or contradiction). In other words, statutory language must always be given presumptively the most natural and ordinary meaning which is appropriate in the circumstances. [71]

---

[68] Calabresi, G.A. Common Law for an Age of Statutes.

[69] *Stock* v. *Frank Jones* (Tipton) Ltd. (1978) 1 WLR 231 at 236.

[70] Hughes T. in The Poet's Rich Resource: Issues in Statutory Interpretation. http://www. lawlink.nsw.gov.au/lawlink/SupremeCourt/11 Sc.nsf/pages/SCO speech spigelman 070801.

[71] Maunsell v. Olins (1975) AC 373 at 391. See also Farrell v. Alexander (1977) AC 59 at 84; Black Clawson International Ltd v. Papiewerke Waldtrof – Aschaffenburg AG (1975) AC 591 at 645; Spigelman "Statutory Interpretation: Identifying the Linguistic Register" (1999).

Meaning is functional and generic, the meanings given to a word today may vary tomorrow. This poses a danger to interpretation. As Fish S, observed:

> All shapes are interpretatively produced, and since the conditions of interpretation are themselves unstable... the possibility of seeing something in a "new light" and therefore of seeing a new something, is ever and unpredictably present... the shapes that seem perspicuous to us now may not seem so or may seem differently so tomorrow. This applies not only to the shape of statutes, poems, and signs in air plane lavatories, but to the disciplines and forms of life within which statutes, poems, and signs become available to us. [72]

In accounting for our understanding of statutes, Fish posits an act of interpretation interposed between the object of our understanding and our grasp of its meaning. The interpretive act is the mediator between the thing we seek to understand and our grasp of its meaning. Interpretation makes understanding possible. Of course, there is often disagreement over the meaning of texts, especially legal texts. Fish thinks interpretation account for this phenomenon. In accounting for the divergent prospective of the majority and dissenting opinions in Riggs v. Palmer, Fish said:

> If it is assumed that the purpose of probate is to ensure the orderly devolution of property at all costs, then the statute in this case will have the plain meaning urged by the defendant; but if it is assumed that no law ever operates in favour of someone who would profit by his crime, then the "same" statute will have a meaning that is different, but no less plain. In either case the statute will have been literally construed, and what the court will have done is prefer one literal construction to another by invoking one purpose (assumed background) rather than another. [73]

The court often faced the problem of interpreting the law. The law is like a sign post which merely indicates directions to follow without indicating the distance to be followed. As Wittgenstein explained:

> A rule stands there like a sign-post- Does the sign post leave no doubt open about the way I have to go? Does it show which direction I am to take when I have passed it; whether along the road or footpath or across-country? But where is it said which way I am to follow it; whether in the direction of its finder or (e.g) in the opposite one? – And if there were, not

---

[72] Fish, S. Is there a Text in this class? (1980) developing the theory of "effective stylistics".
[73] Ibid. at p. 280.

a single sign-post, but a chain of adjacent ones or of chalk marks on the ground – is there only one way of interpreting them? – so I can say, the sign – post does after all leave no room for doubt? [74]

Wittgenstein's point is that interpretation cannot explicate the very idea of understanding of the words of a statute because it gives rise to an infinite regress of interpretation. Interpretation obscures rather than illuminates the phenomenon of human understanding.[75]

On the need for the court to adopt Parliamentary history of the statute as aid to interpretation, the reliability of Parliamentary history has its disadvantages. It has been said that the purpose of debating a Bill is to secure consent to its terms and to explain the intent and meaning of its precise language only to the extent that the explanation will further be the object of getting consent to its passage; that the process of enacting legislation is not "an intellectual exercise in the pursuit of truth but an essay in persuasion or perhaps almost reduction, and that, in these circumstances, to appeal from the carefully pondered terms of the statute to the hurly-burly of Parliamentary debate is to appeal from Philip Sober to Philip drunk,[76]Justice Jackson[77] and Professor Henri Capitant[78] have alike pointed out the disadvantages of this extrinsic aid from which so many diverse constructions can find support somewhere in the varying statements made during the progress of a Bill through the stages of its enactment.

Curtis, C.P. said:

The courts used to be fastidious as to where they looked for the legislative intention. They used to confine the enquiry to reports by committees (of the legislature) and statements by the member in charge of the Bill. But now the pressure of the orthodox doctrine has sent them fumbling about in the eshcans of the legislative process for the shoddiest unenacted expressions of intention.[79]

Apart from these general dangers, there is the particular danger that if Parliamentary history can be appealed to as evidence of intention, such evidence

---

[74] Wittgenstein, Philosophical Investigations GEM. Anscombe trans, 3rd ed. 1958.
[75] Ibid.
[76] See Corry, J.A. The Use of Legislative History in the Interpretation of Statutes (1954) 32 Can. Bar. Rev. 624 at pp. 621-2.
[77] Jackson, J. The Meaning of Statutes: What the congress says or what the Court says (1948) 34 AB A Journal 535.
[78] Capitant, H. L'interprītation des lois d'agrīs les travaux preparatories in Le Recevil d'etudes sur les sources du Droit en l'honneus du doyen Francois Gǔry, Sirey, 1935 pp. 204-216.
[79] Curtis, C.P. A Better Theory of Legal Interpretation (1949) 4 The Record of the Association of the Bar of the City of New York 321.

can be deliberately manufactured during the legislative process by those with an axe to grind. [80]

The framers of a Constitution who want to make it a charter of liberties and not just a set of constitutive rules face a difficult choice. They can write specific provisions and thereby doom their work to rapid obsolescent, or they can write general provisions, thereby allowing substantial discretion to the authoritative interpreters who are the judges.

Many provisions of the Constitution are drafted in general terms. This creates flexibility in the face of unforeseen changes, but it creates the possibility of alternative interpretations, and this possibility is an embarrassment for a theory of judicial legitimacy that denies judges any right to exercise discretion. A choice among semantically plausible interpretations of a text in circumstances remote from those contemplated by its drafters, requires the exercise of discretion and the weighing of consequences.

The decision to read the Constitution narrowly, and thereby to "restrain" judicial interpretation, is not a decision that can be read directly from the text. For example this Constitution does not say, "Read me broadly," or, "Read me narrowly". The decision to do one or the other must be made as a matter of political theory and will depend on such things as one's view of the springs of judicial legitimacy and the relative competence of courts and legislatures in dealing with particular type of issue.

In criminal prosecutions, this sentence "in all criminal prosecutions, the accused shall enjoy the right --- to have the assistance of counsel for his defence" Read narrowly, this just means that the accused can't be forbidden to retain counsel. If he cannot afford counsel, or competent counsel, he is out of luck. Read broadly, it guarantees even the indigent the effective assistance of counsel. It becomes not just a negative right to be allowed to hire a lawyer but a positive right to demand the help of the government in financing one's defence if one cannot do it by oneself. Either reading is compatible with the semantics of the provision, but the first better captures the specific intent of the framers.

The word "ambiguity" is not without its own difficulty. Frequently in the context of statutory interpretation, the word "ambiguity" is used in a more general sense. It is applied, not only to situations in which a word has more than one meaning, but to any situation in which the intention of Parliament with respect to the scope of a particular statutory situation is, for whatever reason doubtful, Cross[81] stated thus:

---

[80] Ibid. at p. 328.
[81] Cross Statutory Interpretation (3rd ed.) 1995 at pp. 83-84

In the context of statutory interpretation the word most frequently used to indicate the doubt which a judge must entertain before he can search for, and if possible, apply a secondary meaning is "ambiguity". In ordinary language this term is often confined to situations in which the same word is capable of meaning two different things; but in relation to statutory interpretation, judicial usage sanctions the application of the word "ambiguity" to describe any kind of doubtful meaning of words, phrases, or longer statutory provisions.

Also in *Bowtell* v. *Goldborough Mort and Co. Limited*[82] O' Connor, J. said:

If has been contended in this case that an ambiguity must appear on the face of a statute before you can apply the rules of interpretation relating to ambiguities. In one sense that is correct, and in another sense it is not. You will frequently find an Act of Parliament perfectly clear on the face of it, and it is only when you apply it to the subject matter that the ambiguity appears. That ambiguity arises frequently from the use of general words. And wherever general words are used in a statute there is always a liability to find a difficulty in applying general words to the particular case. It is often doubtful whether the legislature used the words in the general unrestricted sense, or in a restricted sense with reference to some particular subject matter.

Allegiance to a strictly formal approach is a major constraint to statutory interpretation. With the rise of positivism, courts were increasingly emphasizing the specific operative words of an Act, rather than other evidence of the "intention of the legislature" which was less quantifiable. Mason J. directly criticized this narrow literal approach:

Problems of legal interpretation are not solved satisfactorily by ritual incantations which emphasize the clarity of meaning which words have when viewed in isolation, divorced from their context. The modern approach to interpretation insists that the context be considered in the first instance---[83]

Courts are often faced with many statutes to interpret, thus making their application and interpretation more problematic. As Lord Denning M. R. puts it:

---

[82] (1996) 3 CLR 444 at pp. 456-457.
[83] *K & S Lake City Freighters Pty Ltd.* v. *Gordon & Gotch Ltd.* (1985) 157 CLR 309, 315.

In almost every case on which you have to advise you will have to interpret. There are stocks and stocks of them. For worse for you than for me. When I was called in 1923 there was one volume of 500 pages. Now in 1978 there are three volumes of more than 3,000 paper. Not a single page but it can give rise to argument. This flood of legislation has not abated. In 1992, there are three volumes of more than 3,500 pages, plus a fourth volume of various tables and in 1996 there were four volumes running to 4, 096 pages not including substantial tables and indices, themselves running to hundreds of pages. In 1998 (the most recent year for which my college library has a complete bound set) there are again 3 volumes running to xxx pages. [84]

One of the difficulties which sometimes faces the courts in interpreting statutes is the lack of material about the underlying policy of the statute in question. When the meaning of a provision may vary according to the view taken of the general purpose of the legislation, such a lack of information may put the court in an invidious position, it may have to make a choice between rival social assumptions, argued before it, with little fuller guidance than can be derived from those matters of which it can take judicial notice and such indications, which may be indecisive, as can be gathered from the language of the statute. In the result the interpretation of a provision may seem to depend on the choice and pattern of the language of the Act, when these may in fact have been chosen in the light of instructions to the draftsman which did not, and perhaps could not, anticipate the point being argued. In reality, the court may have had to reach its decision as best it can, even if it is expressed in terms of an analysis of the language used. Thus the question arises whether the courts and the public should, where appropriate and practicable, be provided with some further authoritative aid to the construction of statute.

The Constitution of the United Kingdom is said to be uncodified. That is, its Constitution is not in a single, written document, but is drawn from legislation many hundreds of years old, judicial precedents, convention, and numerous other sources[85]. This means that the British Constitution is an ever - changing one, and so is said to be fluid. The way in which the British Constitution has developed, comes from centuries of conflicts between the monarchy, the aristocracy, religious institutions, and the British people.

---

[84] Denning, M.R. The Discipline of Law pp. 17-19.
[85] The key documents of the United Kingdom's Constitution are the Chanter of Liberties (1100), Magna Carta (1215), The Petition of Right (1628), English Bill of Rights (1628), English Bill of Rights (1689), Act of Settlement (1701), Acts of Union (1707), Act of Union (1800), Scotland Act of 1998 and Associated Legislation, Government of Wales Act of 1998 and Associated Legislation, Northern Ireland Act of 1998 and Associated Legislation. The Belfast Agreement (1998) and the Human Rights Act (1998).

One of the major problems of statutory interpretation in Great Britain is that of statutory language. In *Maunsell* v. *Olins,* Lord Simon of Glaisdale in a case concerned with the meaning of the word "premises" in the British Rent Act 1968 said:

> Statutory language, like all language, is capable of an almost infinite graduation of "register" i.e. it will be used at the semantic level appropriate to the subject matter and to the audience addressed (the man in the street, lawyers, merchants, etc.). It is the duty of a court of construction to turn in to such register and so to interpret the statutory language as to give it the primary meaning which is appropriate in that register (unless it is clear that some other meaning must be given in order to carry out the statutory purpose or to avoid injustice, anomaly, absurdity or contradiction). In other words statutory language must always be given presumptively the most natural ordinary meaning which is appropriate in the circumstance.[86]

Lord Simon of Glaisdale also in the case of Farrell v. Alexander said:

> If a court of construction places itself in the position of the draftsman, acquires its knowledge, recognizes its statutory objectives, tunes into its linguistic register, and then ascertains the primary and natural meaning in their context of the words it has used, that will generally be an end of the task of construction. But occasionally something will go wrong. It may become apparent that the primary and natural meaning cannot be what Parliament intended; it produces injustice, absurdity, anomaly or contradiction, or it stultifies or runs counter to the statutory objective. [87]

Parliament does not legislate on blank sheet. In the case of Britain, it legislates for a European Liberal democracy. General words in statute should not be allowed to abrogate fundamental rights. This principle has a considerable common law pedigree but in practice judges often failed to observe it.

Lord Hoftimann in Simms[88] explained the rationale of the principle:

> Parliamentary sovereignty means that parliament can, if it chooses, legislate contrary to fundamental principles of human rights --- The constraints upon its exercise by Parliament are ultimately political, not legal. But the principle of legality means that parliament must squarely confront

---

[86] *Maunsell* v. *Olins* (1975) AC 373 at p.291
[87] *Farrell* v. *Alexander* (1977) AC 59 at p 84 see also *Black-Clawson International Ltd.* v. *Paplerwerke Waldhof - Aschafenburg AG.* (1975) AC 591 at 645 per Lord Simon of Glalsdale
[88] R. v Secretary for the Home Department Ex. P. Simms (2000) 2 AC 131.

what it is doing and accept the political cost. Fundamental rights cannot be overridden by general or ambiguous words. This is because there is too great a risk that the full implications of their unqualified meaning may have passed unnoticed in the democratic process. In the absence of express language or necessary implication to the contrary, the courts therefore presume that even the most general words were intended to be subject to the basic rights of the individual. [89]

For most of its history the British judiciary has tended to maintain "the law-is-the-law approach" to legal language. [90] On this model of decision-making: Judges are supposed to find out what the law is (eschewing any inquiry into what it ought to be) by consulting the "plain meaning" of statutory words and common law precedents.

In the United Kingdom, highly trained legislative drafters draft statutes and stylistically legislation tends to be detailed. Nevertheless, there are many problems of statutory interpretation. This is inevitable because it would be humanly impossible for the drafter or the legislator to draft legislation that would cover every situation that might arise. Sometimes legislation is passed in a hurry or an amendment is inserted at a later stage that has not been fully considered.

The principles of statutory interpretation are not codified in Britain. They are governed by the common law and are therefore capable of endogenous development by the courts to meet new technical problems or social needs. Since the principles of interpretation are governed by the common law, it might be thought that statutes mean what judges say they mean, rather than what Parliament may have intended. But that is not theoretically so, in general, the court's function is to ascertain the intention of Parliament and that is done from the language that Parliament has used. Thus we can say that the basic model for statutory interpretation is an "Agency Model". The essential feature of this model is that the judge sets out to interpret what is written in front of him, rather than to think about constitutional issues. In doing this, he is fulfilling as faithfully as he can the will of the democratically elected Parliament.

It follows naturally from this that judges in Britain can not rewrite statutes. Moreover, they must always act within judicial constraints. But, in practice, there are situations where it is not clear what Parliament would have intended if it had thought about the situation that has emerged and presents itself in the case before the court. Parliament may have intended one thing but the language which it has used may not bear that meaning. The court has to find the meaning of the statute

---

[89] This principle is now firmly entrenched in English Law see R v. Special Commissioner and Another, Ex. Morgan. Grenfell & Co. Ltd. (2002) UK HL 21.

[90] Stevens Robert, The English Judges: Their Role in the Changing Constitution Oxford: Hart, 2005.

from the language used and the indications given in the statute read as a whole. This means that it is possible that its interpretation will turn out not to have been what Parliament intended.

After a statute is passed, changes often occur, for example, changes in social conditions or technological developments. Exceptionally, a statute is limited to a state of affairs existing at a particular point in time, but more generally it is silent about its effect in changed circumstances. The courts cannot fill gaps in legislation and so they have to determine whether the existing statute applies to the changed state of affairs. The legislation may express a clear purpose that can only be fulfilled if it is applied to a new state of affairs. The House of Lords in *R (Quitavalle)* v. *Health Secretary* held that this was the case:

> Where the statute provided for a process of statutory licensing for in vitro fertilisation of human embryos and a new method of creating embryos outside the human body was discovered. [91]

In other cases, it may be that the legislation refers to a concept, which is sufficiently wide to embrace changes in circumstances. This is the case, for example, where companies legislation require company accounts to show "a true and fair view". The content of the concept of a true and fair view may change over the course of time but the concept itself is unaltered.

In England, the use of legislative history as an aid to the interpretation of the statute was not permitted prior to 1993. It can now be used as an aid to interpretation if the statute is ambiguous and if a government minister, or other promoter of the Bill, made a statement in Parliament dealing clearly with the point of dispute.[92] But this is a very limited exception to the general rule excluding legislative history. The court cannot, for example, use legislative history to show that a particular change in the law was considered and rejected in the course of pre-legislative scrutiny.

There have also been notable clarifications of the principles of interpretation where the British courts have had to interpret domestic legislation against the background of international treaties. In *Salomon* v. *Commissioners of Customs and Exercise*[93] the Court made it clear that where there is cogent extrinsic evidence of a connection between an international treaty and an Act under

---

[91] (2003) 2 AC 687.

[92] (1993) AC 573.

[93] (1967) 2 Q.B 116 The Act in question was the Customs and Excise Act 1952, S.258(1) and Schedule 6, paras. 1(1) and 2. See also *Samuel Montagn and Co. Ltd.* v. *Swiss Air Transport Co. Ltd* (1966) 2 Q.B 306 where the treaty was made part of the Act (Carriage by Air Act 1932) and the Court emphasised that strict interpretation should not be given in view of its effect on the conduct of business and the importance of avoiding conflict between decisions of British courts and foreign courts interpreting the treaty.

interpretation, a court may look at the convention in elucidating the Act, although the Act nowhere makes mention of the treaty. And in Post Office v. Estuary Radio Ltd[94] the court held that, where the meaning of the domestic legislation is not clear, it should be construed in the light of the treaty to which it is giving effect, having regard to the presumption that the national authority (here the Crown) intends to carry out its international obligations.

However, the criticism of the interpretation of statutes by the British courts cannot, even so far as modern times are concerned, be altogether dismissed. Frankfurter J. in spite of his recognition of the interactable elements in the interpretation of statutes said:

> These current English rules of construction are simple. They are too simple. If the purpose of construction is the ascertainment of meaning, nothing that is logically relevant should be excluded. The rigidity of English courts in interpreting language merely by reading it disregards the fact that enactments are, as it were, organisms which exist in their environment. One wonders whether English judges are confined psychologically as they purport to be legally. The judges deem themselves limited to reading the words of a statute. But can they really escape placing the words in the context of their minds, which after all are not automatically applying legal logic but repositories of all sorts of assumptions and impressions? [95]

Allen, C., although emphasising the importance of an intangible judicial factor, has also said:

> Whether or not...our whole doctrine of statutory interpretation rests upon false foundations, it is certain that this branch of our law exhibits inconsistencies which suggest radical weakness somewhere. [96]

Evershed, M.R. said:

> ...heritage of a multiplicity of so-called "rules" and of an accretion of case law in which some judicial utterance can be cited in support of almost any proposition relevant to the problems of statutory interpretation. [97]

---

[94] (1968) 2 Q.B 740.

[95] Frankfurter, J. Some Reflections on the Reading of Statutes (1947) 2 The Record of the Association of the Bar of the City of New York 213 at pp. 231-2.

[96] Allen, C. *Law in the Making*, 7th ed., 1964 at pp. 58 and 529.

[97] Evershed, M.R. The Impact of Statute on the Law of England, Maccabean Lecture in Jurisprudence, (1956) XL 11 Proceedings of the British Academy 247 at pp. 260 and 528.

One of the major problems of Constitutional interpretation in Nigeria is that of filling the gaps in the provisions of the Constitution when the need arises. In situation where there is a 'gap' in the constitutional provision, the exercise of discretion by the court is often more extensive. In such instances, the court may claim the furtherance of the constitutional intent in the gap filling process; but it cannot deny that it has written something new into the provision or "legislated" to fill the gap in the law. There is usually no doubt or debate as to the existence of the "gap" even when the court is reluctant to initiate any judicial legislation. As observed by Justice Owolabi in *Onabanjo* v. *Concord Press*:

> It is because learned counsel for the applicant appreciates that the Constitution makes no provision for what he has proposed that he has boldly asked me to fill in the gap. [98]

Interpreting tax laws is a major problem in Nigeria. The Nigerian courts consider themselves incapacitated using statutory interpretation to fit against tax schemes that are obviously structured to "avoid" tax, provided the provision(s) being construed is/are to them "clear" and "unambiguous". Unfortunately, the strict construction, which is the obvious choice of interpretation, lay no basis to fight such avoidance once the scheme literally fall within the confine of the provision of the law.[99] In *7Up Bottling Company* v. *Lagos State Revenue Board* the court said:

> It has often been the view of courts here and elsewhere that if a person sought to be taxed, comes within the letter of the law, then such a person must be taxed. On the other hand, if the tax authority seeking to recover tax from a person is unable to bring him within "the letter of the law", the person will be free, "however apparently within the spirit of the law his case ought otherwise appear to be" see Comprehensive Aspects of Taxation by R. Glynne Williams 32nd Edition p. 2. The foregoing is in essence one way of expounding the view that taxation provisions are strictly interpreted...[100]

In tandem with the common law approach which views taxation as an invasion of taxpayers' property right, the courts in Nigeria resolves all "ambiguous" provisions in favor of taxpayers of any person whose property right is considered to be expropriated. In *Hon. John O. Fasogbon* v. *Prince Adewale A. Layade* the court said:

---

[98] *Onabanjo* v. *Concord Press* (1981) 2NCLR 4 at p. 408
[99] The courts in several occasions have ruled that the bequeathed model of strict/literal approach to interpretation should be followed, or rather is the general rule for deconstructing tax legislation.
[100] (2003) 3 NWLR pp. 565-591.

...it is necessary to have a recourse to the rule of interpretation of statute that a legislation that takes away or abridge the right of a citizen including one that imposes penalty on him should be construed *fortissimo contra-proferentes*, that is to say, it should be construed strictly against any one claiming benefit see Peenok Investment Ltd v. Hotel Presidential Ltd. (1983) NCLR 122, (1982) 12 SC 1, 12. [101]

It is apparent from the above, that one major difficulty Nigerian courts face using the literal rule is the determination of the "clarity" of the words used. This task still boils down to the individual training, bias or discretion of the judge. Proponents of the literal rule never advocated giving judges such discretion.

Nigerian courts see taxation as a burden and an infringement of tax payer's property right, it shows clearly that courts are out to protect tax payers on the pretext that for any tax to be imposed there must be a clear and unambiguous provision imposing such. Unfortunately, this approach contradicts the idea that all adult members of a society are obligated to contribute to the maintenance of the society they live in; for there is a general or public good that cannot be individually provided for, but by the government through publicly generated revenues.[102] Adopting an approach that seeks to put more money in the purse of tax payers defeats the public good theory and denies government access to financial resources that would have been used for the good of all.[103]

The literal interpretation can be a double-edge sword because it does not favor tax payers at all time. Sometimes it could constitute a real problem to them. The application of the literal rule could operate like the old English common law system, which prior to the advent of Equity constituted serious difficulties to litigants.

---

[101] (1999) 11 NWLR pp. 543-561.

[102] Murphy, L & Nagel, T., *The Myth of Ownership: Taxes and Justice* (New York: Oxford University Press, 2002) p. 46.

[103] Unfortunately, the so-called favour to tax payers is, in my view defeatist. It serves no long-term advantage because taxation is one of the major sources of revenue generation to most governments. And it is also the constitutional responsibility of most government, even when the government has no welfarist agenda, to provide security, enabling environment for the operation of business and also the provision of basic social amenities to the generality of people within the society. If a millionaire tax payer is helped by the court through strict interpretation of tax provisions to keep more money in her pocket, and by the same breath denies the government of substantial amount of money that could have helped it carry its programs such as the provision of security, definitely the millionaire who succeeds in keeping more money in her pocket may lose her life when criminals go on rampage. This is exactly what is happening in Nigeria today. Criminals are invading peoples' homes, maiming and killing people because the police is under-funded. Without going into trouble polemics of determining whether or not the lack of financial muscle or a change in the interpretative approach used by the court will make more money available to the state for the provision of security, it should be taken that when state fails to live up to its constitutional responsibility everybody suffers including the tax payer who succeeds in keeping more money to herself.

The Indian Constitution is basically federal in form and is marked by the traditional characteristics of a federal system, namely supremacy of the Constitution, division of power between the Union and State, and the existence of an independent judiciary in the Indian Constitution. The three organs of the State – Executive, Legislature and Judiciary have to function within their own spheres demarcated under the Constitution. In other words, the doctrine of Separation of Powers has been implicitly recognized by the Indian Constitution. The basic structure of the Constitution is unchangeable and only such amendments to the Constitution are allowed which do not affect its basic structure or rob it of its essential character. The Constitution of India recognizes certain basic fundamental rights for every citizen of India, such as the Right to Equality, the Right to Freedom, the Right against exploitation, the Right to Freedom of Religion, Cultural and Educational rights, and the Right to Constitutional Remedies. Any infringement of fundamental rights can be challenged by any citizen of India in the court of law. The Constitution of India also prescribes some fundamental duties on every citizens in India.

Language more often is not an imperfect instrument of expression of human thought. Though it would be idle to expect every statutory provision to be drafted with divine prescience and perfect clarity.

In *Oxford University Press (India)* v. *Commissioner of Income Tax*,[104] The assessee, Oxford University Press, is engaged in the business of printing, publishing and selling of books. It has been assessed to income-tax as a company from the assessment year 1952-53 onwards on the basis of the notification issued by the Central Board of Revenue. The said notification was issued on the application filed by the assessee. For the assessment year 1976-77. The assessee filed a return showing income of Rs. 19.94 lakhs. It claimed exemption from payment of tax under Section 10 (22) of the Act[105] mainly on the basis that it is a part of the Oxford University incorporated in the United Kingdom. The assessing officer did not accept the claim of exemption and passed the order of assessment under Section 144 – B of the Act[106]. On Appeal the Commissioner of Income-tax (Appeals) accepted the assessee's contention that being a part and parcel of the University of Oxford of U.K it is entitled to the exemption under Section 10 (22) of the Act. On the said finding, the appeal was allowed and the assessment order was set aside. A further appeal filed to the Tribunal proved futile and the Tribunal referred the issue to the High Court. The High Court accepted the contention raised on behalf of the Central Board of Revenue that the assessee, on the facts

---

[104] (2001) SOL Case No. 053 delivered on 24th January, 2001.
[105] Income Tax Act, 1961.
[106] Ibid.

and circumstances of the case, did not qualify for the exemption provided under Section 10 (22) of the Act.

Section 10, clause (22) provides that

> Income not included in total income in computing the total income of a previous year of any person, any income falling within any of the following clauses shall not be included (22) any income of a University or other Educational institution, existing solely for educational purposes and for purposes of profit. [107]

The main issue is whether Oxford University Press, Bombay, which is part of Oxford University, England is exempted under Section 10 (22) of the Income-Tax Act, 1961 from paying tax. In this respect it was the contention of the appellant, that only a person can be assessed to income-tax as provided in Section 4 of the Act[108] and such a person in the present case is the Oxford University of which Oxford University Press is a part, any income earned by the Oxford University Press has to be taken as the income of the University and in that event the entire income is totally exempted from tax under Section 10 (22) of the Act and that in the case of a University the nature of the activities under-taken by it in India and the form and character of the establishment of the University in India are not relevant. The Respondent on the other hand contended that the expression "existing solely for educational purpose etc" qualifies the expression "income of a university or other educational institution." Therefore even assuming that the Oxford University Press is a part of the Oxford University still it does not qualify for exemption since the Oxford University does not exist solely for educational purposes in India and that Oxford University Press is engaged in commercial activities like printing, publishing and selling of books from which the amount has been earned during the assessment year in question.

On the interpretation of the language used in section 10 clause 22 of the Act, the Supreme Court of India by a majority decision held that Oxford University Press in India is profit oriented and cannot enjoy the exemption to pay tax as claimed. Sabharwal, J said:

> The imparting of education is a service to the society. From the language of section 10 (22), it does not appear that without any such service in India, the legislature intended to exempt to total income of the assessee. I do not think that from the language of section 10 (22), it can be said that the

---

[107] Ibid.
[108] Ibid.

hands of the Court are so tied that it cannot read into this provision, the requirement of imparting education or some other educational activity in this country. A University or other educational institution which exists solely for educational purposes and not for purposes of profit though not established in India but having some educational activities in this country alone would be entitled to claim exemption. Such a University or educational institution having educational activity in India but being established or constituted in some other country would not be denied the benefit of exemption only on the ground that it has not been established or constituted in India. The imparting of education or existence of educational activity in India is the basic assumption of section 10 (22) and the place of the establishment of constitution of a university or other educational institution is of no consequence. Similar phraseology has also been used in clause (22 A) in relation to the income of a hospital or other institution for the reception and treatment of the ailments referred to in the said provision. [109]

In Orissa State Warehousing Corporation v. Commissioner of Income – Tax[110], the question involved was about the interpretation of Clause (29) of Section 10 of the Act. The assessee appealed against the decision of the High Court to the Supreme Court of India contending that the High Court was not justified in holding that the interest received by the assessee from the banks on fixed deposits was exempt under section 10 (29) of the Act. The contention on behalf of the assessee Warehousing Corporation was that regard being had to sections 16 and 24 of the Warehousing Corporations Act, 1962, all moneys coming into the hands of the Corporation have to be deposited in the bank account maintained by the Corporation and the same being a statutory obligation, the question of income, therefore, cannot but be termed to be a part of the functioning of the unit and as such exempt under section 10 (29). Rejecting the contention, the court said:

Having due regard to the language used, the question of exemption would arise pertaining to that part of the income only which arises or is derived from the letting of god owns or the warehouses and for the purposes specified in section 10 (29) of the Act – as noticed above. The statute has been rather categorical and restrictive in the matter of grant of exemption: storage, processing or facilitating the marketing of the commodities are definitely regarded as three different forms of activities which are entitled to exemption in the event of there being any income there from. We do lend our concurrence to the view expressed by the Madlya Predesh High

---

[109] *Oxford University Press (India)* v. *Commissioner of Income Tax* (2001) op. cit.
[110] *Orissa State Warehousing Corporation* v. *Commissioner of Income-Tax*, 1999 (237) ITR 589.

Court and record that in the event the letting of godowns or warehouses is for any other purpose or if income is derived from any other source, then and in that event such an income cannot possibly come within the ambit of section 10 (29) of the Act and is thus not exempt from tax. The facts in issue pertaining to the interest income on fixed deposit or ascribing the activities of the assessee being termed and cannot arise Mr. C.S. Vaidyanathan, Addle, Solicitor General rightly contended that the language being clear and there being no ambiguity, the question of there being any integrated activity and reading the same into the statutes would be a violent departure from the intent of the legislature. [111]

After considering some of the decisions pertaining to the interpretation of the fiscal statutes, the court said:

A fiscal statute shall have to be interpreted on the basis of the language used therein and not be hors the same. No words ought to be added and only the language used ought to be considered so as to ascertain the proper meaning and intent of the legislation. The court is to ascribe the natural and ordinary meaning to the words used by the legislature and the court ought not, under any circumstances, to substitute its own impression and ideas in place of the legislative intent as is available from a plain reading of the statutory provisions. [112]

In *K.P. Varghese* v. *Income Tax Officer, Ernakulam and Another,*[113] Section 52 (2) of the Act[114] provides thus:

Without prejudice to the provisions of sub-section (1), if in the opinion of the Income Tax Officer the fair market value of a capital asset transferred by an assessee as on the date of the transfer exceeds the full value of the consideration declared by the assessee in respect of the transfer of such capital asset by an amount of not lees than 15 percent of the value declared, the full value of the consideration for such capital asset shall, with the previous approval of the inspecting Assistant Commissioner, be taken to be its fair market value on the date of the transfer.

The assessee was the owner of a house which he had purchased in 1958 for Rs. 16,500. On December 25, 1965 the assessee sold the house for the same price of Rs. 16,500 to his daughter-in-law and five of his children. The assessment of the

---

[111] Ibid.
[112] Ibid.
[113] 1981 (4) SCC 173.
[114] Income Tax Act, 1961.

assessee in respect of the assessment year 1966-67 was completed in normal course and in this assessment no amount was included by way of capital gains in respect of the transfer of the house since the house was sold at the same price at which it was purchased and no capital gains accrued or arose to him as a result of the transfer. On April 4, 1968, however, the Income – tax officer issued a notice under section 48 of the Act seeking to reopen the assessment of the assessee for the assessment year 1966-67. The Income-tax officer proposed to fix the fair market value of the house sold by the assessee on 25th December, 1965 at Rs. 65,000 as against, the consideration of Rs. 16,500 for which the house was sold and assessed, the difference of Rs. 48,500 as capital gains in the hands of the assessee. The Income tax officer rested his decision to assess the sum of Rs. 48,500 to tax on section 52(2) taking the view that the said section did not require as a condition precedent that there should be understatement of consideration in respect of the transfer and it was enough to attract the applicability of section 52(2) if the fair market value of the property as on the date of the transfer exceeded the full value of the consideration declared by the assessee by an amount of not less than 15% of the value so declared, which was indisputably the position. The Full Bench by a majority decision did not accept the contention of the assessee that the understatement of consideration in respect of the transfer was a necessary condition for attracting the applicability of section 52(2). The case proceeded on the basis that admittedly there was no understatement of consideration and it was a perfectly bona fide transaction. The contention of the Revenue Board was that the consideration paid was more than the stated consideration of Rs. 16,500. The contention was that the payment of consideration was not a relevant ground for attracting section 52(2) and what was relevant was only the fair market value of a capital asset at the time of the transfer which was found at Rs. 65,000 and therefore, as on the date of the transfer, it exceeded the full value of the consideration declared by the assessee in respect of the transfer of such capital asset by an amount of not less than 15%.

On the interpretation of section 52(2) as argued by the revenue, the High Court observed that on a plain and natural construction the only condition for attracting the applicability of the said provision is that the fair market value of the capital asset transferred by the assessee as on the date of the transfer exceeds the full value of the consideration declared by the assessee in respect of the transfer by an amount of not less than 15% of the value so declared. Once the Income-tax officer is satisfied that this condition exists it can proceed to invoke the provisions in section 52 sub-section (2) and take the fair market value of the asset transferred by the assessee as on the date of the transfer as representing the full value of the consideration for the transfer of the capital asset and compute the capital gains on that basis. The revenue contended that no more is necessary to be proved and to introduce any further condition such as understatement of consideration in respect of the transfer would be to read into the statutory provisions something which is not there. Indeed it would amount to rewriting the section. On the language used in Section 52(2). the Supreme Court of India said:

> This court noticed the basic principle of interpretation of statutory provisions. Noticing the words of Judge Learned Hand, it was said that the task of interpretation of statutory enactment is not a mechanical risk. It is more than a mere reading of mathematical formulae because few words possess the precision of mathematical symbols. We must not adopt a strictly literal interpretation of Section 52 (2) but construe its language having regard to the objects and the purpose which the legislature had in view in enacting the provision and in the context of the setting in which it occurs. The literal construction would lead to manifestly unreasonable and absurd consequences. It is a well recognised rule of construction that a statutory provision must be so construed if possible that absurdity and mischief may be avoided. [115]

The Court observed further:

> The construction suggested on behalf of the Revenue would lead to a wholly unreasonable result which could never have been intended by the legislature. It was said that literalness in the interpretation of section 52(2) must be eschewed and the court should try to arrive at an interpretation which avoids the absurdity and the mischief and makes the provision rational and sensible, unless of course, the hands of the court are tied and it cannot find any escape from the tyranny of literal interpretation. It is said that it is now a well-settled rule of construction that where the plain literal interpretation of a statutory provision produces a manifestly absurd and unjust result which could never have been intended by the legislature, the court may modify the language used by the legislature or even do some violence' to it, so as to achieve the obvious intention of the legislature and produce a rational construction. [116]

In *State of Tamil Nadu* v. *Kodaikanal Motor Union (P) Ltd* the court observed thus:

> As Lord Denning has said, the judge has to perform the constructive task of finding the intention of Parliament, and he must supplement the written

---

[115] *K.P. Varghese* v. *Income Tax Officer, Ernakulam and Another* 1981 *op. cit.*
[116] Ibid.

word so as to give 'force and life' to the intention of the legislature. Primarily, it is always the duty to find out the intention of the Legislature and if it can be done without doing much violence to the language as we find it can be done in this case, though as we have noted that when the purpose was written in the scheme of the section "some violence" is permissible here we are of the opinion that the construction put by the assesses cannot be accepted and the contention urged on behalf of the Revenue in this case should be preferred. [117]

In *Luke* v. *Inland Revenue Commissioners* the court observed thus:

The courts must always seeks to find out the intention of the legislature. Though the courts must find out the intention of the statute from the language used, but language more often than not is an imperfect instrument of expression of human thought. As Lord Denning said, it would be idle to expect every statutory provision to be drafted with divine prescience and perfect clarity. A judge out of a dictionary cannot but remember that statutes must have some purpose or object whose imaginative discovery is judicial craftsmanship. We need not always cling to literalness and should endeavour to avoid an unjust or absurd result. We should not make a mockery of legislation. To make sense out of an unhappily worded provision, where the purpose is apparent to the judicial eye, "some" violence to language is permissible. [118]

In *Keshvji Ravij and Co. and others* v. *Commissioner of Income Tax*, the Supreme Court of India held that in a taxation statute where literal interpretation leads to a result not intended to sub serve the object of the legislation another construction in consonance with the object should be adopted. Referring to the words of Thomas M. Cooley[119] the court said:

Artificial and unduly latitudinarian rules of construction which, with their general tendency to "give the tax payer the breaks," are out of place where the legislation has a fiscal mission. Indeed taxation has ceased to be regarded as an "impertinent intrusion into the sacred right of private property" and it is now increasingly regarded as a potent fiscal tool of State

---

[117] 1986 (3) SCC 91.

[118] 1964(54) ITR 692 (IIL).

[119] Cooley, M. Law of Taxation vol. 2, He observed that "Artificial rules of construction have probably found more favour with the courts than they have ever deserved their application in legal controversies has oftentimes been pushed to an extreme which has defeated the plain and manifest purpose in enacting the laws. Penal laws have sometimes had all their meaning constructed away and in remedial laws, remedies have been found which the legislature never intended to give something akin to this has befallen the revenue laws..."

policy to strike the required balance required in a context of the felt needs of the times-between citizen's claim to enjoyment of his property on the one hand and the need for an equitable distribution of the burdens of the community to sustain social services and purposes on the other. [120]

---

[120] *Keshvji Ravij and Co. and Others* v. *Commissioner of Tax,* 1990(2) Ibid.

Chapter Two

Canons, Theories and Principles of Interpretation

Introduction

We shall here attempt examine the canons of interpretation such as Literal Rule, Mischief Rule, and the Golden Rules; the theories of interpretation such as Naturalist Theory, Positivist theory, sociological theory, Realists' theory, Textualist theory, and Critical Legal Movement; and the Principles of interpretation such as Internal aids, External aids and presumptions.

The Courts adopts the same principles of interpretation of statutes to also interpret the constitution. Thus the constitution is a special statute.

The Canons of Interpretation

The paramount guiding principle in interpretation of statutes is that the intention[1] of the legislature predominates. Every statute is to be expounded according to its manifest and expressed intention. It is not easy to discover the intention of the legislature. In *Salomon* v. *Salomon,* Lord Watson described the '*intention of the legislature*' as '*a common but slippery phrase*'.[2]

One basic method of discovering the intention of the legislature is to look at the words of the statute itself, and their plain meaning. The meaning of a statute or of a particular part of it is therefore to be sought for in the statute itself. It should not be found in presumed intention. Hence, the meaning to be ascribed to an expression must of necessity be restricted to the meaning given to it by the statute containing the expression. The meaning cannot be conditioned in the face of specialized statutorily provided definition[3]. To read into the provision of any document or legislation words or meanings that are not there more so when the words used are plain and unambiguous is to defeat the intention of the maker of the document.[4]

---

[1] Badaiki, A.D. Interpretation of Statutes. Tiken Publishers, Lagos p. 18, Lord Reid in *Westminster Bank Ltd.* v. *Zang* (1966) AG p. 182 at 222, *Utih* v. *Onoyivwe* (1991) I NWLR (pt. 166) p. 166.
[2] (1897) A.Gp.22 at 38. See also Badaiki ibid
[3] Badaiki Ibid.
[4] Badaiki, Ibid pp. 18-19.

To discover the intention of Parliament the court often adopts rules of Interpretation. The common rules of statutory interpretation, which dominate the historical perspective, are the Literal Rule, the Golden Rule and the Mischief Rule. In recent times, the court also adopted other rules of interpretation such as the beneficial construction, construing previous legislation, *ures magis valeat quam pareat rule, ejusdem generis rule,* internal aids and presumptions.

Literal Rule

According to the literal approach to statutory interpretation, effect is given to the "plain meaning" of the words even if the result would be absurd or contrary to the spirit of the legislation.[5]

Like the formalization of precedent in the nineteenth century, this approach according to Lord Tenterten CJ in Brandling v. Barrington could not:

> Forbear observing that...there is always danger in giving effect to what is called the equity of a statute, and that it is much better and safer to rely on and abide by the plain words, although the Legislature might possibly have provided for other cases had their attention been directed to them.[6]

The literal approach, or what is often called the Plain Meaning Approach, involves two stages. First of all, if the words in their immediate context (the actual section or subsection in question, or some would say, after reading the whole text) are found to be "plain" or " clear", you apply this meaning to the situation in question, without reference to purposes of the legislation or consequences of doing so. The second stage, if necessary, is that if the words are not "plain" or "clear", you must now interpret them using limited textual techniques of ascertaining legislative meaning and purpose.

So if the words are "precise and unambiguous" then you just formalistically apply the assigned plain meaning of the statute to the facts, and you should not care about or consider the justice or injustice or reasonableness of the result. As Lord Atkinson in Vacher's case puts it:

> If the language of a statute be plain, admitting of only one meaning, the legislature must be taken to have meant and intended what it has plainly expressed, and whatever it has in clear terms enacted must be enforced

---

[5] Badaiki ibid, Esau, A. The Basic Approaches to Statutory Interpretation, University of Manitoba, Faculty of Law, Legal Systems Course Materials Index
http://www.cc.umanitoba.ca/faculties/law/Courses/esau/legalsyetems/CM-5. htm.

[6] (1827) 6B & C 467. The case which is often cited as an authority for this approach is the Succex Peerage Case (1844) 11 Cl. & F. 85, 8 E.R 1034 where Chief Justice Tindal said "If the words of the statute are in themselves precise and unambiguous, then no more can be necessary than to expound those words in their natural and ordinary sense".

though it should lead to absurd or mischievous results. If the language of this subsection be not controlled by some of the other provisions of the statute, it must, since its language is plain and unambiguous, be enforced, and your lordships' House sitting judicially is not concerned with the question whether the policy it embodies is wise or unwise, or whether it leads to consequences just or unjust, beneficial or mischievous.[7]

The primary and basic concern of the courts in their interpretative function, as it relates to the construction of statutes, is that they ascertain the intention of the legislature or lawmaker from the words that are used in the statute. This starting point in every interpretation is the literal rule.[8] It demands that the words used in a statute must be interpreted according to their literal or plain meaning, especially where they appear to be unambiguous and logically complete. According to Tridal, CJ in the Sussex Peerage case,

> The only rule for the construction of Acts of Parliament is that they should be constructed according to the intent of the Parliament which passed the Act. If the words of the statutes are in themselves precise and unambiguous, then no more can be necessary than to expand those words in their natural and ordinary sense. The words themselves alone do, in such case, best declare the intention of the lawgiver.[9]

In applying the literal rule of interpretation, words are given their ordinary dictionary meanings or where they are trade or business terms, they are construed in the light of the particular trade or business to which they belong. So, where a word is alleged to have a technical meaning, evidence with regard to that meaning is unquestionably admissible and that meaning is generally preferred to any other information gleaned from other sources.

It is an accepted canon of interpretation that a statute must be construed *ut res magis valeat quam pareat*[10] so that the intention of the legislature may not be treated as if in vain or left to operate in the air.[11]

---

[7] (1913) AC 107 at 121 see also Professor Zander, in The Law Making Process said "The most rigorous expression of it was Lord Halsbury's Statement in Hilder v. Dextex (1902) AC 474 that the draftman of a statute was the worst person in the world to interpret a statute because he was unconsciously influenced by what he meant rather than by what he had said. He had himself drafted the statute in that case and refused to give judgment on the ground that he might not fully appreciate the literal, objective meaning of the words he had used .

[8] Niger Progress Ltd. v. North East Line Corporation (1989)3 NWLR. 68, Uhunmwangbo v. Okojie (1989)5 NWLR 471.

[9] (1844) H.cl. & Fin. p. 85 at 143.

[10] "It is better for a thing to have effect than to be made void" Earl Jowiff – The Dictionary of English Law 1959 at p. 1819 see p. 93 infra.

[11] Odger. Construction of Deeds and Statutes (5th ed.) 297, Udoh v. OHMB (1993) 7NWLR (pt. 304) 139 at 147, African Newspapers v. Federal Republic of Nigeria (1985)2 NWLR (pt. 6), Okumagba v. Egbe

Hence in *Chief Obafemi Awolowo* v. *Alhaji Shehu Shagari*[12] Eso JSC while interpreting the provision of Section 34 (A) (1) (C) of the Electoral Decree 1977, observed that in all cases of interpretation of statutes, the interpretation should be according to the intent of the statute, that is, statutes should be constructed *ut res magis valeat quam pareat,* so that the intentions of the legislature may not be treated as if vain or left to operate in the air.

Also in *Savannah Bank* v. *Ajilo,* Kolawole JSC in considering the effect of the Land Use Act, 1978 said:

> I approach the object by a declaration that the object of all interpretation is to discover the intention of the Legislature which is deducible from the language used. Once the meaning is clear, the court has to give effect to it...[13]

Furthermore, in *Animashaun* v. *Osuma*[14], following a consent judgment in 1934, the Appellant and the 2nd Respondent (co-lessors) executed a lease in respect of a landed property at Onitsha in favour of the 1st Respondent for a period of 125 years. Clause 5(2) of the said agreement provided that "*after the expiration or sooner determination of the lease to deliver up the said piece of land peaceably to the lessors.*

The lease expired in 1962, the 1st Respondent decided to renew the agreement with the 2nd Respondent alone. It was the contention of the Appellant that the 2nd Respondent could not without his consent renew the agreement with the 1st Respondent in view of clause 5 (2) thereof. On the interpretation of clause 5 (2), the 2nd Respondent urged the court to read 'lessor' for the words 'lessors' used in clause 5 (2). He did not give any reason as to why the plural should be construed as singular. In response Fatayi Williams JSC said:

> ... It is one of the established canons of construction that no gloss should be put on any of the words used. The function of the court is to ascertain what the parties meant by the words which they used...In ascertaining what the parties meant, the court must declare the meaning of what is written in the instrument, not what was intended to have been written...It

---

(1965) ALL NLR 62, Nafiu Rabiu v. State (1980)5-11 SC 130 at 148, Atuyeye v. Ashamu (1987) SC 58, Gonkow v. Ugochu (1993) 6SCNJ 263 at 274, Obomhense v. Ehanon (1993) 7SCNJ 473 at 497, Ejelikwe v. State (1993) 9 SCNJ 152 at 170.

[12] (1980) PLR. Vol. 1 p. 189, see also Atuyeye v. Ashamu supra at 353, African Newspapers v. Federal Republic of Nigeria supra at p. 662, Nokes v. Doncaster Amalgamated Collieries Ltd (1940) AC 1014 (PC) p. 1022.

[13] Savannah Bank v. Ajilo, op. cit. p. 26.

[14] (1972) 1 ALL NLR p. 363 see also Adejumo v. Governor (1972) 3 SC 45, Minister v. Akpagu (1964) 1 ALL NLR 208, Ayo v. Henshaw (1972) 5 SC 87, 370, Udoh v. Okudo (1979) 6 – 7 SC 32, Egbe v. Yusuf (1992) 6 SCNJ 263 at 370, Udoh v. Orthopedic Hospitals (1993) 7 SCNJ 436 at pp. 443 – 444, Solicitor-General Western Nigeria v. Adebanjo (1971) 1 ALL NLR 198.

must be remembered, however, that where same words, such as the word "lessors" in the lease (exhibit C), have for many years received a judicial construction, it is not reasonable to suppose that parties have contracted upon the belief that their words will be understood in what we will call the accepted sense, therefore in the instant case, the only interpretation that can be put on the provisions of clause 5 (2) of exhibit C, and which we now put, is that at the expiration of the term in the deed of lease exhibit C the land thereby demised should be delivered to the co-lessors.[15]

As stated earlier on, statutes are to be interpreted literally under the literal rule. Words used in statutes are to be construed in their usual grammatical sense. If the words are used in relation to a trade or business they are to be given their usual meaning in the trade or business. It is immaterial that hardship would result from literal interpretation.

The ordinary meaning of the words was applied in *Okotie-Eboh* v. *D.P.P.*[16] In the case, the court considered the use of the word '*actual*' and '*peaceable*' within Section 74 of the Criminal Code of Western Nigeria. The Federal Supreme Court held that the word '*actual*' means '*physical*', and the word '*peaceable*' contemplates entry other than by means of physical force. And a person in peaceable possession means a man in possession of land otherwise than by means of '*physical force*'. The court adopted the literal rule using *Stroud's Judicial Dictionary*, (3rd Edition) to get the meaning of '*actual*' and adopted ordinary meaning of '*possession*'. The words '*null and void*' used in Section 26 of the Land Use Act, as well as other sections thereof have been construed to bear their natural and ordinary meaning and no more, and when the sections are applicable to any case, involving their interpretation, they should be interpreted to be mandatory and not directory.[17]

In *Ogwuche* v. *Mba*[18] it was held that the word '*must*' used in Order 1 Rule 3 and Order 2 Rule 2 of the Fundamental Rights (Enforcement Procedure) Rules 1979 is a word of absolute obligation and occurs in a section which is concerned with fundamental principles of justice.

From the foregoing, the aim of the literal rule is that, effect must be given to the words used in the statutes by the lawmaker. However the literal rule has been subjected to judicial scrutiny where its application would deprive a citizen of his constitutional rights to personal liberty.

---

[15] Ibid. p. 376.
[16] (1962) 1 ALL NLR 352.
[17] Awojugbagbe Light Industry Ltd. v. Chinukwe (1995) 4 NWLR (Pt. 39) 379.
[18] (1994) 4 NWLR (pt. 336) 75.

In *Abioye* v. *Yakubu*,[19] the Supreme Court while interpreting the provision of Section 36 of the Land Use Act, 1978 on the customary tenants vis-a-vis customary owners, was of the view that although customary tenant has right to obtain a certificate of occupancy over land in which he is in possession and need for agricultural purposes but such right does not divest the customary owner of his ownership of the land or extinguishes same. The provision of Section 36 of the Act was strictly construed to preserve the right of the customary owner.

In *Bello* v. *Diocesan Synod of* Lagos,[20] the Supreme Court declared as oppressive the action of the Respondent a statutory body in abuse of compulsive powers for taking over the property of the Appellant.

The object of the principle is that where there is any ambiguity in the construction of a statute, that construction which preserves the individual's right to his property is to be preferred. Another implication of this approach to construction of statutes is the presumption that a person's right to his property will not be taken away without provision being made for adequate compensation.

The principle in Abioye v. Yakubu (*supra*) would not be applicable in a situation where the law enabling a compulsory forfeiture of a citizen's property also provides for certain methods or formalities for the forfeiture, the prescribed formalities must be complied with.[21]

In *Adegbenro* v. *Akintola*[22] the provision of Section 33 (10) of the Constitution of the then Western Nigeria which empowered the Governor to remove the Premier if '*it appears to him that the Premier no longer commands the support of a majority of the House of Assembly*' was interpreted by the court as vesting an absolute discretion in the Governor in the determination of whether or not the Premier still enjoyed majority support of the House of Assembly. It is submitted that such a decision ought to have been confirmed or determined on the floor of the House. In this case it was not.

In *Okumagba* v. *Egbe,* the court was to decide whether there had been a breach of Regulation 60b of the 1960 Parliamentary Regulations which read:

> Every person who before or during an election knowingly or recklessly publishes any false statement of the withdrawal of a candidate at such

---

[19] (1991) 6 SCNJ p. 69, see also Bello v. The Diocesan Synod of Lagos (1973) 1 ALL NLR (pt.) p. 247, Peenok Investment Ltd. v. Hotel Presidential (1982) NSCC 477, Din v. Federal Attorney-General (1988) 4 NWLR 147.

[20] (1973) 1 ALL NLR 176, see also Re: Bowman South Shields (Thames Street) Clearance Order (1932) 2 KB 621 at 633, Maxwell, Interpretation of Statutes (12th ed.) p. 258, East Riding Country Council v. Park Estate (Bridlington) Ltd. (1957) AC 223, Major of West Minister v. London and North Western Railway Company (1905) A.C. 426 at 430.

[21] Westminster Bank Ltd. v. Bverley Borough Council (1968) 3 WLR.

[22] (1991) 6 SCNJ p. 69, see also Bello v. The Diocesan Synod of Lagos (1973) 1 ALL NLR (pt. 1) 247, Penok Investment Ltd. v. Hotel Presidential (1982) NSCC 477, Din v. Federal Attorney-General (1988) 4 NWLR 147.

election for the purpose of promoting or procuring the election of another candidate shall be guilty of an offence.[23]

The appellant, having been rejected as a candidate, changed his symbol to that of N, another candidate, and falsely told his supporters that N had withdrawn his candidature, with the aim of inducing them to vote for N's symbol thereby swelling N's votes. The use of the phrase *another candidate* did not implicate the appellant. But the Magistrate felt that the appellant should not be allowed to evade the law by such an ingenious machination. In order to bring him within the ambit of the law, therefore, the phrase *another candidate* was interpreted to mean any candidate. On appeal to the Supreme Court, it was decided that the regulation contemplated lying to help a different candidate win. Since it did not cover the appellant's trickery, the inconvenience and apparent loophole would not justify derogation from the literal and grammatical interpretation of that phrase. In the words of Bairamian, JSC,

> It may be unfortunate that the draftsman used the words "another candidate", but they are the words which the legislature enacted, and admitted in view of those words the regulation contemplates the case of a lie that a candidate had withdrawn his name being published to help a different candidate to win ... Feeling that the appellant deserved to be punished, the Chief Magistrate replaced the words "another candidate" by the words "any candidate" and thus enabled himself to punish the appellant. In effect, he amended the regulation; but amendment is the function of the legislature, and the courts cannot fill a gap which comes to light by altering the words of a regulation to make it read in the way they think it should have been enacted.[24]

Also in *R. v. Bangaza*[25] the Federal Supreme Court attempted to interpret Section 319 (2) of the Criminal Code[26] which ran thus. '*where an offender who in the opinion of the court has not attained the age of seventeen years has been found guilty of murder, such offender shall not be sentenced to death but shall be ordered to be detained ...* Applying the literal rule, the court decided that the relevant period was the time of conviction. The effect of this was to punish a person for an offence committed when he was a juvenile, that is, retroactively. The provision was later amended by the Criminal Justice (Miscellaneous Provisions) Decree.[27]

---

[23] (1965) 1 ALL NLR 62.
[24] Ibid.
[25] (1960) 5 FSC 1.
[26] Cap 42 Laws of the Federation and Lagos, 1958.
[27] Decree No. 84 of 1966.

Assuming A and B both 15 years old, committed murder and their trial commenced when they were both 16years old. If A's trial was concluded before he attained the age of 17 and B's was prolonged until after he had attained 17, the chances are that, going by this interpretation, B could be sentenced to death while A might not, being under 17 at the time of conviction. The conviction or sentence could have been delayed with the intention of denying the juvenile the benefit of that section, leaving room for abuses by prosecuting officials. This anomalous situation was only rectified by a subsequent amending statute reiterating that the relevant age is the age at the time the offence was committed and not at the time of the conviction.[28]

Since words in themselves have no *'proper'* meaning, it is logical to look further a field into the context in which they have been used by the legislature. After all, a word is known by the company it keeps. A contextual approach to the interpretation of statutes is, therefore, necessary. An otherwise ambiguous section may be clearer when read in the context of the whole statute. But besides this, no extraneous matter should be introduced to a statute unless justified by the perceived intention of the legislature.[29]

The plain meaning approach cannot survive modern hermeneutic understandings of how we read texts. No words are simply "plain in themselves". The words are just scratches on a page. They are said to be plain only because the interpreter is deciding to treat them as such and giving a particular connotation to them, a connotation that the judge claims to be the connotation intended by the legislator. The judge in dividing up the words into plain categories or ambiguous categories is really doing so by supplying a context and assigning a connotation, even unconsciously, for the words.

The Literal rule has also been subjected to several criticisms:

i)   the most fundamental objection to the rule is that it is based on a false premise, namely that words have plain, ordinary meanings apart from their context;

ii) those who apply the literal approach often speaks of using the "dictionary meaning" of the words in question, but dictionaries normally provide a number of alternative meanings;

iii) the plain-meaning approach cannot be used for general words, which are obviously capable of bearing several meanings;

---

[28] See The Criminal Justice (Miscellaneous Provisions) Act 1966, Attorney-General of Ondo State v. Attorney-General of the Federation (1983) 2 SCNLR 269, Lawal v. Ollivant (1972) 3 SC 124, Animashaun v. Osuma (1973) ALL NLR 363, Teriola v. Williams (1982) INCLR 263 at 257 – 261, Isagbe v. Alagbe (1981) 2 NCLR 424 at pp. 427 – 428, Ogbuyiya v. Okudo (1979) 6 – 9 SC 53 at 74, Aya v. Henshaw (1972) 5 SC 87.

[29] See Attorney – General v. Prince Ernest Augustus of Hanoter (1957) A. C. 436, Krucblack v. Kruchlak (1958) 2 Q.B. 32.

iv) not infrequently the courts say that the meaning of the words is "plain" but then disagree as to their interpretations;

v) the plain-meaning theory may be acceptable outside the courtroom, since it could be true that a high proportion of statutory materials and other legal documents can in fact be interpreted without recourse to any mischief or golden rule. But in the court room there are by definition two parties, usually represented by counsel, arguing over the meaning of the relevant passage. It makes little sense to dispose of the issue between them by reference to the plain meaning when there are two meanings in issue.[30]

The literal rule makes too little allowance for the natural ambiguities of language, for the frailties of even the most skilled of draftmen and for the impossibility of fore-seeing future events. According to the English Law Report Commission of 1969:

> To place undue emphasis on the literal meaning of the words of a provision is to assume an unattainable perfection in draftsmanship; it presupposes that the draftsmen can always choose words to describe the situations intended to be covered by the provision which will leave no room for a difference of opinion as to their meaning. Such an approach ignores the limitations of language, which is not infrequently demonstrated even at the level of the House of Lords where Law Lords differ as to the so-called "plain meaning" of words.[31]

The literal approach is based on a narrow perception of the actual words used, to the exclusion of the surrounding circumstances that might explain what the words were actually intended to mean. The Report continues thus:

> A final criticism of the literal approach to interpretation is that it is defeatist and lazy. The judge gives up the attempt to understand the document at the first attempt. Instead of struggling to discover what it means, he simply adopts the most straightforward interpretation of the words in question – without regard to whether this interpretation makes sense in the particular context. It is not that the literal approach necessarily gives the wrong result but rather than the result is purely accidental. It is the intellectual equipment of deciding the case by tossing a coin. The literal interpretation in a particular case may in fact be the best and wisest of the various alternatives, but the literal approach is always wrong because it amounts to an abdication of responsibility by the judge. Instead of decisions being

---

[30] Esau, A. The Basic Approached to Statutory Interpretation, op. cit.

[31] The Interpretation of Statute, The Law Report Commission, 1969.

based on reason and principle, the literalist based his decision on one meaning arbitrarily preferred.[32]

Apart from the literal rule, all other rules of interpretation apply only when the wording of a statute is unclear.[33]

Mischief Rule

One of the most useful guides to interpretation of statutes is the mischief rule which considers the state of the law before the enactment, the defect which the legislation sets out to remedy or/and prevent, the remedy adopted by the legislature to cure the mischief and the true reason of the remedy. The duty of the court therefore is to adopt such interpretation that will enable the suppression of the mischief and to promote the remedy within the true intent of the legislation.[34]

This rule was first formulated in *Heydon's Case*[35] and forms the basis for the purposive approach enunciated by Lord Denning M.R in *Seaford Court Extates Ltd* v. *Asher*[36] where it was formulated that when a defect appears in an enactment, a judge cannot simply fold his hands and blame the draftsman. He must set to work in the constructive task of finding the intention of parliament, and he must do this not only from the language of the statute but also from a consideration of the social conditions which gave rise to it, and of the mischief which it was supposed to remedy.

This approach finds its historical roots way back prior to the formalist period, just as the more flexible conventions of precedent may be seen as being as much a return to the past as they are a modern phenomena. The classic statement of the mischief rule is that given by the Barons of the Court of Exchequer in Heydon's case where it was laid down as follows:

> "That for the sure and true interpretation of all statutes in general (be they penal or beneficial, restrictive or enlarging the common law) four things are to be discerned and considered; 1[st.] What was the common law before the making of the Act; 2[nd.] What was the mischief and defect for which the common law did not provide, 3rd What remedy the Parliament hath resolved and appointed to cure the defect of the common law and 4th The true

---

[32] Ibid. at p. 54.

[33] Edger, S.G.G. Craies on Statute Law London. 1971 p. 10, Badaiki, op. cit. p. 26.

[34] *(1963) AC 614, Liversidge v. Anderson (1942) 1 AC 206,* see also Oba, A. A. Judicial Attitude to Notice of Revocation under the Land Use Act Revisited, Journal of Commercial Private and Property Law, 1999 Vol. 2.

[35] (1984) 3 Cal. Rep. 78, 76 ER. 638, IBWA v. Imano (Nig.) Ltd (1988) 2 NWLR (pt. 85) 633, Idehen v. Idehen (1991) 7 SCNJ 222 at 243 Akerele v. IGP (1955) 2 NLR 37.

[36] (1949) 2 KB 481.

reason of the remedy; and then the office of all the Judges is always to make such construction as shall suppress the mischief, and advance the remedy, and to suppress subtle inventions and evasions for continuance of the mischief, and *pro-privato commodo,* and to add force and life to the cure and remedy, according to the true intent of the makers of the Act, *pro bono publico.*[37]

The Approach in Heydon's case, emphasizing as it does the need to find the purpose or object or spirit of the statute and to advance that object in interpretation, nevertheless is expressed in the somewhat archaic language reflecting the view that statutes were a mere appendix to the common law. Today, the tables are reversed, and common law is increasingly being swallowed up by an orgy of legislation. Thus, the modern rule in Heydon's case might be expressed better as to find four points, this way:

(i) what was the state of the law, if any, on the relevant subject matter before the legislation in question was passed?;

(ii) what was the social, political, economic or other problem that gave rise to the need for the statute?;

(iii) what was the solution that was to be embodied in the statute?;

(iv) what was the purpose aimed at by this solution?

The court, in applying the mischief rule, should therefore be guided by the following considerations:

(a) what was the law before the statute was passed?;

(b) what was the mischief for which the law did not provide?;

(c) what remedy did the legislature resolve and appoint to cure the mischief?;

(d) what was the true reason for the remedy?[38]

In *Akere* v. *Inspector-General of Police*[39], Ademola, J., in interpreting the word *accused as used in Section 120b of the Criminal* Code noted that the short history behind that section of the code was to prohibit indiscriminate accusation of witchcraft and to stop the practice of trial by ordeal and the like. In view of this mischief, he interpreted the section to advance only the appropriate remedy thereby holding that the section could not have contemplated a formal accusation under oath. The rule is not appropriate in those cases where the words of a

---

[37] In Coke's Institutes, similar effect was given thus "Equity is a construction made by the judges, that cases out of the letter of a statute, yet being within the same mischief, or course of the making of the same, shall be within the same remedy that the statute provideth; and the reason hereof is, for that the law-makers could not possibly set down all cases in express terms.

[38] Per Lindley, M. R. in Re: Mayfair Property and Co. (1898)2 Ch. 28 at 35 and approved in Balogun v. Salami (1963) 1ALL NLR 129 see also Kolawole v. Albelto (1989)1 NWLR 382 at 416, Onyeanusi v. Miscellaneous Offences Tribunal (2002) 41 WRN 49 SC 76

[39] (1995) 21 NLR 37.

statute, looked at as a whole are clear, devoid of any ambiguity. In such cases no extrinsic aid would be needed[40].

In *Emelogu* v. *The* State,[41] the court was called upon to ascertain the intention of the legislature in the Repeal and Modification of Certain Decree, 1979[42]. That Decree, *inter alia*, amended the Robbery and Firearms (Special Provisions) Decree, 1970[43], by repealing Section 6 of the 1970 statute, which gave the State Attorney – General or an appropriate officer in the Ministry the power to prosecute under it. The Supreme Court, in determining the *locus standi* of the State Attorney – General in the instant case, relied on the history behind the 1979 Decree. As Nnaemeka-Agu, JSC, puts it:

> Unless I put legislation on armed robbery in their proper historical setting ... I cannot reach a correct decision in the matter...I feel entitled to call in aid the historical background of the enactment in order to correctly comprehend the true import thereof.[44]

In *Savanna Bank* v. *Ajilo*[45] the Appellant contended that Section 32 (2) of the Land Use Act, 1978 envisaged two rights in respect of developed land in an urban area, the first granted by the Military Governor after the commencement of the Act and subject to all the provisions of the Act, and the second by the operation of the law before the Act came into effect, and not within the control and management of the Governor was held not to conform with the purpose of the Act which was to effectively harmonize the land use system in the country and correct the mischief of the past where there were broadly two different and distinct land systems in the North and South Nigeria. Karibi Whyte JSC held that,

> The purpose of the provision of Section 34(2) is to bring lands holding in existence before the creation of the Land Use Act in line with the Act for uniform control and management, hence the holders of such title are to be deemed to be holders of statutory right of occupancy issued by the Military Governor. Thus, the contention that the Act envisaged two categories of rights holders...is clearly wrong and inconsistent with the express words of the Act, and the mischief intended to prevent.[46]

The rule has also been applied in hire-purchase transaction regulated by the Hire-Purchase Act.[47] In *Omoijuanfo* v. *Nigerian Technical Company Limited*[48]

---

[40] Ugu v. Tabi (1997) 7 NWLR 368.
[41] (1988) 2 NWLR (pt.78).
[42] Decree No. 105 of 1979.
[43] Decree No 47 of 1970.
[44] Emelogu v. The State, supra.
[45] (1987) NWLR (pt. 57) 421.
[46] ibid at p. 26.
[47] Cap 168, Laws of the Federation of Nigeria, 1990.

after the hirer has made instalmental payments totalling over three fifths of the hire-purchase price of the hired vehicle under the hire-purchase agreement between the parties, he defaulted with three consecutive instalments. The owners repossessed the vehicle under Section 9 of the Hire-Purchase Act 1965 pursuant to sub-section (5) thereof, which was inserted by the Hire-Purchase (Amendment) Decree 1970[49]. The hirer sued for money heard and received, contending that as he had already paid three fifths of the hire-purchase price, the owners could not lawfully repossess. It was held that the mischief aimed at by the amending Decree is the considerable hardship worked by Section 9 of the Principal Act on the owner of a hired vehicle, who, as the law then stood, was unable to repossess the vehicle from a defaulting hirer until he could bring an application to court pursuant to the provisions of sub-section (1) of Section 9 of the Principal Act. Accordingly, the Defendants/Respondents were entitled to repossess the hired vehicle.

In Interpreting the Registration of Titles Act, the mischief rule was applied in *Balogun* v. Salami.[50] There it was held that Section 10 (3) of the Act was intended to provide a remedy for the well-known bane attendant on dealings with family land. Also in *Idehen* v. *Idehen*[51] the Supreme Court delved into the history of the Wills Act in Nigeria in interpreting Section 3 (1) of the Wills Law of the then Bendel State and held inter alia that it is permitted to consider the mischief which the statute was designed to prevent.

In *Abioye* v. Yakubu,[52] the Supreme Court examined the Land Tenure Law that prevailed in the country before the Act, the relationship between the customary landowner and his customary tenant before the Act came into effect and the mischief that the Act was designed to correct in this respect. It was held that although the Land Use Act has removed the radical title in land from individual Nigerian and vested the land in the Military Governor of each state in trust for the use and benefit of all Nigerians, the Act never sought to disturb existing relationships or extinguish the incidents of customary ownership of land; the Act preserved the customary rights of both the customary landlord and customary tenant in respect of land used for agricultural purposes by its provisions in Section 36 (1-4) relating to the rights of occupier and holder. It has not robbed the holder of his right to tributes from the occupier of land used for agricultural purposes.

---

[48] (1976) 1 ALL NLR 294, Salami v. Balogun (1963) 1 ALL NLR 128.
[49] Decree No. 3 of 1965.
[50] (1963) 1 ALL NLR 294.
[51] (1991) 6 NWLR (pt. 198) 382.
[52] (1991) 5 NWLR (pt. 190) 130.

Also in *Akerele* v. *IGP*[53] the court applied the mischief rule in construing the word 'accuse' in Section 210 (b) of the Criminal Code. The court viewed the mischief sought to be prohibited by parliament in the '*indiscriminate accusations of witchcraft and to stop the practice of trial by ordeal and the like by making them punishable*'. The court therefore rejected the argument that the word '*accuse*' meant making a formal accusation by swearing to an information under oath.

In *Ifezue* v. *Mbadugha*[54] the Supreme Court while considering the effect of Section 258 (1) of the 1979 Constitution which made it mandatory for the court to deliver its judgment within three months after the close of evidence and final address, were of the view that the mischief aimed at by the said Section 258 (1) was clearly against delays in the delivery of judgments after conclusion of hearing of cases, that some judges form the habit of delaying judgments leading to a deprivation by them of the advantage of forming fair impressions of the witness and evaluation of evidence.

The application of the mischief rule as applied in the case of *Ifezue* v. *Mbadugha*[55] may instead of being a vehicle for expeditious administration, be a shackle to the administration of justice and hinder its speed with the consequential inconveniences and inflation in the cost of litigation as a result of a misfortune of the court itself to which the parties have nothing to do, and which they cannot control. To correct this injustice, the legislature amended the said provision by enacting further sub-sections 4 and 5, the effect of which was to save judgments delivered outside the time limit, provided there was no substantial miscarriage of justice.[56]

The mischief rule is a vast improvement over the literal rule in that it acknowledges that we give meaning to words by supplying the context and that rules in statutory form are more than ends in themselves. Rules are a means to an end. However, the use of the mischief rule has difficulties associated with it.

One difficulty that is often raised deals with the concept of "legislative intent". Much of the criticism of the mischief rule results from a confusion over what we mean by legislative intent. Some commentators speak of the intention of the legislature; others of the intention of the legislation. Some commentators speak of legislative intent as backward looking – what was in the minds of individual lawmakers, or collectively in the minds of lawmakers, when the legislation was passed? Other commentators look at intent as forward looking –

---

[53] (1955) 21 NLR 37.

[54] (1984) 1 ALL NLR p. 256, see also Odi v. Osafile (1985) 1 ALL NLR p. 20, Ariori v. Muraimo Elemo (1983) 1 SC 13.

[55] Ibid.

[56] See Third Schedule Constitution (Suspension and Modification) (Amendment) Decree No 17 of 1985, see also Ojokolobov. Alamu (1987) NWLR (pt. 61) p. 377.

what is the aim of the legislation? Some commentators talk about intention as to meaning – that is, what specifically did the legislators or the draftsperson or the party proposing the legislation think a particular word or phrase meant? Other commentators speak about intention as to goal-what did the lawmaker hope to achieve in the world by this legislation?

The mischief rule does not require us to believe that "legislative intent" can be found and "exists" in some of the senses that this term is used. Rather the point could be made that the judiciary should be trying to establish what the goal of the legislation is. In finding evidence for or against various proposed goals, the court might turn to materials associated with "legislative intent" as used in the other senses, but these are not definitive in and of themselves. Rather than trying to get into the head of some mythic legislature as a corporate body to find specific answers to what meaning to give a phrase, we should rather be thinking about using evidence from the context of the making of the legislation to help us establish what the legislation was meant to accomplish.

The second problem of the mischief rule is how much constraint is placed on any interpretation by the text itself. Thus once we move to a much wider contextual search for purpose, we give too little consideration to the text itself.

The third problem is how to interpret the so called purpose? One of the limitations in the use of the purposive approach has been the judicial unwillingness to expand the use of so-called "extrinsic materials" like records of legislative debate etc.

The fourth problem relates to the overall justification of the mischief rule in terms of the role of the judiciary. The judge simply advance his or her idiosyncratic and undemocratic views under the guise of "purpose".[57] The pitfall of the mischief rule are elaborated in Twining and Myers, thus:

> From the standpoint of a rule-maker the concept of purpose is indispensable: it is pointless to make purposeless rules. We have also seen that people are often called unto interpret rules that appear to them to have no discernible purpose or to have outlived their original purpose or to be purposeless for some other reason; and that there is an approach that favours treating rules as things in themselves, without regard to, perhaps even in spite of, their purposes, however clear and attractive these may be. Thus, notions such as purpose and goal are not an absolutely essential precondition for interpreting a given rule. Yet it is also a widely held view, which we share, that careful examination of the purpose(s) of a rule is one of the most important aids to resolving doubts in interpretation.

---

[57] Esau, A. The Basic Approaches to Statutory Interpretation, University of Manitoba, Faculty of Law, Legal Systems Course Materials Index
http://www.cc.umanitoba.ca/faculties/law/courses/esau/legalsystemu/CM-5 htm.

Golden Rule

The golden rule was formulated in the case of *Beck* v. *Smith*[58] but was also reiterated in Gray v. Pearson by Lord *Wensleydale*[59] thus:

> ... the grammatical and ordinary sense of the words is to be adhered to unless that would lead to some absurdity or some repugnance or inconsistency with the rest of the instrument in which case the grammatical and ordinary sense of the word may be modified, so as to narrow the absurdity and inconsistency, but no further[60].

The golden rule can only be invoked when there is internal disharmony in the statute. The golden rule allows for a departure from the literal rule when the application of the statutory words in the ordinary sense would be repugnant to or inconsistent with some of the other provisions in the statute or even when it would lead to what the court considers to be an absurdity. The usual consequence of applying the golden rule is that words, which are in the statute, are ignored or words, which are not there, are read in[61].

The golden rule seems to apply only in three types of cases.

(a)   Where alternative interpretations are possible, the court should choose the one that will avoid absurdity.

(b)   A statutory provision may be amended by interpretation to prevent it being unintelligible, totally unreasonable, unworkable, or totally irreconcilable with the rest of the statute[62]. So in the clear case "and" may be read as "or", and vice versa. The words of the statute are amended because it cannot possibly be believed that parliament meant what it said.

(c)   A statute may be read against the background of presumptions and general legal principles, which may be used both to qualify it and to extend it beyond its words, examples of general principles impliedly qualifying the interpretation of statutory words are the principle that a person cannot bring an action based on his own wrong[63], and that a police officer cannot claim special rights and privileges unless he is acting in the execution of his duty.[64]

Accordingly, where the words to be interpreted are ambiguous, it is the court's duty to interpret the words in such a manner as to avoid absurdity.

---

[58] 50 ER724, see also Adler v. George (1964)2B.7.

59 (1964) 6 HCL 106.

[60] Ibid. p. 108.

[61] Awolowo v. Federal Minister of Internal Affairs (1962) 11R p. 177, Sheffield v. Ratchliff (1616) Hob. 334 at 346.

[62] Rupert C. Statutory Interpretation 84 -98.

[63] See R. v. Chief National Insurance Commr, ex parte O' Cannor (1981) 2 WLR 412, R v. Home Secretary, ex parte Puttick.

[64] Morris v. Beardmore (1981) AC 446, see also Glanville, W. The Meaning of Literal Interpretation 11 Butterworth Publication, Thursday Nov. 12 Vol. 131 No. 6027, 1981 p. 1150.

In *R.* v. Princewell,[65] the court held that the word "*marries*" in Section 370 of the Criminal Code was not to be construed as contracting a valid marriage but as going through a form of marriage known to or recognized by the law. To hold otherwise would have negated the intention of the legislature.[66] By Section 370 of the Criminal Code, the offence of bigamy is committed where any person, having a husband or wife, marries in circumstances where such marriage is void by reason of its taking place during the life of such husband or wife. But strictly speaking, a married person cannot under English Law marry again, since a marriage can only be conducted between two parties who are unmarried.[67] The literal meaning of the word 'marries', therefore, becomes an absurdity. To avoid this result, the court in *R.* v *Princewell*[68] rightly read the expression to mean going through the form of marriage.[69]

Similarly, where it is impossible to comply with the provisions of a statute when they are construed literally, the general rule is that the court would not adopt the literal interpretation[70]. The court would interpret the provisions in such a way as to avoid the absurdity and at the same time reflect the intention of the legislature.[71]

In applying the Golden Rule, the courts sometimes construe the word 'or' as 'and' in such a way as to avoid absurdity.[72] It must be emphasized, however, that the primary object of the court in adopting such construction is to give effect to the intention of the legislature. Although the interpretation enactments contain a presumption that the word "or" is to be construed as a disjunctive word, that presumption is subject to any contrary intention in the statute being interpreted.[73]

The principle is applicable only where the meaning of the statutory provision is ambiguous. In *Balogun* v. Salami,[74] the court considered the history of the Registration of Titles Act[75] and said that the ban on dealings in family land was sale of such land by some members of the family followed by repudiation of transaction by other members of the family on grounds of absence of the family's

---

[65] (1963) 2 ALL NLR 31.
[66] See also Akinosho v. Enigbokan (1955) 21 NLR 88.
[67] See Hyde v. Hyde (1966) L. R 1 P & D 130.
[68] R. v. Princewell supra.
[69] See also R. v. Allen (1872) 26 LR 644.
[70] Commissioner of Police v. Okoli (1966) NNLR 1 at p. 4.
[71] Ibid. See also Awe v. Alabi (1970) 2 ALL NLR 16.
[72] Ejor v. I.G.P. (1963) 1 ALL NLR 250, R v. Eze (1950) 19 NLR 110.
[73] See e.g. Interpretation Act 1964 No 1 of 1964, SS1 and 18(3), Jammal Steel Structures Ltd. v. Africac Continental Bank Ltd. (1973) 1 ALL NLR 208, 11 SC 77.
[74] (1963) I ALL NLR 129, see also Jammal Steel Structures Ltd v. African Continental Bank Ltd. supra at 208.
[75] Federation and Lagos Laws 1958, cap. 181.

consent. The court said that the purpose of the Act was to remove the ban. It then interpreted the provision in the light of this history.

In *Akerele* v. *I.G.P.*,[76] the court had to interpret the word 'accuse' in Section 210 (b) of the Criminal Code. Rejecting the argument that the word meant making a formal accusation by swearing to an information under oath, Ademola J. (as he then was) said:

> It appears to me the short history behind this chapter of the code is to prohibit indiscriminate accusations of witchcraft and to stop the practice of trial by ordeal and the like by making them punishable.

The Golden Rule is a canon of construction which is yet another exception to the literal rule. Where literal rule does not meet the purpose of statute for any reason, such as absurdity, inconsistency or ambiguity, the courts are obliged to take a second step of resorting to another well-known canon of interpretation.[77] Thus, the literal rule will be modified for the purpose of bringing out the purpose of the provision that is being construed. The use of 'shall' to sometimes mean 'may' and vice versa illustrates this position.[78] In this context also, the word 'or' can be construed as a conjunctive word and 'and' construed as a disjunctive word[79]. The word 'void' can in certain statute be interpreted to mean voidable.[80]

In *Alhaji Awe* v. *Afolabi*[81], the word 'same' had to be interpreted within the provision of Section 47 of the Magistrates' Court (Lagos) Ordinance. It provides:

> A Magistrate, at the same time or any subsequent sitting of the court, may set aside any judgment or order given or made against any party in the absence of such party, and the execution thereupon, such terms, if any, as he may think just, on application and on sufficient cause shown to him for that purpose.

The court held that the words 'at the same or in any subsequent sitting of the court' or a Magistrate in order to make sense can only have reference to the 'same sitting' or 'subsequent sitting' of the magistrate or court that gave judgment. Any other interpretation, it was pointed out would not fit in the word 'same'.

In *The Council of The University of Ibadan* v. *N.K.* Adamolekun,[82] The Supreme Court had to determine whether an Edict made by Military Governor of

---

[76] (1955) 21 NLR 37.
[77] Okeke v. A.G. Anambra State (1992) I NWLR (pt. 215) 164, Ogwuche v. Mba (1994) 4 NWLR (pt. 336) 75, COP v. Obasi (1976) I ALL NWLR 28.
[78] Queen Ex Parte (1961) I ALL NLR 29.
[79] Tarka v. DPP. (1961) I ALL NLR 355 it was held that the word "or" which appears at the end of each of paragraph (A) and (B) of S. 341 (2) CPC should be read conjunctively, R. v. Eze 19 NLR interpreting S.2 Criminal Procedure Ordinance, the word "and" in the section was construed disjunctively.
[80] Kolawole v. Alberto (1989) INWLR (pt.98) 382.
[81] (1970) I ALL NLR 351.
[82] (1967) I ALL NLR 225.

Western Nigeria could be declared void by the court. By virtue of Section 3(4) of the Constitution (Suspension and Modification) Decree 1966[83] where an Edict was void to the extent of the inconsistency. But Section 6 of the same Decree provided that *"No question as to the validity of this Decree or any Edict shall be entertained by any court of law in Nigeria'.* It was the contention of the respondent counsel that even if the Edict in question was void, the court could not declare it void in line with Section 6 of the decree. The court in order to resolve the absurdity declared the said Edict void and inconsistent with the Constitution.

A literal interpretation would have precluded the court from questioning the validity of the edict but the application of the golden rule enabled the court to arrogate to itself implied powers to enquire into the validity of an edict when it was found to be in conflict with the provisions of the Decree.[84]

Also in *Awolowo* v. *Federal Minister of Internal* Affiars,[85] *the court* in interpreting Section 21(5) (c) of the 1960 Constitution which provided that *'an accused person is entitled to defend himself in person or by legal representatives of his own choice ... ',* held that under the provision, the legal representative chosen if outside Nigeria must be a person who could enter Nigeria as of right.

The golden rule allows the court to avoid the rigours of the literal rule, by making it possible for the judge to determine first that certain words are unclear in the context or that injustice or absurdity is manifested. However, this rule has a restricted sphere of operation because it applies only in cases of obvious slips and inconsistencies.[86]

Where the application of the plain grammatical interpretation of a particular provision will produce absurd, inconsistent or ambiguous results, the court may, instead, apply the words with a secondary meaning that they are capable of bearing. The assumption is that the legislature could not have intended an absurd result.

The rule cannot be invoked for every imaginable inconvenience or absurdity. It envisages the presence of some internal disharmony or logical inconsistency either between parts of the same statute or between a statute and some other principle of law. Any other form of inconvenience resulting from other circumstances, e.g. that the party concerned would thereby be under a burden or

---

[83] Decree No. 1 of 1966.

[84] Olagbiye, T. *'Justice and Judicial Interpretation of Statute'',* in Omotola, J.A. On Issues in Nigerian Law. The Caxton Press (West Africa) Ltd., Ibadan, 1991 p. 17, see also Badaiki, A.D. Interpretation of Statutes. Tiken Publishers 1996 pp. 1-2, Glanville, W. "Language and the Law" (1945) 6 LQR 71, 179, 293, 384, (1946) 62 LQR 381.

[85] (1966) LLR 177, see also Awolowo v. Sarki (1966) INLR178.

[86] Olagbaiye op. cit. p. 23.

suffer any personal discomfort, would not suffice.[87] The usual implication of the application of this rule is that words in the statute are ignored or those not there are read into it. The court is always careful to ensure that where the words are plain and clear, than they should bear their natural signification or import, unless a contradiction or inconsistency would arise therein by reason of some subsequent clause from whence it might be inferred that the intention of the law-makers was otherwise.[88] In *Re* Signsworth,[89] a son who had murdered his mother was disallowed from succeeding to the estate of the deceased as 'the issue' in order to ensure that he did not profit from his crime. The word 'and' as used in Section 7 of the English Official Secrets Act, 1911, had been taken to mean 'or' to make sense of the section[90] while 'owner or master' was interpreted conjunctively, to render both the owner and master liable under the Oil in Navigable Waters Act, 1955[91].

In *R*. v. Eze,[92] the court construed the disjunctive article 'or' immediately before clause (c) in Section 2 of the Criminal Procedure Act conjunctively as 'and' to make sense of the definition of an indictable offence.[93] This interpretation was also adopted by the Supreme Court in *Ejor* v. *Inspector–General of Police*[94] and given legislative endorsement by a subsequent amendment of the offending section[95].

The Golden Rule can be criticized:

i)   it suffers from the same difficulties as the literal approach via lack of wider contextual understandings of "meanings";

ii)   The idea of 'absurdity' covers only a very few cases. Most cases involve situations where difficult choices have to be made between several firmly plausible arguments, not situations where the words lead to obvious absurdities;

iii)   The use of the "absurdity" safety value can be very erratic.[96]

---

[87] Awolowo v. Shagari supra.

[88] Mitchell v. Torrup (1766) Park 277 per Perk, C.B.

[89] (1935) Ch. 89.

[90] Re Lockwood (1958) Ch. 231.

[91] *R*. v. *Federal Stream Navigation Co. Ltd. (1974) IWLR 505, (1974) 2 All ER 97.*

[92] (1950) 19 NLR 110.

[93] But see Onyemachi v. Okeugo (1958) 2 ER NLR 29 for a contrary decision.

[94] (1963) INLR 250.

[95] See Section 2 of the Criminal Procedure (Amendment) Act 1966.

[96] Willis Statute Interpretation in a Nutshell (1938) 16 C.B. Rev. 1 pp. 13-14 said "What is an "absurdity"? When is the result of a particular interpretation so "absurd" that a court will feel justified in departing form a "plain meaning"? These is the difficulty "Absurdity" is a concept no less vague and indefinite than plain meaning. You cannot reconcile the cases upon it. It is infinitely more susceptible to the influence of personal prejudice. The result is that in ultimate analysis the "golden rule" does allow a court to make quite openly exceptions which are based not on the social policy behind the Act, not even on the total

Beneficial Construction

The beneficial construction is often adopted when the court is faced with a choice between a wide meaning which carries out what appears to have been the object of the legislature more fully and a narrow meaning which carries it out less fully or not at all.[97]

In *Rabiu* v. *State*, Udoma JSC said:

> In my view, this court should whenever possible and in response to the demands of justice, lean to the broader interpretation unless there is something in the text or in the rest of the constitution to indicate that the narrow interpretation will best carry out the objects and purposes of the constitution ... I do not conceive it to be the duty of this court to construe any of the provisions of the constitution as to defeat the obvious end the constitution was designed to serve where another construction equally in accord and consistent with the words and sense of such provisions will serve to enforce and protect such ends.[98]

In *Savanna Bank of Nigeria Limited* v. *Ajilo*[99] the Supreme Court in their interpretation of Section 34 (2) of the Land Use Act, 1978, which was deemed to give the owner of a developed land in an urban area prior to the commencement of the Decree a right to a Statutory Right of Occupancy outside the Act, were of the view that the said Section 34 (2) is narrow and restrictive in view of the provisions of Sections 1, 2, 5, 9, 34 (2) and 39 of the same Decree which vested the control and management of all lands in the Governor of that state and also provides for the requirements to obtain an 'actual' certificate of occupation in respect of any part thereof.

Construing Previous Legislation

The principle on which a previous legislation may be relevant to the interpretation of later legislation is based on two factors.

First, the course which legislation on a particular point has followed often provides an indication as to how the present statute should be interpreted. It is in such cases presumed that the interpretation in the former must have been known to those who drafted the latter.

---

effect of the words used by the legislature, but purely on the social and political views of the man who happen to be sitting on the case..."
[97] Shannon Real Properties Ltd. v. De St. Michael (1924) AC 185.
[98] (1980) 8-11 SC p. 130.

[99] *Savanna Bank* v. *Ajilo supra.*

Secondly, it is accepted that light may be thrown on the meaning of a phrase or word in a statute under construction by reference to a similar phrase or word in an earlier statute dealing with the same or cognate subject matter.

In *Ifezue* v. *Mbadugha*,[100] the Supreme Court while giving effect to Section 258 (1) of the 1979 Constitution which made it mandatory for a judge to deliver its judgment within three months after the close of evidence and final address made references to Section 21 (1) of the 1960 Constitution and Section 22 (1) of the 1963 Constitution which provide for a fair hearing within a reasonable time by a court as too wide to cure the mischief resulting from the delay in the delivery of judgments by the courts and that the object of the maker of the 1979 Constitution was to find solution to the tenuous and tortuous judicial interpretation of the phrase *'within a reasonable time'*.

Reliance on previous legislation may be injurious in the dispensation of justice especially where the two legislation have different socio-cultural background. In *Auqua Eyo Okon* v. *The State*[101], the Supreme Court rejected the view of the Respondent that Section 38 (1) of the (English) Children and Young Persons Act, 1993 is the same with Section 182 (1) of the Nigerian Evidence Act[102] on the unsworn and uncorroborated evidence of a child. Nnaemeka – Agu, JSC said:

> In my judgment this line of reasoning clearly exposes the danger of placing undue reliance upon foreign decisions, especially when, as in the instant case they are based on a legislation differently worded from our own which is in point in a case in hand...Nigerian Courts are obligated to give a Nigerian Legislation its natural and ordinary meaning, taking into account our own sociological circumstances as well as other factors which form the background of our local legislation in question. A 'copy-cat' transposition of an English decision may in some circumstances turn out to be inimical to justice in our own courts[103].

Other Canons of Interpretation

It is a general principle that a statute is to be construed in such a manner as not to command doing what is impossible[104] – *Lex non cogit ad impossibilia*[105]. Other rules of Interpretation of statutes are ut res *magis valeat quam pareat* rule and ejusdem generis rule.

---

[100] *Ifezue* v. *Mbadugha supra.*
[101] *(*1988) I ALL NLR p. 173.
[102] Cap. 62, Laws of the Federation, 1958.
[103] Asugua Eyo Okon v. The State supra.
[104] COP v. Okoli (1966) NNLR 1.
[105] i.e. the law does not compel the doing of impossibilities.

The ut res magis valeat quam pareat rule

In principle, where a provision is reasonably susceptible of two interpretations and it is found that by one interpretation the provision would be valid and by the other it would be invalid, the provision ought to be construed in such a manner as to make it valid, in other words the statute is to be construed *ut res magis valeat quam pareat*[106]. Provisions being interpreted should not be read in isolation[107]. Thus, words are to be construed in their context and any section or part there of which is being interpreted must be read as whole[108]. In general, a statute must be read as a whole[109]. Sometimes, it is only by doing so that the court can discover from the statute the intention of the legislature. Where a section being interpreted is not clear, all relevant sections must be considered[110]. Where a provision is ambiguous, earlier statutes *in pari materia*[111] may be referred to in interpreting it[112].

The Ejusdem Generis Rule

This is the rule of construction of documents that where general words used after the enumerations of particulars forming a category are deemed to refer only to persons, words, things, articles etc. coming within that category. For example the English Sunday Observance Act, 1677, enacts that no tradesman, artificer, workman, labourer, "or any other person whatsoever," shall carry out his ordinary calling on Sunday. Here, the phrase 'any other person whatsoever" was held to be confined to those callings of the same kind as those specified by the preceding words so as not to include an estate agent.[113]

Similarly, it will not include lawyers, bankers, doctors etc. For instance, in *Nasr* v. Buari,[114] the question before the court was whether premises used partly as living accommodation and partly as a night club were premises within the meaning of Section 1 (1) of the Rent Control (Lagos) Amendment Act 1965[115]. The Act defined *'premises'* as *'a building of any description occupied or used by persons for living or sleeping or other lawful purposes, as the case may be, whether or not at any time it is also occupied or used under any tenancy as a shop or a store …"*. The premises in question were not used as a shop or store'. The court had to determine whether *'other lawful purposes'* meant any lawful

---

[106] i.e. that it may rather have effect than be destroyed, see Osho v. Philips (1972) I ALL NLR 276.
[107] Council of the University of Ibadan v. Adamalekun (1967) I ALL NLR 213.
[108] See Nabhan v. Nabhan (1967) 1 ALL NLR 47 at 54.
[109] Ibid.
[110] Akintola v. Aderemi (1962) I ALL NLR 442.
[111] i.e. upon the same matter.
[112] Nasr v. Bouari (1969) I ALL NLR 37 at 55.
[113] Gregory v. Fearn (1953) 1 W.L.R. 974.
[114] (1969) I ALL NLR 35, see also Jammal Steel Structures Ltd v. African Continental Bank Ltd. (1973) I ALL NLR 208, (1973) II SC 7.
[115] No. x of 1965.

purposes other than premises for living or sleeping, or only any lawful purposes of the class of living or sleeping. The court held that '*other unlawful purposes*' must be confined in meaning to purpose similar to living or sleeping. Accordingly, it was held that premises used partly as a night club were not premises within the meaning of the provision notwithstanding the fact they were also partly used for living[116]. The courts have stated that the doctrine should be applied with caution[117]. It should be applied only where the application would be consistent with the intention of the legislature[118]. Where the history and structure of the statute strongly indicate that the intention of the legislature would be given effect only by applying the doctrine, the doctrine ought to be applied[119].

In *Palmer* v. *Snow*[120], the court had to interpret the provisions of the Sunday Observance Act, 1677, which prohibited the doing of certain acts on Sundays. The class of people so prohibited were '*trades men, artificers, workmen, labourers, or other person whatsoever*'. The court held that the phrase other person whatsoever should be limited to persons of the same genus as those expressly mentioned and could not include farmers and barbers. This is a re-affirmation of the legal maxim *expressio unius est exclusio alterius*; the express mention of one person or thing is the exclusion of the other.

Also in *Brown Sea Heaven Properties* v. *Poolle Corporation*[121], a local authority had been empowered to make orders concerning traffic routes and the prevention of obstruction '*in all times of public processions, rejoicings and illuminations, and in any case when the streets are thronged or liable to be obstructed*'. The phrase in any case was held not to justify the prescription of one way traffic for six months under normal conditions.

A prohibition with respect to '*house, office room or other place*' for betting with persons resorting thereto has been held not to include an uncovered enclosure adjacent to a race course[122] while '*signal, warning sign posts, direction posts signs and other device*' was interpreted to exclude a white line painted on the road[123]. The rule is to be applied cautiously only to give effect to the intention of the legislature[124]. Thus, in *R.* v. *Payne,*[125] a crowbar was included in the interpretation of a statute under which it was an offence to convey into prison

---

[116] See also Onasile v. Sani (1962) 1 ALL NLR 272.
[117] Board of Customs and Excise v. Viale, supra at p. 61.
[118] Ibid.
[119] Onasile v. Sani, supra at p. 276.
[120] (1900) 1 Q.B 725. See also Gregory v. Fearn (1953) 1.WLR 974.
[121] (1958) Ch. 574.
[122] Powell v. Kempton Park Race Course Co. (1899) A.C. 143.
[123] Evans v. Cross (1938) KB 694.
[124] See Board of Customs and Excise v. Viale supra.
[125] (1866) 35 LJMC 170.

with intent to facilitate the escape of any prisoner, *'any mask, dress or other disguise, or any letter, or any other article or thing'*.

In *Eton Rural District Council* v. *River Thames Conservators*[126], the court considered the provisions of Section 9 (1) of the English Land Drainage Act, 1930. That section imposed a duty on catchments boards to take steps for the communication of all obligations imposed on persons *'by reason of tenure, custom, prescription or otherwise, to do any work … in connection with the main river'*. The general words or otherwise were limited to the particularized circumstances thereby excluding purely contractual obligations[127]. Similarly, the word otherwise as used in Section 22 of the Land Use Act, has been confined to any of the means by which legal title or possession of real property can be transferred from one person to another[128].

It would appear that the court has some discretion in the application of the rule to specific instances. In *Buhari* v. Yusuf,[129] the appellants, General Buhari and the All Nigeria Peoples Party (ANPP) had sought for their names to be struck out as respondents in an election petition brought by Alhaji Yusuf and the Movement for Democracy and Justice, one of the registered political parties that participated at the 2003 presidential elections, against the PDP and others. In considering whether they were properly joined as parties to the action, the court was invited to interpret Section 133 (2) of the Electoral Act, 2002. Section 133 (1) and (2) provides:

> An election petition may be presented by one or more of the following persons:
> (a)   A candidate at an election;
> (b)   A political party which participated at the election.
> (2) The person whose election is complained of is, in this Act, referred to as the respondent, but if the petition complains of the conduct of an Electoral Officer, Presiding Officer, a Returning Officer or any other person who took part in the conduct of an election, such officer or person shall for the purpose of this Act be deemed to be a respondent and shall be joined in the election petition in his or her official status as a necessary party.

The appellants urged the court to apply the *ejusdem generis rule* to interpret the phrase *'or any other person who took part in the conduct of an election'*. The court conceded that in applying the rule, *'general words or terms*

---

[126] (1950) Ch. 540.
[127] See also Hobbs v. C.G. Robertson Ltd (1970) I WLR 980.
[128] Okuneye v. First Bank of Nigeria Plc. (1996) 6 NWLR 749.
[129] (2003) 4 WRN 124.

are to be read as comprehending only things of the same kind as that designated by the preceding particular expressions, unless there is something to show that a wider sense was intended[130]. Nevertheless, it rejected the argument that the rule was helpful in the interpretation and proper understanding of the section in question, noting that applying the rule would restrict the phrase to the INEC officials who took part in the conduct of an election; a restriction which the court felt could not be justified in the present instance.[131]

Ejusdem generis rule helps to confine the construction of general words within the genus of special words which they follow in a statutory provision or in a document.

In *Ashbury Railway Carriage and Iron Co.* v. *Riche*[132] the statement in a Memorandum of Association was that one of the object of the company was "to carry on the business of mechanical engineers and general contractors "The House of Lords, per Lord Cairms L. C. said that the expression "general contractors" was limited by the previous words "mechanical engineer", and that it ought to be confined to the making of contracts connected with that business.

In Attorney - General v. Seccombe[133] Section 11 (1) of the Customs and Inland Revenue Act 1889 which referred to gifts "retained to the entire exclusion of the donor or of any benefit to him by contract or otherwise" come up for interpretation as to what "or otherwise" delimited. It was held that those words must be confined to an enforceable arrangement of a sort which was *ejusdem generis* with contract.

Noscitur a Sociis Rule
A man is known from his associates. So also the meaning of a word can be gathered from the context: where there is a string of words and the meaning of one of them is doubtful, that meaning is given to it which it shares with the other words. So if the words "*horse*", *cow*, or other animal occur, "*animal*" is held to apply to brutes only. This is therefore similar but not identical to the *ejusdem generis* rule. Simply put, a word is known by the company it keeps.[134]

Principles of Interpretation
The Principle of Interpretation include, Internal aids, External aids and Presumptions.

---

[130] Per Uwaifo, JSC, at p. 136.
[131] For illustration, the court had reasoned that a police office for instance, who contrary to his official assignment at an election had stuffed ballot boxes with unlawful ballot papers should, under the section, qualify as a respondent even though he is not an INEC official.
[132] (1875) L.R.H.L. 653.
[133] (1911) 2. K.B. 6
[134] See Earl Jowitt – The Dictionary of English Law 1959 at p. 1238

Internal Aids

A statute can sometimes be the best instrument to employ in interpreting itself, for the contents of a statute consist of what has been described as internal aids to interpreting statutes. The internal aids include, long and short titles, preamble, definition sections, headings or marginal notes, punctuation marks, text of the sections, commencement section, provisos, schedules and explanatory notes.

Long and Short Titles

Statutes generally have two titles, these are long and short titles. An Act is cited using the short title. For example *'The Interpretation* Act'[135], is the short title of the Act, while the long title is *'An Act to provide for the construction and interpretation of Acts of the National Assembly and certain other instruments; and for purposes connected here with.* [136]

Traditionally, short titles have little relevance to the meaning of statutes for brevity, rather than precision, is the virtue in short title. The long title is different. It is part of the legislation and is included in the debate by the Parliament. The long title can be useful in throwing light on ambiguous words in the statute[137]. If the text of a statute is unambiguous, then the long title has no relevance. The short title must be given effect[138]. In *Bello and Ors* v. *A.G. Oyo State,* Karibi-White J.S.C said:

> 'The long title of a statute is now accepted as an important part of it and may be relied upon as explaining its general scope and aids in its interpretation... where the meaning of the words used in the section are clear and unambiguous that meaning governs. Resort is only to be had to the long title to resolve ambiguity'[139].

Where there is ambiguity, it is better to work at the scope of the long title to modify the interpretation of the plain words of the section[140].

The long title usually delimits the purpose of the statute and may be relied upon as explaining its general scope. It is, however, never allowed to affect or restrain the plain meaning of the statute.[141]

---

[135] Oba, A.A. Statutes as their own interpretation: Internal Aids to Interpretation of Statutes in Nigeria, UDUS Law Journal, vol. 1 no.5, 2004 p. 23, Obilade, A.D. Nigerian Legal System. London: Sweet and Maxwell, 1979 pp. 56-60, Niki. T. *Sources of law. Lagos.* MIJ Professional Publishers Ltd. 1996 pp. 83-88. Asein, J.O. *Introduction to Nigerian Legal System.* Ibadan: Sam Bookman Publishers 1997 pp. 46-57, Denning, M.R. The Disciplines of Law. London: Butterworths 1979 pp. 9-22, *Attorney General Lagos State* v. *Attorney-General of the Federation & Ors (2003) 6 SCNJ p. 1.*

[136] See the heading to the Interpretation Act and Section 39 for the long and short titles respectively.

[137] Osawara v. Ezeiruka (1978) NSCC vol. 11, 390, UTC (Nig.) v. Pamotel (1989) 3 SCNJ 79 at p. 9 citing R. v. Survey (North-Eastern Area) Assessment Committee (1948) 1 KB 29 at pp. 32-33.

[138] Ibid. p. 871.

[139] (1986) 5 NWLR 828 at 871.

[140] ibid

Preamble

A preamble is an amendable, descriptive component of a statute, and it is generally placed after the long title and before the enacting words and the substantive sections. It is a useful guide to the intention of the Parliament in that it may detail the mischief to which the Act is directed; explain the reason, purpose, object or scope of the Act; and detail facts or values which are relevant to the Act[142].

Preambles can be seen to have both a contextual and a constructive roles in statutory interpretation. The contextual role is where the preamble assists with confirming the ordinary meaning of the enactments, and assists with determining if there is any ambiguity in the Act. The Constructive role is where the preamble is effectual in clarifying or modifying the meaning of ambiguous enactments. While there is substantial consensus on the function of a preamble in relation to the latter role, the contextual role of a preamble has had the more contested history.[143]

The Constructive Role of the Preamble

The use of preambles in legislation is like that of a recital in deed. The preamble does not normally constitute an operative part of the statute[144]. Preambles are relevant to interpretation of statutes where there is ambiguity or difficulty in ascertaining the intention of the statute. The legal effect of preambles was set out by Tindall, C.J. in Sussex Peerage Claim as follows:

> If any doubt arises, from the terms employed by the legislature it has always been held a safe means of collecting the intention to call in aid the ground and cause in making the statute and to have recourse to the preamble which according to Chief Justice Dyser in Stowe v. Lord Zouch is

---

[141] Ibid.

[142] Winckel, A. The Contextual Role of a Preamble in Statutory Interpretation (1999) MULR 7; (1999) 23 Melbourne see also Bennion, FAR Statutory Interpretation: A Code (2nd ed.) 1992 p. 483. The Preamble is part of the Act A.G. v. Prince Ernest Augustus of Hanover (1957) AC 436, 467. Powell v. Kempton Park Racecourse Co. Ltd. (1899) AC 143, 184, Brett. v. Brett (1826) 3 Add 210; 162 ER 456, John Bell and Sir George Engle, Cross on Statutory Interpretation (3rd ed.) 1995 pp. 126-7.

[143] A Preamble can play both constructive and contextual role in statutory interpretation. Some commentators and judges have disagreed over the contextual role. A small number have advocated that a preamble could not even be referred to a part of the context of an Act without an ambiguity being independently identified in the substantive enactments. Evidence suggests that this "rule" has never been the favoured view of the courts, and it is certainly not an accurate statement of the current law. Misconceptions about the contextual role of a preamble can be traced to both mistaken assumptions about the legal status of preambles, and the imperfect methods of statutory interpretation commentators.

[144] Eramus Osawe & Ors v. Register of Trade Unions (1985) INWLR (pt. 4) 755.

to open the minds of the makers of the Act and the mischief which they intended to redress.[145]

The Constructive role of a preamble in statutory interpretation relates to the effect that a preamble may have in modifying the ordinary meaning of substantive enactments in a statute.

If there is an ambiguity in the text, the text may be clarified through reference to the preamble[146]. If the preamble is quite clear[147], then it may "throw light upon" the preferred meaning[148]. As a guide to legislative intent and the object of the Act, the preamble may indicate how various ambiguous enactments may be restrained[149] or enlarged[150] to better reflect the intentions of Parliament. This intention may be discovered through various types of information provided in preambles, such as information about the mischief to be remedied, the motives behind the legislation, and the purposes, objects and scope of the Act.

However where there is no ambiguity, where the text is plain and clear, the preamble cannot affect the interpretation of the words, either to narrow or enlarge the meaning. But the words must be construed according to their ordinary meaning[151]. There is a well-known rule that "where the words of a statute are plain and clear, their meaning cannot be cut down by reference to the preamble[152], similarly, the plain and clear enactment cannot be controlled[153], restrained[154], restricted[155], qualified[156], confined[157], or limited[158] by a narrow preamble. Likewise, the preamble may not broaden a clear substantive section.[159]

---

[145] Ibid p. 143, see also Income Tax Commissioners v. Persel (1981) AC 531 at p. 542, Commissioner of Lands v. Oniru (1961) 2 NLR 72, Chief E.J.P. Operola v. S.O.O. Opadiran & Anor. (1994) 5 NWLR (pt. 344) AC 463 at p. 382.

[146] Ibid.

[147] Eton College v. Minister of Agriculture, Fisheries and Food (1964) 1 Ch. 274.

[148] Mason v. Armitage (1806) 13 Ves Jun 25;33 ER 204, 208 (Lord Erskine CJ).

[149] Powell v. Kempton Park Rececourse Co. Ltd. (1899) AC 143, where the word "place" in the Betting Act 1853 (UK) 16 & 17 Vict, C119, was interpreted narrowly, in line with the object of the Act expressed in the preamble, so as not to prohibit the conduct of bookmakers in an open inclosure at race meetings.

[150] Eart of Halsbury, Laws of England, vol. 27 (1913).

[151] Powell v. Kempton Park Racecourse supra.

[152] Bowtell v. Goldsbrough, Mort & Co. Ltd. (1906) 3 CLR 444, 451 (Griffith CJ). This Statement was affirmed by Gibbs CJ in Wacando v. Commonwealth (1981) 148 CLR1, 16 see also Powell v Kempton Park Racecourse Co. Ltd. (1899) AC 143, 157 (Earl of Halsbury LC).

[153] Emanuel v. Constable (1827) 3 Russ 436; 38 ER 639, 640 (Sir John Leach MR); Powell v. Kempton Park Racecourse Co. Ltd. (1897) 2 QB 242, 290 (Rigby LJ), 299 (Chitty LJ), Powell v. Kempton Park Racecourse Co. Ltd. (1899) AC 143, 193 (Lord James); Ward v. Holman (1964) 2 QB 580, 587 (Lord Parker CJ).

[154] Ryall v. Rowles (1749) 1 Ves. Sen 348; 27 ER 1074, 1084 (Lord Parker CB).

[155] Powell v. Kempton Park Racecourse Co. Ltd. Supra (Lindcey LJ).

[156] Ibid. (Earl of Halsbury LC)

[157] Mason v. Armitage, Supra (Lord Erskine LC)

The Contextual Role of the Preamble

The contextual role of a preamble in statutory interpretation relates to the manner in which, as part of the context of a whole Act, a preamble may assist in confirming the ordinary meaning of enactments, or indeed, be suggestive of alternative meanings which are consistent with the intentions of the legislature.

Where the preamble forms part of the text of the statute by being expressly incorporated into the statute or expressly declared to be part of the statute, it must be read as part of the statute[160]. This was fairly common during the defunct military regimes in Nigeria. A good example of this is the Federal Military Government (Supremacy and Enforcement of Powers) Decree, 1970[161] where the preamble was expressly declared to be part of the statute. Another example is the Federal Military Government (Supremacy and Enforcement Powers) Decree, 1984[162]. The preambles in both sections were taken to be part of the statutes and were so interpreted by the courts.[163] Where the preamble is declared by the statute to be part of the enactment, it ought to be examined in case of ambiguity.[164]

Preambles are not normally a part of the operative section of the statute. They however, assume a different status if they are expressly incorporated[165]. Where the preamble to a statute is incorporated into its main body it must be read as part of the provisions of the Act. For instance, in Okeke v. Attorney General of Anambra State[166] the preamble to Decree No. 13 of 1984 was interpreted to form a part of the Decree in order to understand its provisions.

Maxwell on Interpretation of Statutes commented that there was now little to be said about preambles in interpretation. However, the House of Lords in A.G. v. Prince Ernest Augustus of Hanover[167] made references to the preamble's role as part of the context in statutory interpretation. The court was of the view that Act cannot be said to be unambiguous until it is read as a whole, including the preamble if there is one[168] Viscount Simonds argued that words could not be

---

[158] Halton v. Cove (1830) IB & Ad 538; 109 ER 887, 895 (Lord Tenterden CJ)

[159] Wilson v. Knubley (1806) 7 East 128; 103 ER 49, 51-2 (Lord Ellenborough CJ).

[160] Adejumo v. Military Governor, Lagos State (1971) l ALL NLR 159.

[161] Decree No. 28 of 1970.

[162] Ibid. Section 1 (1). See Criticism of this approach to legislative drafting in Karibi – White A.G. "The Federal Military Government Supremacy and Enforcement of Powers" Decree No. 28 of 1970.

[163] See Adejumo v. Military Governor, Lagos State Supra. Professor Christian Nwachukwu Okeke v. Attorney – General Anambra State (1992) l NWLR (Pt. 215) at p. 60.

[164] See Adejumo v. Military Governor, Lagos State *Supra*. Federal Military Government Supremacy and Enforcement Powers) Decree, Supra.

[165] See e.g section 1 of the Federal Military Government (Supremacy and Enforcement of Powers) Decree *Supra*

[166] (1992) l NWLR (pt. 215) at p. 60.

[167] P. St. J. Langan, Maxwell on the Interpretation of Statutes (12th ed., 1969) p.7.

[168] Cross on Statutory Interpretation (3rd ed., 1995) pp. 126-7

read in isolation, but "their colour and content (were) derived from their context"[169]. He said:

> No one should profess to understand any part of a statute --- before he had read the whole of it. Until he has done so he is not entitled to say that it or any part of it is clear and unambiguous[170].

Lord Norman puts it as follows:

> In order to discover the intention of Parliament, it is proper that the court should read the whole Act, inform itself of the legal context of the Act --- and of the factual context, such as the mischief to be remedied --- it is the merest commonplace to say that words abstracted from context may be meaningless or misleading --- No part of a statute can be regarded as independent of the rest.[171]

The contextual role of the preamble requires a purposive approach to statutory interpretation. In the interpretation of an Act, a construction that would promote the purpose or object underlying the Act (whether that purpose or object is expressly stated in the Act or not) should be preferred to a construction that would not promote that purpose or object[172]. In CIC Insurance Ltd. v. Bankstown Football Club Ltd.[173] the court said:

> The modern approach to statutory interpretation (a) insists that the context be considered in the first instance, not merely at some later stage when ambiguity might be thought to arise, and (b) uses "context" in its widest sense to include such things as the existing state of the law and the mischief which --- one may discern the statute was intended to remedy.[174]

Thus, in determining the ordinary meaning of a provision, it is necessary to have regard to the purpose of the legislation and the context of the provision as well as the literal meaning of the provision. The purpose of legislation could sometimes be discovered by an examination of the legislation as a whole.

A preamble is used like the rest of the context, to help establish the ordinary meaning of the substantive words and to be a guide to the intention of the

---

[169] A.G. v. Prince Ernest Augustus of Hanover Supra, at pp. 436, 461.
[170] Ibid at p. 463.
[171] Ibid at pp. 465, 467
[172] Australian Interpretation Act (1901) (C th) Section 15AA (1)
[173] (1997) 187 CLR 384, 408 (Brennan C.J., Dawson, Toohey and Gummow JJ) see also Saraswati v. The Queen (1991) 172 CLR 1, 20-1 (Mc Hugh J).
[174] Ibid.

legislature.   A preamble assist in identifying ambiguities in the Act where an alternative construction could better enact the intention of the Parliament.

The preamble is a key to open the minds of the makers of the Act, and the mischief's which they intended to redress. The preamble is a good mean to find out the meaning of the statute. As Sir John N.Cholla puts it in Brett v. Brett:[175]

> The key to the opening of every law is the reason and spirit of the law-it is the 'animus imponentis', the intention of the law-maker, expressed in the law itself, taken as a whole. Hence, to arrive at the true meaning of any particular phrase in a statute, that particular phrase is not to be viewed detached from its context in the statute: it is to be viewed in connection with its whole context. It is to the preamble more especially that we are to look for the reason or spirit of every statute rehearsing this, as it ordinarily does, the evils sought to be remedied, or the doubts purported to be removed by the statute, and so evidencing, in the best and most satisfactory manner, the object or intention of the legislature in making and passing the statute itself.[176]

Lord Thring[177] comments on the importance of a preamble when his lordship said:

> The proper function of a preamble is to explain certain facts which are necessary to be explained before the enactments contained in the Act can be understood. The preamble as part of the context plays an even larger role where the statute concerned is a penal statute, for such Acts are interpreted narrowly.[178]

The contextual role of the preamble is evident in the series of cases dealing with the making of a will. For instance words like "any will or codicil" may raise such question as to whether it relates to real property only or "any" wills including personal property. Lees v Summersgill[179] decided that the words "any will or codicil" were perfectly plain, and could not be limited by reference to the preamble. Lees v. Summersgill was not followed in Brett v. Brett.

---

[175] (1826) 3 Add 210; 162 ER 456, Emanuel v. Constable (1827) 3 Russ 436; 38 ER 639.
[176] Ibid.
[177] Lord Thring, Practical Legislation: The Composition and Language of Acts of Parliament and Business Documents (2nd ed) 1902 p. 92.
[178] Ibid.
[179] (1811) 17 Ves. Jun 508; 34 ER 197.

It is clear from the latter two cases that the words "any will or codicil" were found to be general, indefinite words, and capable of a more limited meaning. In Emanuel v. Constable,[180] John Leach MR said:

> I agree that the preamble of a statute cannot control a clear and express enactment, but the plain intent of the legislature is expressed in the preamble, and the nature of the mischief, which is sought to be remedied, may serve to give a definite and qualified meaning to indefinite and general terms.[181]

In the Sussex Peerage case[182], the case involved the interpretation of the Royal Marriage Act, 1772 (IMP)[183] and particularly whether overseas marriages had to comply with the rule requiring marriages of the king's descendants to be given royal consent. The words "contracting marriage" were found to be general and universal, but they were nevertheless given their plain meaning. The preamble was used in its contextual role to confirm the ordinary meaning of the words.

The preamble may throw light on the purpose and object of an enactment. As Mason J. in *Wacando v. Commonwealth*[184] puts it:

> It has been said that where the enacting part of a statute is clear and unambiguous it cannot be cut down by the preamble. But this does not mean that a court cannot obtain assistance from the preamble in ascertaining the meaning of an operative provision. The particular section must be seen in its context; the statute must be read as a whole and recourse to the preamble may throw light on the statutory purpose and object.[185]

Though the preamble cannot control the enacting clause, it should be compared with the rest of the Act, in order to ascertain the intention of the legislature.

The preamble may assist to resolve an ambiguity in the text of an Act. According to Lord James in Pwell v. Kempton Park Racecourse Co. Ltd.,[186]

> If the wording of the statute gives rise to doubts as to its proper construction, the preamble can be and ought to be referred to in order to

---

[180] (1826) 3 Add 210; 162 ER 456, 458
[181] ibid at p. 640
[182] (1844) ll CI & Fin. 85; 8ER 1034
[183] 12 Eeo 3, C II
[184] (1981) 148 CLR 1, 23.
[185] Ibid
[186] (1899) AC 143, 192 – 3.

arrive at the proper construction to be put upon the enacting portion of the statute.[187]

The preamble has been held to be part of the statute and thus allow the court, where ambiguity in the text exists, to examine it from the colour and context of the whole statute.

The preamble has a variety of roles. As a declaration of information, the preamble constantly informs the reader of legislation throughout the life of the Act, perhaps never becoming subject to litigation at all. However, when a dispute arises about the meaning of a substantive section, then there may be argument about what role the preamble should play. In the event of an ambiguity, it is natural that the mischief to be remedied or the legislative intent will be sought, thus immediately focusing attention on the preamble. But one could argue that reference to the preamble to throw light on an ambiguity is not the preamble's primary role. Preambles are not put unto place only to assist when things become unclear. Fundamentally they are there to inform the community throughout the operation of the law. It is a narrow view to always consider the role of preambles in terms of disputed meanings.

A preamble is clearly identified in the Act of Parliament.[188] An Act of Parliament can be divided into three main parts; the operative components (including the sections and schedules); the amendable descriptive components (including the long title, the preamble, and the short title); and the unamendable descriptive components (including the marginal notes, the punctuation and the sectional headings). Traditionally, unamendable components have had less significance in relation to statutory interpretation, as these sections of the Act are not formally discussed by the Parliament (they are generally finalized by the legislative drafters after the Bill has been passed). In comparison, the preamble has been seen as a reliable source of the intention of Parliament, as it is subject to parliamentary debates.

Historically, preambles have been used by the courts, not only to aid the interpretation of ambiguous sections and to assist in determining the mischief to be remedied by the Act, but also to determine the intentions of Parliament, as context for clarifying the possible meaning of substantive sections. Suggestions that the preamble could not be referred to without an ambiguity in the Act seem not to be tenable.

A preamble can play both constructive and contextual roles in statutory interpretation. The belief that a preamble could not be referred to as part of the context of an Act without an ambiguity being independently identified in the

---

[187] Ibid

[188] A.G. v. Prince Ernest Augustus of Hanover (1957) AC 436.

substantive enactments is a misconception. The misconceptions about the contextual role of a preamble can be traced to both mistaken assumptions about the legal status of preambles and the imperfect methods of statutory interpretation.

Notwithstanding the various misconceptions about the contextual role of a preamble, the common practice of judges has been to have recourse to the preamble even when the meaning is plain. This is the contextual role of the preamble. If the meaning of the enactments remained unambiguous in the context of the preamble and the whole Act, then there was no need to employ the preamble in its constructive role to refine the meaning of the Act.

Preambles have a contextual as well as a constructive role in statutory interpretation. Preambles are part of the wider context of a statute, and should be referred to during the initial reading of an Act as a whole. The preamble may, in that role, confirm the plain and ordinary meaning of the words, or it may in fact raise or confirm alternative constructions which suggest an ambiguity in the substantive sections. An Act cannot be said to have a clear meaning until it has been read through as a whole document, including the preamble if one exist.

While the contextual role of a preamble is consistent with English common law, current Acts Interpretation Legislation, and recent High Court precedents, the past existence of a contextual role for a preamble has been contested by those who advocate the rule that a preamble cannot be referred to if there is no ambiguity already evident in the text. These advocates of the "no recourse rule" can be understood to some extent in the context of misleading assumptions and misleading commentaries on statutory interpretation.

Definition Sections or Statutory Definitions

One of the most common instances of term definition is when there is need to specify the scope of a non-specific term in the statute. The use of the qualifier, '*reasonable*', for persons, time and actions, usually gives rise to such a definitional process. A good example of this occurred when the question of '*reasonable time*' for pre-arraignment detention was raised in *Folade* v. *Attorney-General of Lagos State*[189]. In this instance, the court acknowledged the relativity of the term and adopted the definition offered in an earlier case which had held that in defining the term '*reasonable time*', '*each case must therefore depend on its own facts*'[190]. The court affirmed that the term could be '*consistent with delays and should depend on circumstances*'. Balogun J. explained:

---

[189] (1992) 1 NWLR (pt. 215) at p. 60.
[190] (1981) 2 NCLR 771 at 779.

It has to be remembered that each case of this nature must depend on its own peculiar facts; and that no length of time is per see too long to pass scrutiny under the right guaranteed under Section 33 (1)[191]

In an earlier case, the court had held that since the expression, '*reasonable time*', was not defined under Section 21 (3) and 22 (2) of the Constitution, 1963,

Each case must therefore depend on its own facts. The accused has now been in custody for a year. The prosecution knew all along the witnesses to be called ... in my judgment the accused has not been brought to trial within a reasonable time having regards to the facts of the case ...[192].

In *M. A. Akinwunmi* v. *Mrs. Diet Spiff and 30 others*[193] and *Oloyo* v *Alegbe*, attempts were made by the trial courts to define the meaning of the term, '*full time employment*' under paragraph 2(b) of Part 1 of the 5th schedule to the Constitution, 1979:

Without prejudice to the foregoing paragraph, a public officer shall not engage or participate in the management or running of any private business, profession or trade but nothing in this sub-paragraph shall apply to any public officer who is not employed on full time basis.[194]

In almost startling contrast, the court in *M.D. Oloyo* v. *Alegbe (Supra)* dismissed the issue when a similar preliminary objection was raised as to the competence of counsel who was the Speaker of the State House of Assembly, to appear before the court. In a rather effective obiter, R.A. Ogbobine, F. stated:

I do not consider that this is a proper forum to discuss whether or not a member of the House of Assembly who is a lawyer has a right of audience to any court but when one considers the privilege given to a member to sit for only two-thirds of the statutory life of the House one is constrained to hold that the office of a member of a House of Assembly is not meant to be a full time affair[195].

In *Okogie* v. *Attorney-General, Lagos State*[196], the FCA was faced with the need to interpret the word '*medium*' as used in Section 36 (2) of the 1979 Constitution. As Mamman Nasir PCA., pointed out, the basic issue was:

Whether the word 'medium' is to be limited in its import as 'mass medium' as contended by the Attorney-General or to be broadly interpreted by

---

[191] Ibid
[192] State v. Mathematical Nasamu (unreported) (1976) High Court of Lagos State Charge No. LCD/1/76
[193] *(1981) 2 NCLR 345*
[194] *(1981) 2 NCLR 347.*
[195] Ibid.
[196] *Okogie* v. *Attorney General of Lagos State (1981) 2 NCLR 337 at 353.*

giving the word the ordinary dictionary meaning so as to include any intermediate agency for the dissemination of knowledge, information and ideas.[197]

The court opted for the broad interpretation rather than the limited one, citing acknowledged canons of constitutional interpretation to support its choice of definition.

The Interpretation Act[198] contains the definition of some specific words or concepts. For example, the Act says '*words importing the masculine gender include females*[199]. The Act defines *'Chief'* as *'a person who, in accordance with the law in force in any part of Nigeria, is accorded the dignity of a chief by reference to that part or to a community established in that part.*[200] Such definitions are applicable to all statutes provided that specific statutes do not contain special definitions of the words in the statute.[201] Such specific definitions are generally placed in a definition section at the beginning or end of the statute[202]. When the meaning of the words used in a statute can be ascertained by reference to the definitions given in the statute, it is not correct to look for their meaning in other statutes independent of the statute containing them.[203] For example, it was held that where a statute defines *'public office'* by adopting the definition contained in part II of the Fifth Schedule to the 1979 Constitution, the court should not go beyond this in defining a *public officer.*[204] The particular definition so given is applicable throughout the legislation.[205]

But where the definition in the specific statute is *'inclusive'* and not *"exclusive"* such definition can be supplemented with that in the Interpretation Act. For example, the Chiefs (Appointment and Deposition) Law says:

> For the purposes of sections 2 and 3 of this law the words 'chief' and 'head' chief mean a chief or a head chief who has been appointed to the office of native authority under the provisions of the Native Authority Ordinance or the Native Authority Law or which office is deemed to be constituted thereunder or who is a member of a native authority constituted under provisions of that ordinance or law or, where the office of native authority

---

[197] Ibid.
[198] Interpretation Act.
[199] Ibid. Section 14(a)
[200] Ibid. Section 18.
[201] Ibid. Section 1.
[202] For example see the definitions in Section 50 (1) of the Land Use Act, cap. 202 Laws of the Federation of Nigeria, 1990.
[203] Anowey v. Iherere & ors (1991) I NEPAR 56, Wilson v. Attorney General Bendel State (1985) NSCC vol. 16 (pt. 1) p. 191.
[204] *Anowey* v. *Ihekere & ors supra.*
[205] *Kalu* v. *Odili, supra.* at p. 119.

so appointed or deemed to be constituted, is a chief associated with a council, any chief or head chief who is a member of an advisory council'[206].

In *Alhaji Salami Olaniyi* v. *Gbadamosi Aroyehun and Ors*[207] the Supreme Court, in deciding whether the Onira of Ira who had been so turbaned by the Emir of Ilorin is a Chief for the purpose of the Chiefs (Appointment and Deposition) Law, fell back on the definition in the Interpretation Act. The court held that the turbanning brings the Onira within the definition of a Chief within the definition in the Interpretation Act. The Court distinguished *Akanbi* v. *Yakubu*[208], where it was held that the Bara of Ijagbo is not a Chief for the purposes of the Chiefs (Appointment and Deposition) Law, on the ground that there was no evidence in the case to bring the Bara within the definition in the Interpretation Act.

The definition in the definition section may not be exhaustive. This is particularly so if the list of definitions given is said to *'include'* the stated definitions. For example in *Madam Okesuji* v. *F.A. Lawal*[209], the Supreme Court considered the definition of *'probate action'* which was defined under the Lagos High Court (Civil Procedure) Rules as including *'actions or other matters relating to the grant or recall of probate or of letters of administration other than common form business*[210]. The court held that *'the use of the word definition is not exhaustive.*[211] The court per, Apata JSC, then proceeded to extend the meaning of *"probate action"* to include the construction of wills:

> I am in agreement with the views held by Taylor, C.J. in the case of Okoya v. Ojule and Ors (1968)2 NLR 55 at pages 58 to 59 that the construction and interpretation of a will and its contents are matters within the Jurisdiction of the High Court of Lagos State and being probate matter is governed by the law and practice for the time being in England, that is, the 1925 Settlement Act.[212]

Definitions contained in definition sections of statutes can sometimes be ambiguous or even misleading in which case the court will have recourse to other means of interpreting the words.[213]

---

[206] Cap. 28 Laws of Kwara State 1994.
[207] *(1991) 7 SCNJ (pt. 1) 76 at p. 119.*
[208] *(1973) NSCC 701 at 704.*
[209] *(1991) 2 SCNJ p. 1.*
[210] Order 1 Rule 2, Lagos High Court (Civil Procedure) Rules, Cap 52, Law of Lagos State of Nigeria 1973.
[211] *Okesuji* v. *Lawal supra.*
[212] Ibid.
[213] *Aluko* v. *D.P.P Western Nigeria (1963) I ALL NLR 378.*

Headings and Marginal Notes

Headings, like preambles are useful in the interpretation of ambiguous sections. For instance, the heading of Section 10 of the English Naturalization Act, 1870 was considered relevant in interpreting the meaning of *'child'* as used in that section. Since it reads *'National Status of Married Women and Infant Children*[214]. The relevant section in the body of the statute must indeed be ambiguous for the heading to be used in aid of interpretation[215]. In *U.T.C (Nig) Ltd* v. *Pamotel*[216] the question was whether Order 24 Rule 15 of the High Court of Lagos State (Civil Procedure) Rule[217], headed; *'Default Pleadings'*, applied to summary judgments. The Court of Appeal answered in the affirmative, relying on the heading. The Supreme Court disagreed and held that as a trite principle of statutory interpretation, the heading cannot be used to interpret any of the provisions of Order 24 unless the provisions are found to be ambiguous[218].

Sections sometimes have headings and marginal notes. Marginal notes are also referred to as side notes. These are not parts of the parliamentary text and are thus not parts of the statute[219]. They are intended only for *'convenience of reference only*[220]. Marginal notes are not necessarily comprehensive of the matters in the section to which it relates Kalgo JCA, brought this out thus:

> The marginal note to any section or provision of the law gives an indication or information of what one may find mentioned in the particular section or provision. It does not necessary mean that the marginal notes will in all cases cover what the section or provision is all about. It only gives an idea of what the section or provision is dealing with[221].

Traditionally, marginal notes are inadmissible as aids in interpreting the text of the statute. In *Chandler* v. *D.P.P.*, the House of Lords per Lord Reid enunciated the reasons for this position:

> In my view side notes cannot be used as an aid to construction. They are mere catchwords and I have never heard of it being supposed in recent times that an amendment to alter a side note could be proposed in either House of Parliament. Side notes in the original Bill are inserted by the draftsmen. During the passage of the Bill through its various stages amendments to it or the reasons may make it desirable to alter a side note.

---

[214] *(1992) INWLR 60 at 83.*
[215] Being the age of majority then, see Re Certain (1945) I Ch. 280.
[216] Ondo State University v. Folayan (1994) 7 NWLRI.
[217] (1989) 2 NWLR 60 at 83.
[218] Cap. 52, Laws of Lagos State, 1973.
[219] Section 3 (2) Interpretation Act.
[220] Ibid.
[221] Financial Merchant Bank Ltd. v. Nigerian Deposit Insurance Corporation (1995) 6 NWLR (pt. 400) 266 at pp. 244-245.

In that event, I have reason to believe that alteration is made by the appropriate officer of the House – no doubt in consultation with the draftsman. So side notes cannot be said to be enacted in the same sense as the long title or any part of the Act.[222]

A distinction is sometimes drawn between marginal notes that form part of the legislative text of the statute. This point was brought out vividly in respect of the revised laws of some states. For examples, the statutes contained in the Laws of Northern Nigeria 1963 where by legislation *'substituted for the enactments which are replaced by the enactments included in such (revised) volumes'*. The Supreme Court ruled that the marginal notes contained in the statutes in this collection of statutes in the said revised laws are part of these statutes[223].

Nowadays, marginal notes are regarded as useful guides when considering the general purpose of a section and the mischief at which it is aimed with the marginal notes in mind[224]. In *Paul Yabugbe v. Commissioner of Police*[225], the question was whether or not the protection offered to public officers by the Public Officers Protection Laws in civil cases also extends to criminal cases. The Court in interpreting the word 'pr*osecution'* in the act as not extending to criminal cases, relied inter-alia on the side note to Section 2 of the Law which read *'action against public officers'.* The Court held that this by implication excludes criminal prosecution.

Marginal notes cannot control the plain words of the statute or give different effect to clear words where there can be no doubt as to their ordinary meaning.[226]

Marginal notes have been described in recent times as useful guides when considering the general purpose of a section and the mischief at which it is aimed[227] with the marginal notes in mind. It is permissible to consider the purpose of a section and the mischief at which it is aimed. Since they are not binding as laws, they may be ignored in those cases where the express provisions in the body of the enactment are clear. For instance, Section 1 of the Official Secrets Act, 1911 was interpreted to cover sabotage and espionage, notwithstanding the narrow reference to *'penalties for spying'* in the marginal notel.[228]

---

[222] (1964) AC 763. 789 quoted with approval in Nigerian Tabacco Co. Ltd v. Alloysius Olumba Aquanne (1995) 5 NWLR (pt. 394) 541.
[223] *Nigerian Tobacco Co. Ltd v. Alloysius Olumba Agunanne, supra.*
[224] Oloyo v. Alegbe (1983) 2 SCNLR 35 at p. 57, Uwaifo v. Attorney-General Bendel State (1982) 7 SC 124, Adewunmi v. Attorney-General Ondo State,
[225] *(1996) 8 NWLR (pt. 234) 152 at 171.*
[226] *(1992) 4 NWLR (pt. 234) 152 at 171.*
[227] *Oba, A.A. op. cit.*
[228] *Chandler v. Director of Public Prosecution (1964) AC 763.*

Punctuation Marks

Punctuation forms part of the enactment and it must be considered in constructing a statute[229]. In *Shell B.P.* v. *Federal Board of Inland Revenue*[230] the Federal High Court was faced with the construction of the definition of *'petroleum operations'* under Section 2 of Petroleum Profits Tax Acts, 1959. The commas used in the definition turned out to be crucial in giving meaning to the definition. The court reasoned thus:

> Looking at the definition of 'petroleum operations' ... the effect of the comma before and the one after the clause "not including refining at a refinery" is to put that clause in a bracket and making it a parenthesis. A parenthesis is being defined as a clause placed as an explanation or comment within an already complete sentence. The explanation or comment always qualifies or amplifies the preceding word or phrase. If one takes away the clause between the two commas in the definition one will find that the remaining sentence reads smoothly and sensibly[231].

It is a rule of law that minute points of punctuation are not to be read as making major changes in the law[232].

The old rule, borrowed from English law, was that punctuation is not part of the statute and that courts will disregard the punctuation, if need be, to read the true meaning of the statute.[233] The modern court recognizes that punctuation often clarify meaning, and that skilled drafters can be expected to apply good grammar.[234]

However in Hammock v. Loan and Trust Co. the court remains relunctant to place primary importance on punctuation. The court said "A statute's plain meaning must be followed..., and the meaning of a statute will typically heed the commands of its punctuation"[235] The court said further that "a purported plain meaning analysis based only on punctuation is necessarily incomplete and run the risk of distorting a statute's true meaning"[236]

---

[229] Oba, A.A. op. cit.

[230] (1976) 1 FNR 197, see the analysis of use of punctuation in this case in Badaiki op. cit. 84 – 85.

[231] (1976)1FRN 197 at p. 202.

[232] Tonge v. Wilkinson (1957) CLY 3054 confirmed in Piper v. Harvey (1958) 1 QB 439, Kiralfy op. cit. p. 124.

[233] Hammock v. Loan and Trust Co. IO5 US (15 OHO) 77,84-85 (1881) (Disregarding a comma) see also United States v. Shreveport Grain and Elevator Co 287 US. 77, 82-83 (1932) (also disregarding a comma).

[234] See, e.g Arcadia v. Ohio Power Co. 498 US. 73, 78 (1990) ("In causual conservation, perhaps such absentminded duplication and omission are possible but Congress is not presumed to draft its laws that way").

[235] United States Nat'l Bank of Oregon v. Independent Ins Agents, 508 U.S 439, 454 (1993).

[236] Ibid see also Constanzo v. Tillinghast 287 U.S 341, 344 (1932) ("it has often been said that punctuation is not decisive of the construction of a statute ... upon like principle we should not apply the rules of syntax to defeat the evident legislative intent").

It should be noted that the refusal to be bound by the rules of punctuation gives the court some flexibility in construing statutes. This is not to say, however, that punctuation rules should be disregarded in statutory drafting since such rules are ordinarily strong guides to meaning.

Text of the Sections

All the parts of a statute are construed as a whole rather than a part only by itself[237]. Every word or clause of the statute should be construed with reference to the content and other clauses of the statute as far as possible so as to make a consistent enactment of the whole statute or series of statutes relating to the subject matter[238]. Special or specific provisions in a statute prevails over general provisions[239], the rule being *generalia specialibus non derogant*[240]. Each section of a statute must be interpreted without calling in aid other sections unless there is a conflict in their provisions[241]. Where part of a legislation is good and part is invalid, the *"blue pencil"* rule may be applied to sever the good from the bad in order to preserve the good part. As Ogundare JSC, explains:

> The 'blue pencil rule' is applied to sever a part of a legislation that is good in a sense that it is valid, from the part that is bad, in that it is invalid. That is, the blue pencil is run over the part that is bad, if what remains of the impugned legislation, that is the part that is good, can stand, then it is applied. But if what remains cannot stand on its own the impugned legislation is declared invalid.[242]

The *'blue pencil'* rule is also applied to excess words in statutes.[243]

Commencement Date

Statutes usually contain a commencement date. The date specified therein is the date on which the statute comes into operation.[244] This is given effect subject to the important limitation that the Constitution does not allow retrospective legislation in respect of criminal offences[245].

---

[237] Chief Chuba Egolum v. Chief Olusegun Obasanjo & Ors (1999) 5 SCNJ 92 at p. 121.
[238] Ibid.
[239] Martin Schroder & Co. v. Major and Co. (Nig.) Ltd (1989)2 SCNJ 210 at pp. 215 – 216. Hon. Justice E. O. Araka v. Justice Don. Egbue (2003) 7 SCNJ 114 at pp. 124.
[240] This is "general thing do not derogate from special", p. 215 see also James G. Oruba v. National Electoral Commission & Ors (1989) 2 NEPLR 24 at p. 39, (1988) 12 SCNJ254, Alhaji Hashimu Garba Matari & Ors v. Ahmadu Dangaladima and Anor (1993) 2 SCNJ 122.
[241] Eze Lambert Okoye Akuneziri v. Chief PDC Okenwa & Ors (2000) SCNJ 242 at p. 269.
[242] Attorney – General of Abia State & Ors v. Attorney –General of the Federal (2002) SCNJ 158 at p. 248, see also Attorney-General Abia State v. Attorney-General of the Federation (2006) 6NWLR (pt. 763) 284.
[243] See Balewa v. Doherty (1963) 1 WLR 949 per Lord Devilin at p. 960.
[244] Kotoye v. Saraki (1994) 7 - 8 SCNJ 524 at p. 578.
[245] Section 4 (9) 1999 Constitution.

Proviso

Proviso to a section forms part of the section. It is established that where the main part of the section is plain, a proviso cannot alter the plain meaning[246], but where the words used in the main part are reasonably susceptible of more than one meaning, a proviso ought to be examined for it may show the meaning which the words are intended to bear[247].

The proviso of a statute must be construed as a whole and proviso must be read with them[248]. The object of a proviso in a statutory enactment is to qualify or whittle down the enacting clause which precedes it. It is in reality an exception to the main rule.[249]

A proviso cannot alter the plain meaning of a section in a statute[250]. The court will not modify, enlarge or contract the scope and meaning of any enactment merely because of the proviso to that enactment[251]. But where a section is capable of two meanings, a proviso can give a particular meaning to it[252]. Examples of proviso include the use of words like *'provided that'* and *'subject to'*. Where the expression *'subject to'* is used at the commencement of a statute as is the case with the Wills Law, it is an expression of limitation. It implies that what the section or sub-section is *'subject to'* shall govern, control and prevail over what follows in that section or sub-section of the enactment.[253]

Illustrations

Illustrations can sometimes be found attached to sections of a statute though this is not a common practice. A prominent example is *penal code*[254] in which illustrations give examples of the offences created under some of the sections while comment and notes on practice and procedure explain the ingredients of the offences. Such illustrations do not form part of the statute but they should not be rejected in interpreting a statute unless they are repugnant to the sections with which they deal or are otherwise not helpful in the working and application of the statute.[255]

---

[246] Anya v. State (1996) NMLR 62, Nabhan v. Nabahan (1967) 1 ALLNLR 47 at p. 54.

[247] Nabhan v. Nabhan. Ibid.

[248] Chief Joseph Odetoye Oyeyemi v. Commissioner for Local Government, Kwara State & Ors (1992) 2 SCNJ 266.

[249] Abasi v. State (1992) NMLR 62.

[250] Anya v. State (1966) NMLR 62.

[251] Kotoye v. Saraki, supra, at p. 567.

[252] Nabhan v. Nabhan (1967) 1 ALL NLR 47 at p. 54.

[253] Joseph Osemwegie Idehen and Ors v. George Otutu Idehen and Ors (1991) 7 SCNJ 196 at pp. 212, 226, 224 – 227, 233 and 243, see comments on the Judicial construction of the phrase "subject to" in the case in I.E. Sagay "Customary Law and Freedom of Testament Power" (1995) NSCC Vol. 3, 310, Alhaji Umaru Abba Tukur v. Government of Gongola State (1989) 9 SCNJ 1 at pp. 17 &54, Taxaco Panama Incorporation v. Shell Petroleum Development Corporation of Nigeria Ltd., (2002) 2 SCNJ 102 at p. 112.

[254] Cap 116, Laws of Kwara State, 1994.

[255] Badaiki, op. cit. p. 88 citing Mahammed Syedo Ariffin v. Yeoh Ooi Gark (1916) 2 AC 575 at p. 581.

Schedules

Schedules form part of the enactment if they are incorporated by the enacting sections[256] and they may be referred to when any enacting section being interpreted is ambiguous.

Schedules are integral parts of a statute and must be given effect as if they are in the main body of the legislation[257]. When there is a conflict between statute and its schedule, the provision in the statute prevails to the extent of the inconsistency and the schedule is invalid to that extents[258].

Forms are often included in the schedules. For example the High Court (Civil Procedure) Rules[259] contain forms to be used in connection with civil litigation in the High Court[260]. General forms included in a schedule are inserted merely as examples and for convenience to be followed as circumstances of each case permit.[261]

Explanatory Notes

Explanatory notes are a common features of most modern statutes in Nigeria. Like side notes, they are inserted after the law has been passed. It is usual for the inserting authority to state expressly that they do not form part of the statute. They are not entirely useless and may, in the absence of any other aid, serve as weak pointers to the intention of the legislature.

Explanatory notes are sometimes added to statute (after the law has been passed) to explain their effect on existing law. These notes which are a regular features of Military Decrees in the country are sometimes expressly stated as not forming part of the statute. The usual style was to declare immediately under the Explanatory Note that 'This note does not form a part of the above decree but is intended to explain its purport.'[262]

External Aids

The application of canons of interpretation of statutes involves the use of external aids. Examples of External Aids are Dictionaries, Interpretations laws, Rules and Orders, Textbooks and Cases.

---

[256] See e.g. Criminal Code Law (Lagos Laws) 1973, cap. 31, Section 2 and schedule.
[257] Egolum v. Chief Obasanjo & Ors, op. cit. p. 147.
[258] Ibid. p. 154.
[259] High Court (Civil Procedure) Rules, 1987 Kwara State.
[260] See the Appendix attached to the rules, Ibid. pp. 188 – 357.
[261] Egolum v. Chief Obasanjo & Ors. supra at p. 130.
[262] See for example the Federal Military Government (Supremacy and Enforcement of Powers) Decree 1984 op. cit.

Dictionary

Dictionaries are generally referred to in ascertaining the usual meanings of words and in determining whether a word is reasonably susceptible of two different meanings.[263]

Of course the application of dictionary definitions is not always a clear course, many words have several alternative meanings[264.] Ambiguity is a creature not of definitional possibilities but of statutory context[265] in *Smith* v. *United States*, the court said that the "use" of a firearm in commission of a drug offence or crime of violence includes trading a gun for drugs[266]. And sometimes dictionary meanings can cause confusion. As Judge Learned Han observed:

> It is one of the surest indexes of a mature and developed jurisprudence not to make a fortress out of the dictionary; but to remember that statutes always have some purpose or object-to accomplish, whose sympathetic and imaginative discovery is the surest guide to their meaning.[267]

Dictionaries have the virtue of appearing neutral, thus gaining greater legitimacy for interpreters concerned about judicial subjectivity.[268]

In *Smith* v. *United* States,[269] the court considered whether a defendant who offered to barter a gun for drugs had "used" the gun in the course of the drug purchase under a statutory penalty-enhancement provision. Justice O' Cannor writing for the majority, based her construction of "use" on definitions from two dictionaries. She concluded that the term did include the petitioner's conduct, because in ordinary palance "use" means "to convert to one's service" or "to employ". Although she conceded that language, of course, cannot be interpreted apart from context, she however rejected the arguments that the statute should be

---

[263] Obilade, A.O. The Nigerian Legal System. Sweet & Maxwell, London 1979 p. 63.

[264] See, e.g MCI Tel. Corp, v. American Tel. & Tel Co 512 US 218, 226-28 (1994) (FCC's authority to "modify" requirements does not include the authority to make tariff filing optional; aberrant dictionary meaning "to make a basic or important change" is antithetical to the principal meaning of incremental change and is more than the statute can bear); and Nixon v. Missouri Municipal League, 541 U.S 125 (2004) (preemption of state laws that prohibit "any entity" from providing telecommunications services means, in context, "any private entity", and does not preempt a state law prohibiting local governments from providing such services). If the court views the issue as one of deference to an administrative interpretation, then the agency's choice of one alternative dictionary definition over another may indicate sufficient "reasonableness" Smiley v. Citibank (South Dakota), 517 U.S 735, 744-47 (1996).

[265] Brown v. Gardner, 513 U.S 115, 118 (1994)

[266] Smith v. United States, 508 U.S 233 (1993) Bailey v. United States 516 U.S 137 (1995) Muscarello v. United States 524 U.S 25 (1998).

[267] Cabell V. Markham, 148 F. 2d 737, 739 (2d Cir 1945) Justice Stevens has expressed a preference for established interpretation over dictionary definitions. "In a contest between the dictionary and the doctrine of stare decisis, the latter clearly wins" Hibbs v. Winn, 542 U.S 88, 133 (2004) (J. Stevens, concurring).

[268] Solan, L., When Judges Use the Dictionary, 68 Am Speech 50 (1993).

[269] 113S Ct. 2050 (1993)

read in context to require the use of the gun as a firearm. She explained that even though both interpretations were acceptable, they were not exclusive and did not indicate the way the term was "most reasonably read". She apparently concluded that her reading of the statute was the most "reasonable" ordinary meaning because it fits the definition in her chosen dictionaries.

However, dictionaries are not necessarily accurate repositories of the ordinary meaning of statutory term. Most obviously, dictionaries are secondary sources, exogenous to the statutory text.

Another problem with dictionary meanings is their fundamental indeterminacy. There are a wide variety of dictionaries from which to chose, and all of them usually provide several entries for each word. The selection of a particular dictionary and a particular definition is not obvious, and must be defended on some other grounds of suitability.

One of the most significant flows of dictionaries as interpretative tools is the imperfect relationship of dictionaries to statutory context. The limited ability of dictionaries to reflect statutory context can lead courts to interpretative blunders. Dictionaries can be pernicious both when their definitions are applied in an inappropriate context and more subtly, when they obscure or prevent an inquiry into the context of a statute.[270]

Interpretation Laws

The External Statutory aids are contained in the interpretation laws which apply subject to the provisions of the enactments being interpreted. For instance, Section 6 (1) of the Interpretation Act states the effect of the repeal of an enactment. It provides, in part, that the repeal of an enactment does not:

> affect any investigation, legal proceeding or remedy in respect of such right, privilege, obligation, legal proceeding or remedy may be instituted, continued or enforced, and any such penalty, forfeiture or punishment may be imposed, as if the enactment has not been repealed.[271]

Interpretation laws also provided that a statute does not bind the State.[272] Furthermore they provide that words importing the masculine gender are to be construed to include females,[273] that words in the singular include the plural and

---

[270] Shapiro, D.L, Continuity and Change in Statutory Interpretation 67 N.Y.U.L Rev 921, (1992).

[271] Interpretation Act, 1964. Section 6 (1) (i), see also Interpretation Law (Lagos Laws, 1973, cap. 57) Section 6 (1) (c), Interpretation Law (WRN Laws 1959, cap. 51) Section 12, Interpretation Law (N.N. Laws 1963, cap 52) Section 12, Interpretation Law (E.N. Laws 1963, Cap 66) Section 13, in re Edewor, 1969 NMLR 273.

[272] See e.g. Interpretation Law (NN Laws 1963, cap 52. 52) Section 65.

[273] See e.g. Interpretation Act, 1964, Section 14 (a).

those in the plural include the singular[274]. By virtue of the Interpretation Legislation, where a punishment is prescribed with respect to an offence, that punishment is the maximum punishment for the offence[275]. The legislation also defines a number of expressions. Section 18 (3) of the Interpretation Act 1964 provides, for instance, that the word *"or"* and the word *"other"* are to be construed disjunctively and not as implying similarity.[276]

Rules and Orders

Rules and Orders are subsidiary legislations, and as such, they are read as part of the enactment.[277] Where rules have been made under the authority of an enactment, recourse may be heard to the rules if the construction of the enactment is doubtful on any point. If a construction has been put on an enactment, a court can adopt and follow that construction[278]. Thus, where a new rule identical in terms with a former rule is continued by a superseding enactment which provides that rules made under the suspended enactment should continue in force as if made under the superseding enactment, the rules may be called in to aid the construction of any doubtful expressions in the enactment. A rule or order must give way if there is a conflict between it and an enactment.

Textbooks

The old view is that the opinion in textbooks of living writers are no authority on the construction of statutes.[279] The modern view is that such extra-judicial opinions by living academic writers can be put forward, accepted and applied especially at the high judicial hierarchy.

In *Osafile* v. *Odi*[280] it was held that an extra judicial opinion may persuade a court which may adopt it or may fail to do so if the court considers the preposition of law which it espouses as incorrect. Therefore, books of authority may be referred to in order to show the accepted meaning of terms used at the time the statute was passed. In order to resort to a textbook to interpret a statute and indeed establish and apply a principle of law, the text-writer may be of established repute. Although textbooks do not make law, they show more or less whether a principle has been generally accepted.[281]

---

[274] Ibid. Section 14 (b).
[275] Ibid. Section 1 and 14 (b).
[276] Obilade *op. cit.* p. 63.
[277] *A.G.* v. *De Keyser's Royal Hotel* (1920) AC 508 at 551.
[278] Ex p. Wier (1871) LR 6 Ch. 875 at 679, Re Andrew (1876) 1 Ch D. 358.
[279] *Re Ryer and Steadman's contract* (1927) 2 Ch. 62 at 74.
[280] (1990) 3 NWLR 130.
[281] *Henty* v. *Wrey* (1982) 12 Ch. D. 332 at 348.

Cases

Cases can be of assistance in construing statutes. Law reports are replete of decided cases effectively construing the words of statutes that are not defined in the statutes and establishing principles and rules where the scope and effect of statutes may be interpreted. As has been pointed out, statutes should be construed primary by the words used in them.

In *Laja* v *I.G.P*[282] the appellant was charged with obtaining by false pretence under Section 419 of the Criminal Code. It was held that the word *'intent to defraud'* in Section 419 of the Criminal Code mean an intent to deceive in such a manner as to expose any person to loss, or the risk of loss.

However care should be taken to ensure that the use of decided cases in statutory interpretation does not enlarge the terms of a statute or defeat the intention of the law-maker by diverting attention from what the state enacted to what had been said about it by judges. This is consistent with the principle that every statute must be interpreted according to its tenor. Thus, the Court of Appeal rightly held in *CBN* v. *Katto*[283] that cases decided under one statute such as the Land Use Act 1978 cannot be useful guides in the interpretation of another statute such as Decree No 17 of 1984.[284]

---

[282] (1961) I ALL NWLR 744.
[283] *(1994) 4 NWLR (pt. 339) 446.*
[284] Badaiki op. cit. pp. 89-114.

Chapter Three

Judicial Approach to the Interpretation of the Constitutions in Australia, Canada and India

Introduction

The various approaches adopted by the courts in Australia, Canada and India will be discussed in this chapter.

The Australian Constitution

The Constitution of Australia was deliberately drafted to embody an ideal of responsible government and representative democracy in which each citizen participates equally with all others. The Australian democracy can be described as "existentialist".

The framers of the Australian Constitution considered the political wisdom of the future generations. Chief Justice Mashall in *McCulloch* v. *Maryland* described the Australian Constitution this way:

> When he spoke of a Constitution, intended to endure for ages to come, and consequently, to be adopted to various crises of human affairs.[1]

The work of the framers of the Australian Constitution reflects an acceptance of the view that, in ages to come, the country would be confronted by crisis, the nature of which could not be foreseen and the solutions for which could not be predicted. Those crises could only be resolved by the collective wisdom of the people of that time. The choice which that generation might make should not be fattered by the supposed wisdom of the past.

Secondly, the Australian Constitution made it easier for the judiciary to maintain the confidence of the public in the work of the Judges as the non-political arm of government.

---

[1] 17 US (4 Wheat) 316, 415 (1819). See also Justice Patrick A.K. In celebration of the Constitution. Presented at the Banco Court in Brisbane 12 June, 2008.

The text of the Australian Constitution, like that of United States and Canada, is written in language which is brief, sometimes obscure and often ambiguous.

By a legislative act of the United Kingdom Parliament[2] the Australian Constitution joined "the people of New South Wales, Victoria, South Australia, Queensland, and Tasmania" to make "one indissoluble Federal Commonwealth"[3] The Australian colonies chose to federate, not out of revolutionary desires to separate from the United Kingdom but instead under the belief that they might benefit from a central government with the power to legislate on matters of common concern.[4] The Australian Constitution was "drafted by a select group of delegates to a series of constitutional conventions held in Australia during the 1890s, and then endorsed by the voters at referenda."[5]

The Australian constitutional framers were influenced by both the English legal tradition, under which the Australian colonies were established and governed, and the United States Constitution.[6] Like the United States Constitution, the Australian Constitution establishes a federal system of government, consisting of the federal government (referred to in the Constitution as "Commonwealth"), States, and Territories[7]. The Australian Constitution gives the federal legislature enumerated powers[8], leaving State parliaments with residual powers.

Like the American counterpart, the Australian Constitution devotes separate chapters to the federal legislature (Chapter 1), executive (Chapter 11) and judiciary (Chapter 111). However, unlike the United States Constitution, the

---

[2] See Commonwealth of Australian Constitution Act, 1900.

[3] Australian Constitution. It should be noted that there are no references to Western Australia in the preamble. There was a good deal of uncertainty about whether Western Australia would join the Federation, and the Western Australian referendum on the question was not held until three weeks after the enactment of Australian's Constitution. Consequently, covering Clause 3 of the Constitution provided for Western Australia's possible late entry. Documenting a Democracy: Australia's story, htt://www.foundingdocs.gov.au/item.asp?dID=11.

[4] John A. La Nauze, The making of the Australian Constitution 1-2 (1972). See also N.K.F. D'Neil, Constitutional Human Rights in Australia, 17 FED. L. REV. 875 (1987).

[5] Peter J. Hanks & Deborah Cass, Australian Constitutional Law: Materials and Commentary 4 (6th ed. 1999).

[6] See Stephen Gageler, Foundations of Australian Federalism and the Role of Judicial Review 17 FED. L. REV. 162, 164 (1987).

[7] Contemporary Australia has six States (New South Wales, Queensland, South Australia, Tasmania, Victoria and Western Australia), two mainland territories (the Australian Capital Territory and the Northern Territory), and a number of external territories CIA   The World Factbook-Australia, http://www/cia.gov./library/pulications/the-worl-factbook//geos/as.html.

[8] Although this Article uses the word "federal", the Constitution itself employs the term "the Parliament of the Commonwealth". AUSTL. CONST Section 51 is the principal provision granting and outlining the federal legislature's powers.

Australian Constitution describes a parliamentary system of government.[9] The Federal Parliament is comprised of the Queen, Senate and House of Representatives.[10] The two Houses of Parliament consist of members "directly chosen by the people,[11] with each State sending an equal number of senators.[12] In accordance with the parliamentary system, section 64 of the Australian Constitution provides that "no Minister of State shall hold office for a longer period than three months unless he is or becomes a senator or a member of the House of Representatives.[13] The framers viewed responsible government as a critical concept underlying the new constitutional framework, creating "the British heart in an otherwise Australian federal body."[14]

Importantly, the Australian Constitution established a federal supreme court, the High Court of Australia..[15] Although modelled on the United States Supreme Court, the High Court differs significantly from its United States cousin in that the Australian Constitution expressly confers jurisdiction on the High Court to hear and determine appeals from both state and federal courts.[16] It should be noted that under the original Australian Constitution, High Court decisions could be appealed to the Privy Council.[17] In fact, the High Court did not truly become the apex of Australia's judicial system until 1986, when the last of a number of legislative enactments aimed for abolishing appeals to the Privy Council was passed[18]. However, the most important connection between Australia and the United Kingdom remains: Australia is a constitutional

---

[9] Simply put this form of government involves 'an executive government chosen from and responsible to Parliament" Sir Anthony Mason, The Role of a Constitutional Court in a Federation: A Comparison of the Australian and the United States Experience, 16 FED. L. 1,3 (1986).

[10] Australian Constitution S.1.

[11] Ibid S.7 (regarding the Senate), S.24 (regarding the House of Representatives).

[12] Ibid. S.7

[13] Ibid. S.64.

[14] Gegeler, op.cit. at p. 172. Bruce Ackerman describes the Australian Constitution as a "fascinating hybrid of British and American elements" Bruce Ackerman, the New Separation of Powers, 113 HARV. L. REV. 633, 674(2000).

[15] Australian Constitution S.71.

[16] Ibid. S. 73 Erin Daly, United States Supreme Court, in Oxford Companion 693 (Tony Blackshield et. al. eds; 2001).

[17] However, cases relating to "the limits inter se of the Constitutional powers of the Commonwealth and those of any State or States, or as to the limits inter se of the Constitutional powers of any two or more States" required, pursuant to S.74 as originally enacted, a Certificate from the High Court to be appealed.

[18] The passage of the Australia Acts, 1986 (Australia) and (U.K) marked the final step in the abolition of appeals from Australian Courts to the Privy Council. This abolition process began with the Privy Council (Limitation of Appeals) Act, 1968 (Australia) and the Privy Council (Appeals form the High Court) Act, 1975 (Australia) Bennett, Establishment of Court, in Oxford Companion 247 (Tony Blackshield et. al. eds., 2001). Although in theory an avenue remains to bring appeals to the Privy Council, the possibility is foreclosed for all practical purposes.

monarchy.[19] Its head of State, the Governor-General, is the representative of the Queen of England in her capacity as Queen of Australia.[20]

The framers of the Australian Constitution did not include a Bill of Rights.[21] This decision, which subsequent generations have left unchanged, leaves Australia an outlier in modern constitutional systems.[22] This does not mean that the Australian Constitution confers no rights. It confers a number of express rights,[23] and has been interpreted to confer implied freedoms.[24]

However, the framers' decision not to include a Bill of Rights has had an enormous impact on the direction of Australian constitutional law. In sharp contrast to other constitutional systems, Australia's Constitution jurisprudence does not include a large body of work in the field of individual rights.[25] Rather, it is principally concerned with the relationships between federal and state parliaments, executives, and courts.[26]

Historical Approach to the Interpretation of the Constitution in Australia

Constitutional Interpretation in Australia started in 1901. Judicial approach to constitutional interpretation started from *coordinate federalism* and then to *centralising legalism, rapid centralisation, political legalism, human rights protection, legal realism* and *judicial activism.*

---

[19] Hank and Cass. op. cit. at p. 28.

[20] Section 61 of the Australian Constitution vests the executive power of the Commonwealth in the Queen, exercisable by the Governor-General as the Queen's representative. Australian Constitution S.61. In a 1999 referendum, Australians voted against amending the Constitution to change Australia from a constitutional monarchy to a republic. Australian Election Commission,
http://www.aec.gov.ue/elections/referendums/1999_referendum_reports_statistics/key_results.htm

[21] Disagreement exists regarding the framers' intentions is not including a written Bill of Rights. The Conventional view is that the framers considered the possibility of including a written Bill of Rights but decided against it, believing that rights would be adequately protected by the common law and legislatures. Tony Blackshield, Bill of Rights, in Oxford Companion 62 (Tony Blackshield et al. eds. 2001). However, some scholars take issue with this view, see e.g. George Williams, Human Rights Under the Australian Constitution 25 (1999).

[22] Blackshield Ibid at pp. 62 and 63.

[23] Adrienne Stone notes that the Constitutional provisions most often categorised as "express rights" include sections 116 (the free exercise of religion), 80 (the right to a jury trial), 51 (xxxi) (the "just terms" requirement of the acquisition power), and 117 (the prevention of discrimination based on state residence) Adrienne Stone, Australia's Constitutional Rights and the Problems of Interpretative Disagreement, 27 Syndey L. Rev. 29, 31 (2005).

[24] An example is the implied freedom of political communication. See e.g. Lange v. Australia Broad Corporation (1997) 189 CLR 520.

[25] See David .S.B The Religion Clauses and Freedom of Speech in Australia and the United States: Incidental Restrictions and Generally Applicable Laws, 46 Drake L. Rev. 53, 56 (1997).

[26] See Collins J.S. Judicial Review and the American Constitution, 17 FED. L. REV. 1,3 (1987).

Coordinate Federalism

Coordinate federation is a concept of federalism in which national, state and local governments interact collectively to solve common problems, rather than making policies separately.

When the Commonwealth of Australia Constitution Act 1900 (UK) took effect on 1st January, 1901, it provided for a Federal Supreme Court, to be called the High Court of Australia.[27] It did not sit, however, until the passage of the Judiciary Act 1903 and the appointment of the first Bench of three judges: Sir Samuel Griffith CJ, Sir Edmoud Barton and Richard Edward O'Connor JJ.[28]

The original Bench comprised a prominent Federalist. Their views informed the High Court's early interpretation of the Constitution, and they were distinctly in favour of a coordinate federation. As Craven argues:

> The critical function of the Court in relation to federalism was to maintain the Commonwealth and the States within their respective spheres, and in particular to ensure that the Commonwealth kept within the ambit of its powers and did not invade the realm of the State.[29]

This federalism was notable in early cases heard by the court. *D' Emden* v. *Pedder*[30] and Deakin v. Webb[31] found that the States could not hinder Commonwealth officers in carrying out their duties and the *Railway Servants' Case*[32] similarly protected the States from Commonwealth legislation. Through this series of cases, the High Court ensured:

> each was to be free to perform its functions and exercise its powers without interference, burden or hindrance from the other government. And so was created and developed the Australian doctrine of the immunity of instrumentalists...[33]

Running alongside this was the doctrine of reserved powers, whose intention was to maintain the exclusive power of the States to manage their domestic concerns.[34]

---

[27] Commonwealth of Australia Constitution Act 1900 (UK) S.71.

[28] The first sitting took place on 6 October 1903 in the Supreme Court building in Melbourme.

[29] Craven, G. The High Court of Australia: A study in the Abuse of Power. Thirty-Five Alfred Deakin Lecture. Melbourme.

[30] (1904) 1 CLR 91.

[31] (1904) 1 CLR 585.

[32] Federated Amalgamated Government Railway and Tramway Service Association v. New South Wales Railway Traffic Employees Association (1906) 4 CLR 488.

[33] Zines, L The High Court and the Constitution of Australia: Butterworths (1908) 6 CLR 469.

[34] Peterwald v. Bartley (1904) ICLR 494.

The workload of the Court increased greatly in the early years as it established for itself a wide appellate jurisdiction. In 1906 two further Justices were appointed, Sir Isaac Isaacs and Henry Bournes Higgins, who were to have a major impact in the constitutional interpretation of the Court due to their differing views on federalism.[35]

Centralising Legalism

With the originalist sentiment of the court come to past, Isaac and Higgins JJ eventually carried with them all the court of 1920 with the exception of Gavan Duffu J.[36]. The Engineers' case[37] rejected the openly federalist principles of the early court in favour of a legalist interpretation of the Constitution that would ultimately lead to a strong centralising trend. Morgan argues that:

> The new post-World War I generation of High Court Justices ...began a process of reducing the effective sovereignty of the States. Some Justices adopted a literalist approach... The doctrine of literal interpretation has enjoyed enormous standing within the legal profession of many generations...The High Court, for over 70 years (in fact since the retirement of Sir Samuel Griffith), has been engaged in this process of reducing the effectiveness of the states.[38]

Indeed, the years immediately following the Engineers' decision seem to reflect the idea that the doctrines of reserved powers and the immunity of instrumentalities had been buried. *Roche* v. *Kronhsimer*[39], *Dignan's case*[40] and *Radio Corporation Pty Ltd* v. *Commonwealth*[41] established the Commonwealth Parliament's ability to delegate legislation. The *Roads case*[42]

> confirmed that specific purpose payments from the Commonwealth to the States could be directed to areas of government responsibility that were not included in formal Constitutional responsibilities.[43]

---

[35] Mr. Justice Isaacs was renowned in his day for supporting pro-Commonwealth Constitutional doctrines because he expressly referred a strong national government. See Gilbert C. Australian and Canadian Federalism 1867- 1984 Melbourme. Melbourme University Press, 1986, 154.

[36] Zines L. The High Court and the Constitution 7

[37] Amalgamated Society of Engineers v. Adelande Steamship Co. Ltd (1920) 28 CLR 129.

[38] Morgan, H. The Australian Constitution: A Living Document. The Samuel Griffith Society, 1992.

[39] (1921) 27 CLR 239.

[40] Victorian Stevedoring and General Contracting Co. Pty Ltd. v. Dignan (1931) 46 CLR 73.

[41] (1938) 59 CRL 170.

[42] Victoria v. Commonwealth (1926) 38 CLR 399.

[43] Bennet, S. Australia's Constitutional Milestone Canberra: Parliamentary Library.

Rapid Centralisation

The increasing international tension in the time leading up to and during World War II saw the High court deal with many disputes over the Commonwealth's defence power. The centralising tendency produced in Engineer's, coupled with the necessities of wartime, led to a continuation of the "expansion of federal power and concurrent downgrading of provincial status that have resulted from the High Court's approach to the Australian Constitution since 1920.[44]

Indeed, many important precedents were decided in this period, which would have massive consequences for the future Australian political and legal landscapes.

According to Kirby, M.:[45]

No clearer illustration of this fact could be found than in the 1935 decision[46]. That the federal Parliament's legislative power in S.51(v) of the Constitution with respect to postal telegraphic and other like services extended to radio (later television) broadcasting services which did not exist (and were not even known to) the framers of the Constitution in the 1890s[47].

Other cases similarly expanded the Constitutional powers of the Commonwealth into areas not explicitly outlined. Attorney-General (V.C) v. Commonwealth[48] allowed a Commonwealth clothing factory, whose primary concern was the production of military uniforms, to also manufacture civilian clothing, despite difficulties establishing a strong link between the activities. *R.* v. *Burgess;* Ex aprte Henry[49] allowed the Commonwealth the power to implement international treaties, establishing a precedent relied on in *Koowarta* v. *Bjelke-Peterson*[50] and other major cases.

Gallingan said:

...the two wars were crucially significant in enhancing both the sense of nationhood and the centralisation of powers. You have a ratchet up of powers to meet the needs of war, and then they don't go down to what

---

[44] Gilbert, C. Australian and Canadian Federalism 1867- 1984. 155.

[45] Kirby, M. Constitutional Interpretation and Original Intent-A Form of Ancestor Worship? 1999 Sir Anthony Mason Lecture, University of Melbourne Law Students' Society.

[46] R.v. Brislan; Ex parte William (1935) 54 CLR 262.

[47] Kirby, M. op. at.

[48] (1935) 52 CLR 533.

[49] (1936) 55 CLR 608.

[50] (1982) 158 CLR 168

they were before the war. Many of the big initiatives, came out of war time-the Commonwealth getting into income tax and so on.[51]

Political Legalism

Legalism is rested on a literal reading of judgement and legislative texts in order to arrive at their meaning. The legalist approach to Constitutional interpretation aims to concentrates on the written text of the Constitution pays little or no attention of a particular legislation or contemporary political expectations.

In 1946, with the financial strain of the war over, the Bench was returned to seven Justices. The Government cited an increased workload and problems with equally split decisions as its reasons for appointing Sir William Flood Webb in May of that year. This was not to be the only change to the court due to the end of World War II; any seeming departure from legalism for policy reasons was to be quickly corrected.

In the years following, the court was reluctant to favour the Commonwealth excessively. In fact, so regular were decisions against the Federal Government that many commentators see political overtones in that period. Howard, said:

> The period since the second World War yields some striking examples. These were the Bank Nationalisation case in 1948, 76 CLR 1, in which the court struck down an attempt by the government of the day to nationalise the Bank. In 1951 there was the Communist Party case, 83 CLR1, in which the court struck down an attempt at the height of the cold war to outlaw the Australian Communist Party. Then there was the long series of cases in which the Court was widely perceived to be on the side of big battalions when it came to tax avoidance.[52]

If the Centralist bias of Engineers' appeared to have been neglected, the legalist approach to constitutional interpretation was stronger than ever. The appointment of Sir Owen Dixon as Chief Justice in 1952 led to his famous praise of legalism. There is no other safe guide to judicial decisions in great conflicts than a strict and complete legalism.[53] This was to be the view of the court for quite some time. Bar-Wick CJ in 1975 appeared to paraphrase Dixon CJ's words: "The only true guide and the only course which can produce stability in constitutional law is to read the language of the Constitution...and to find its meaning in legal reasoning."[54]

---

[51] Galligan, B. in Innes J. Australia's Constitutional Landmarks.
[52] Howard, C. The High Court. The Samuel Griffith Society 1994.
[53] (1952) 85 CLR xiv.
[54] Attorney General (Cth); Ex Pel Mc Kinley v. Commonwealth (1975) 135 CLR 1 at 17.

Indeed, Sir Gar-field Barwick's influence on the court was significant, and not merely in the judicial sense. His efforts in Federal Parliament and later as Chief Justice of the High Court led the push to create a new federal superior courts to ease the burden of both appellate and original cases.

Human Rights Protection
During this time the composition of the Bench changed significantly. Owen, Walsh, Menzies and Windeyer J.J replaced Fullagar, Taylor, Webb and William J.J respectively. The attitudes of the court changed accordingly, and even though a legalistic mindset, they supported legislative protection of human rights within Australia.

According to Bryce, Q.

> "....Key Constitutional landmarks for women included the introduction of the equal pay for equal work principle by the first Equal Pay Case in 1969. The Equal Pay Case of 1972 followed. This case enshrined the principle of equal pay for work of equal value. These cases were possible at a national level because of the conciliation and arbitration power (section 51 (XXXV)) in the Commonwealth Constitution. [55]

Other cases in this period established the ability of the Commonwealth to legislate various rights for all Australians. *Russell* v. *Russell*[56] upheld the Family Law Act 1975. The *Nuclear Text case* saw Australia successful in its litigation of France over environmental issues.

Perhaps the most important subsequent development was the Commonwealth use of its external affairs power to increase its sovereignty over the States. Picking up where the 1936 Burgess case left off, *Koowarta* v. *Bjelke-Peterson*[57] allowed the Commonwealth to legislate nationally for the implementation of international treaties. The Racial Discrimination Act 1975 was upheld as carrying out obligations under the Racial Discrimination Convention. *The Tasmanian Dam care*[58] and *Richardson* v. *Forestry Commission*[59] both found in a similar way.

The court did not limit the power to the implementation of treaties, however, in the *Seas and Submerged Land case*[60] "sovereign rights over territorial seas and the continental shelf was (sic) vested in the Commonwealth," [61] and

---

[55] Bryce, Q in Innes J. Australia's Constitutional Landmarks.
[56] (1976) 134 CLR 495.
[57] (1982) 153 CLR
[58] Commonwealth v. Tasmania (1983) 158 CLR 1
[59] (1988) 164 CLR 261.
[60] New South Wales v. Commonwealth (1975) 135 CLR 337
[61] Bennet J. Australia's Constitutional Milestones.

Strickland v. *Rocla Concrete Pipes Ltd*[62] gave the Commonwealth power over trade conducted by corporations.

Legal Realism

The legalistic approach to the interpretation of the Constitution seems to have been reiterated by Barwick CJ in 1981.

> The rejection of access to the Constitutional debates lasted many generations. As recently at the time of Chief Justice Barwick, the self-denying ordinance was reiterated by a decision of the High Court. But then in Cole v. Whitfield,[63] in an unanimous opinion of the entire Court in 1988, led by Chief Justice Masson, the old legal rule was reversed. The books of the Convention debate were real in open court. [64]

Sir Anthony Mason did indeed lead the move away from Dixon's "strict and complete legalism". Since his appointment as Chief Justice in 1987 and with Dawson, Toohey, Brennan, Deane and Gandron JJ, he has been outspoken in his advocacy of legal realism. "The formulation of legal principle is, and always has been, undertaken in the light of policy considerations.[65] The High Court's more recent decisions have indeed been more liberal with-or at least more honest about-their reliance on policy. The landmark common law decision in Mabo[66] overruled:

> The validity of fundamental propositions which have been endorsed by long-established authority and which have been accepted as the basis of the ...law of the country for more than 150 years. [67]

In Constitutional law the court has returned to a wider reading of the Constitution, including the possibility of implied rights. Craven criticizes:

> the line of cases purporting to discern within the Australian Constitution an implied freedom of political communication, from Australia Capital Television, [68] through Nationwide News,[69] and Theophanous[70] to large and heavy. [71]

---

[62] (1971) 124 CLR 468.

[63] (1988) 165 CLR 360.

[64] Kirby M. Constitutional Interpretation and Original Intent- A Form of Ancestor Worship? 1999 Sir Anthony Mason Lecture.

[65] Mason, A. in Virtue B. High Court is planning New Rules (1993) 28 Australian Lawyer 18.

[66] *Mabo* v. *Queensland* (1992) 175 CLR1

[67] Ibid.

[68] *Capital Television Pty Ltd.* v. *Commonwealth* (1992)177 CLR 106.

[69] Nationwide News Pty Ltd. Wills (1992) 177 CLR 1.

These cases read the right of freedom of political communication into the Constitution as necessary for its operation. Many commentators see this development as a precedent for the process of inventing appropriate rights regardless of whether they exist in the Constitution.

The focus on implied rights has now, however, turned the court away from its Engineers' legacy completely: the sovereignty of the Commonwealth has continued to increase. In *Sue* v. *Hill*[72] the High Court decided that "the United kingdom was, for the purpose of S.44 of the Constitution, a foreign power"[73] *Re The Governor, Goulbum Corrections Centre, Ex Parte Eastman*[74] held that the Territories are not to be treated as States, but are disjointed from Federation.

A significant proportion of lawyers and legal academics are not content with the current trend of "Judicial activism"[75]. Having seen the major shift in judicial reasoning over time, from originalism, through legalism, to realism, one can only speculate on what the future holds for the Australian Constitution. One thing is certain, however, the Commonwealth will gain power at the expense of the States. To borrow from Morgan, "the High Court has become a one-way stop valve".[76]

Judicial Activism is a term used by political scholars to describe a tendency by judges to consider outcomes, attitudinal preferences, and other public policy issues in interpreting applicable existing law. [77] Formally, judicial activism is considered the opposite of judicial restraint, but it is also used pejoratively to denote judges who are perceived to endorse a particular agenda. Although alleged activism may occur in many ways, the most debated cases involve courts exercising judicial review to strike down statutes as unconstitutional. Views about constitutional interpretation abound, ranging from strict constructionist to the living constitution and therefore, in practice, any controversial decision striking down a statute may be labelled by the decision's critics as judicial activism.

---

[70] Theophanous v. Herald Weekly Times Ltd (1994) 182 CLR 104.

[71] Craven G. The High Court of Australia: A study in the Abuse of Power. The Thirty-First Alfred Deakin Lecture 8.

[72] (1999) 73 ALJR 1016.

[73] Kirby M. Constitutional Interpretation and Original Intent- A Form of Ancestor Worship? 1999. Sir Anthony Mason Lecture

[74] (1999) HCA 44 at 87

[75] For example, the Samuel Griffith Society.

[76] Morgan, H. The Australian Constitution: A Living Document.

[77] Merriam – Webster's Dictionary of law defines judicial activism as "the practice in the judiciary of protecting or expanding individual rights through decisions that depart from established precedent or are independent of or in opposition to supposed constitutional or legislative intent. Black's law Dictionary defines judicial activism as "a philosophy of judicial decision – making whereby judges allow their personal views about public policy, among other factors, to guide their decisions, usually with the suggestion that adherents of this philosophy tend to find constitutional violations and are willing to ignore precedent".

Defenders of judicial prerogatives say that many cases of "judicial activism" merely exemplify judicial review and that courts must uphold the Constitution and strike down any statute that violates the Constitution. They say that it is the duty of the courts to protect minority rights and to uphold the law, notwithstanding the political sentiments of the day and that constitutional democracy is far more than just majority rule.

The detractors of judicial activism charge that it usurps power of the legislature, thereby diminishing the rule of law and democracy. They argued that an unelected judicial branch has no legitimate ground to overrule policy choices of duly elected representatives, absent of a real conflict with the Constitution. They argued that neither democracy nor the rule of law can exist when the law is merely what judges say it should be. That the discretion of judges must be limited (e.g. by the intentions of lawmakers), or else any group of people engaged in any behaviour could become a judicially protected minority, and any law could be subverted by the predilections of unelected judges.

Traditional Approaches to Constitutional Interpretation

The traditional theoretical approaches to constitutional interpretation are usually described respectively as *literalism, legalism, texturalism, originalism* and *moderate originalism.* [78]

Literalism

The most frequently quoted enunciation of the doctrine of literalism as the paradigm of constitutional interpretation is to be found in the *Engineers' case:*

> The fundamental rule of interpretation, to which all others are subordinate is that the statute is to be expounded according to the intent of the Parliament that made it; and that intention has to be found by an examination of the language used in the statute as a whole. The question is, what does the language meaning; and when we find what the language means, in its ordinary and natural sense, it is a duty to obey that meaning, even if we think the result to be inconvenient or impolitic or improbable... unless the limitation can be found elsewhere in the Constitution, it does not exist at all. [79]

---

[78] The dominant interpretative paradigm from time of the High Court decision in the Engineers' case until Cole v. Whitfield (1988) 165 CLR 360 has been a combination of literalism and dixonian legalism which together are sometimes labelled textualist, while the dominant paradigm since that time has been moderate originalism, which is also sometimes referred to as "intentionalism" or "semantic originalism" or even "faint-hearted originalism". On the other hand, full-blown originalism properly so-called has never commended itself to Australian judges, and is mostly an American artefact.

[79] Amalgamated Society of Engineers v. The Adelande Steamship Company Ltd & Others (1920) 28 CLR 129 at 161-162. Per Higgins J.

As may be seen, this is a purported application in constitutional setting of the old "golden rule" of ordinary statutory interpretation. Indeed, the Engineer's case emphasizes that ordinary principles of statutory interpretation are applicable to interpreting the Constitution.

The problem with a naive application of a "literalist" approach is that words, even when taken in isolation, simply do not have a single "natural and ordinary" or "essential" meaning. This has been recognized since at least the 16th century by philosophers and linguists as diverse as Thomas Hobbes, Immanuel Kant, Ludwig Wittgenstein and Michel Foucault. Even a cursory glance at any good dictionary will tell us that most words have numerous potential meanings, and the social setting in which they are uttered. Moreover, the meaning of words changes over time. McHugh J gave an example of the changing meaning over time of the word "marriage" as:

> Thus, in 1901 "marriage" was seen as meaning a voluntary union for life between one man and one woman to the exclusion of all others. If that level of abstraction were now accepted it would deny the Parliament of the Commonwealth the power to legislate for same sex marriages, although arguably "marriage" now means, or in the near future may mean a voluntary union for life between two people to the exclusion of others. [80]

In addition, an even more striking example of changing meanings over time is the word "gay", which until recently meant "happy". Indeed the *Oxford Dictionary* does not even mention the current dominant meaning as an alternative, and yet today a person using the word "gay" to mean happy would almost certainly[81] run the risk of being completely misunderstood. Fortunately, the word "gay" does not appear in the Commonwealth Constitution.

The purely linguistic problems of interpretation are still further compounded by the fact that words in the Constitution are commonly found in "compound conceptions." [82]

However, as Kirk suggests, although the majority justices emphasized the necessity to construe the words of the Constitution, their approach is probably better regarded as one of legalism with textualism the instrument of that legalism. The majority justices in the *Engineers' case* emphatically rejected the use of external political principles or policies to interpret the Constitution, and thereby committed the court to the strict legalism of which Sir Owen Dixon became the leading proponent. However, the *Engineers' case* did not rule out of the history or

---

[80] Re Wakin, Ex parte Mc Nally (1999) 163 ALR 270.

[81] And perhaps dangerously depending on the situation.

[82] e.g S. 51 (xxxv) "Conciliation and arbitration for the prevention and settlement of industrial disputes extending beyond the limits of any one State. See Re Pacific Coal Pty Limited; Ex parte Construction, Forestry, Mining and Energy Union (2000) HCA 34 per Mc Hugh J. at pp. 124-128.

background of the Constitution as interpretative aids. The majority justices in that case expressly said in that the Constitution was to be read in the light of the circumstances in which it was made with knowledge of the combined fabric of the common law and the pre-Constitution statute law.

As Kirk has pointed out, the Australian literalist orthodoxy falls within the realm of originalism. Literalism indicates that constitutional words are to be given their full, natural and literal meaning as understood in their textual and historical context. The courts' role is to give effect to the intent of the Constitution's framers, or perhaps that the imperial Parliament, as found "by an examination of the language used in the statute as a whole." This language should be read in its "natural sense"; other considerations should be excluded except "the state of the law as it was when the statute was passed, and the light to be got by reading it as a whole." Provisions are to be understood according to their essential meaning at the time they were enacted in 1900. A distinction has been drawn here between "connotation" and "denotation".[83] In modern philosophical usage this distinction tends to be termed "meaning" or "sense" versus "reference" (or "concept" and "conception").[84] The court seeks the connotation or meaning of the words: the essential qualities or characteristics of the concept referred to, as understood in 1900. The particular matter falling within the scope of those words, the denotations or references, may change over time. The most frequently quoted example of how denotation may change while connotation remains the same is the evolution of the posts and telegraph power in section 51 to include a power to regulate radio and TV broadcasting.[85]

Legalism

The idea that judges should adopt a strictly legalistic approach to interpreting the Constitution was most powerfully enunciated by Dixon C.J on the occasion of his swearing in as Chief Justice of Australia in 1952:

> ...close adherence to legal reasoning is the only way to maintain confidence of all parties in federal conflicts. It may be that the court is thought to be excessively legalistic. I should be sorry to think that it is anything else. There is no safeguard to judicial decisions in great conflicts than a strict and complete legalism. [86]

---

[83] See R v. Commonwealth Conciliation and Arbitration Commission; Ex parte Association of Professional Engineers (1959) 107 CLR 208 at 269 per Winderyer J; Street v. Queensland Bar Association (1989) 168 CLR 461 at 537-538 per Dawson J. for explanations of the connotation/denotation distinction.

[84] A dichotomy used by Mc Hugh J. in Wakim.

[85] Although neither existed in 1901 and therefore were not in the founders contemplation. See R v. Brislan; Ex parte Williams (1935) 54 CLR 262.

[86] Dixon CJ a former Chief Judge of Australia.

The immediate historical context of these remarks was a series of High Court decisions that had been extremely controversial[87] Dixon CJ was in part seeking to modify the outrage of some politicians who had expressed the view,[88] but also expresses His Honour's long held views as to the proper role of the High Court. Dixonian legalism was also the preferred approach to the next Chief Justice Barwick CJ[89] Dixonian legalism has been usefully analysed by Kirk:

> Legalism represents one type of answer to the second basic question of interpretation: the resolution of uncertainty. In its strictest version it signifies that judges neither need make, nor should make, subjective choices; nor should they refer to consequences or policy considerations, when interpreting and applying law. Two elements underpin the approach. One is the declaratory theory of law. The other is the principle that a decision should not depend upon the particular judge hearing in case, which, in turn, reflects the fundamental precept of justice that like cases should be treated alike. Legalism correlates to what Americans often call "interpretivism": the idea that constitutional issues can and should be resolved only by reference to norms and values within the "four corners" of the Constitution. [90]

Legalism was dominant theme of the Engineers decision, with its rejection of subjective "political" judgments. The majority condemned reliance on "necessary implications" by the Griffith High Court in relation to intergovernmental immunities as being vague and elusive, derived from circumstances and hopes external to the Constitution, and "referable to no more definite standard than the personal opinion of the Judge who declares it." By abandoning reliance on such implications, engineers represented a clear step in a legalist direction. Yet even this step was not an unequivocal success in legalist terms. However, the court has subsequently found that one cannot really do without implications when interpreting a document like the Commonwealth Constitution, replete as it is with abstractions and generalities. The modern approach to intergovernmental immunities has re-imposed similar but more limited implications than those abandoned in Engineers.[91] Even more spectacular examples of the failure of a "strict legalism" approach are provided by the case law on sections 90 and 92 of the Constitution. [92]

---

[87] e.g. Bank of New South Wales v. Commonwealth (Bank Nationalisation Case (1948) 79 CLR 1.

[88] Rather like some politicians in the wake of the more recent Mabo and Wik decisions.

[89] See Attorney-General (Cth); Ex rel Mc Kinlay v. Commonwealth (1975) 135 CLR at 17.

[90] Kirk J. Australian Academic.

[91] See Commonwealth v. Cigamatic Ltd (1962) 108 CLR 372; Re Residential Tenancies Tribunal of New South Wales & Others; Ex parte Defence Housing Authority (1996) 146 ALR 495.

[92] Duties of exercise and freedom of interstate trade respectively.

The huge volume of case law generated by the Dixon court's adopted technical and legalistic "criteria of operation" postulates to the characterization of laws alleged to infringe either of these sections was stemmed only by the adoption of a completely different approach in more recent decisions in *Ha* v. *New South Wales*[93] and *Cole* v. *New Whitfield*[94] respectively. State governments who wanted to evade and frustrate the clear intentions of these sections had little difficulty in devising laws whose formal "criteria of operation" took them outside the Dixonian formulae while having exactly the practical effect that the Constitutional drafters clearly wanted to avoid. The High Court's adoption of more subjectively evaluative approaches to both sections is both easier to understand and more intellectually satisfying than the old Dixonian approach. The Court did this by adopting an "intentionalist" or "moderate originalist" approach.

Pure legalism or interpretivism (supposedly neutral interpretation) is an impossible goal[95]. Neither the text nor history will always provide clear answers to a significant number of constitutional questions. That conclusion does concede that language is fundamentally indeterminate. The text may provide clear answers on some matters but not, for example, on issues which are peripheral or unforeseen. However, as Kirk suggests, this ultimate failure of strict legalism need not destroy the whole creed. A legalist judges could, for instance, seek to minimise the number or extent of subjective choices, or could place great weight on past choices made by other judges.

Originalism

It implies strict compliance or reliance on the founders' decisions; it advocates that the meaning of constitutional provisions is fixed as at 1900. Recourse to the Convention Debates has been useful[96] in ascertaining the constitutional intention in some cases, especially relating to sections 90 and 92. But such an approach has been of much more limited value in many other cases, especially those involving section 51 heads of power. As Kirk J. says, there are numerous problems with seeking to ascertain the enactors' intentions from reading the Convention Debates:

> Rarely, in assemblies of any size, will a majority of speakers express clear views. It would be vary rare for most of the winning majority on any particular question to have spoken, let alone an overall majority of the assembly derived first from the winning majority. The Convention Debates are no exception in this regard. Collective intent can then only be gathered

[93] (1997) 189 CLR 465.
[94] (1988) 165 CLR 360.
[95] See L. Zines. The High Court and the Constitution (4th ed.) 1997 Chapter 17.
[96] Since first permitted in Cole v. Whitfield (1988) 165 CLR 360.

by assuming that the silent members agreed with the comments of the leading proponents. Ascertaining group intent from individual statements are expressly endorsed by the group is inherently speculative and may often be wrong. This problem represents one of the main reasons that the courts have long been wary of taking account of extrinsic materials.

Sometimes there may simply be no common intention. Quite different conceptions of the effect of a measure may emerge form its supporters. Some delegates may expect it to be interpreted in one way but actually hope that it is interpreted in another... Indeed, sometimes the framers deliberately left issues to be resolved by the Court, as appears to have been the case with S. 92...

The Australian Convention Debates in particular appear to offer little practical guidance to the resolution of interpretative disputes. Reane J has dismissed the framers' contributions to Convention discussions as "largely extempore and sometimes ill-informed". Brazil described the Debates as "rambling affairs". Zines and Lindell have noted that relatively little time was spent on the extent of the powers granted to the Commonwealth. The framer simply did not directly address certain crucial issues, such as whether, and to what extent, the Constitution incorporates the doctrine of the separation of powers. More generally, the framers' discussion of any issue tended naturally to concentrate on matters of contemporary concern, but it would be erroneous to conclude from this "that the relevant provision was directed to that issue and nothing else. [97]

Another important question here is: whose intentions are relevant? Judges have sometimes talked of what "the Constitution intended". [98] A document cannot have intentions; it can only manifest them. Meaning is what the reader takes from a communication. The random typing of monkeys will eventually produce a work capable of having meaning to us, but it would have no intended meaning and we would have no reason to attach significance to it. Originalism involves seeking the meaning that the speaker intended to convey.

A further problem with seeking to ascertain the enactors' 1900 intentions is to decide whose intentions are important, i.e. is it the intention of the Convention delegates who drafted the Constitution (assuming they even had a collective intention and we could work out what it was)? Or is it the intention of the Australian people who voted for it at referenda in 1899-99 (an intention which Kirby J has labelled as "unknowable")? Or is it the intention of the imperial Parliament which actually enacted the Constitution and gave it legal force?

---

[97] Kirk J. Australian Academic.
[98] e.g Lange v. Australian Broadcasting Corporation (1997) 189 CLR 520 at 577.

However, the imperial Parliament, although it insisted on some minor amendments concerning Privy Council appeals, most simply referred to the wishes of the Australian people as expressed in the text presented to it for enactment. The High Court has never expressed a view on exactly whose intention we are seeking.

The most vocal advocate of "pure" originalism in the US is Supreme Court Justice Antonin Scalia. Justice Scalia said that the Constitution has a fixed meaning, which does not change: it means today what it meant when it was adopted, nothing more and nothing less. Moreover, as Rosen J[99] convincingly demonstrates, Scalia tends in reality only to pay lip service to the task of divining the founder's intentions: he ignores them when they fail to coincide with his own ultra-conservative views and reverts to justifying those views by appeals to what everyone (i.e everyone who agrees with him) traditionally believes. Scalia's minority judgments on abortion and gay rights legislation most clearly demonstrate this methodological inconsistency. Scalia's extreme originalist approach has never commended itself to Australian judges. As Mc Hugh said in Eastman:

> In one very important respect, judicial practice in Australia has departed from Justice Scalia's view of constitutional interpretation and the notion that the meaning of constitutional provisions is fixed as at 1900. Even taking the most favourable view of the Court's interpretation of some constitutional provisions, it is difficult to reconcile some judicial decisions as to their meaning with the theory that the meaning of each constitutional provision is that which it had in 1900. To take one example: Sir Harry Gibbs had noted, the interpretation has assumed a meaning vastly different from that contemplated by the framers of the Constitution.

> The reason for the Court's interpretation is that the relevant intention of constitutional provisions is that expressed in the Constitution itself, not the subjective intentions of its framers or makers. It is an intention that is determined objectively. Indeed until Cole v. Whitfield the court would not even look at the Convention Debates. [100]

Theoretical Approaches to Constitutional Interpretation
The three main constitutional interpretative methods in Australia are *literalism*, *intentionalism* and *progressivism*.

---

[99] Rossen J. Origionalist Sin, New Republic, 5 May 1997.
[100] (2000) HCA 29 (25 May, 2000).

Literalism

Graven G. describes literalism as interpreting the Constitution "by reading the words according to their natural sense and in a documentary context and thus giving them their full effect."[101]

However one of the most persuasive arguments towards the literalism approach is that it is political, it avoid judges making decisions by some other considerations.[102] While others argue it also gives certainty to meaning, it can be shown that the English Language is ambiguous in many instances and this may lead to uncertainty.

Progressivism

Progressivism is an approach to constitutional interpretation which maintains that provisions should be interpreted as to give meaning most consonant with the recognition and satisfaction of the need of contemporary Australian society.[103]

Progressivism does not restrict the interpretation of the Constitution to the intentions of the framers or the plain meaning but allows the Constitution to be interpreted to the needs of an ever changing liberal democracy. [104]

Critics of progressivism suggest that it is political and allows unelected judges to state what they view to be the needs of Australian society. [105]

Intentionalism

Intentionalism holds that the Constitution should be interpreted "to give effect to the intentions of those who formulated the Constitution."[106]

Intentionalist argue that ambiguity can be overcome by analyzing the framers intentions by looking at the Convention Debates and the Constitution Drafts which the High Court has done.[107]

The major criticism of intentionalism is that it does not allow for the nation to progress by restricting the interpretation of the Constitution to that of the founders.[108]

---

[101] Craven G. The Crisis of Constitutional Literalism in Australia in HP Lee and G Winterton (eds) Australian Constitutional Perspectives (1992) 1 at 6.

[102] Ibid at p.10.

[103] Ibid at p.20.

[104] Craven G. *op. cit.* at p. 15.

[105] Mason A. "Interpretation in a Modern Liberal Democracy" in Sampford. C and Preston K (ed.) Interpreting Constitutions – Theories, Principle and Institutions 1996 p. 31.

[106] Ibid at p. 17.

[107] Cole v. Whitfield (1988) 165 CLR 360.

[108] Goldsworthy, J. "Originalism in Constitutional Interpretation" (1997) 25 Fed LR at 27.

Judicial Approach to the Interpretation of the Constitution in Australia

Justice Mason, A[109] though classified the various approaches to the interpretation of the Constitution of Australia as that of originalism,[110] intentionalism,[111] literalism,[112] progressivism or flexible interpretation, the learned jurist does not expressly align himself with any of the doctrines. He said "Australian courts has for a long time, turned its back upon originalism and pure intentionalism.[113] He is of the opinion that a constitutional court, must interpret the constitutional charter in a way that will "reinforce and enhance the concept of a modern liberal democracy.[114] However he cautions:

> Just how far a constitutional court can travel down such a path will be affected by the court's own assessment of legitimacy and perceptions of legitimacy. In other words, much depends upon the court's perception of the underlying political philosophy of the nation, as to the appropriate limits of the law-making function of a non-elected judiciary.[115]

He remarked that the task of a judge is how best he could interpret the Constitution. Each judge is obliged to do more than to stumble about looking for a solution to the particular case. Intuition and instinct about such matters are not enough. Sitting on a desk with the Constitution in one hand and a dictionary in the other, is also not enough. Following blindly judicial opinions written in earlier and very different times may not be enough, as *Sue* v. *Hill*[116] demonstrates that each judge should have a theory of constitutional interpretation. In the absence of a theory, inconsistency will proliferate.

An adequate grounding in the various theoretical bases of constitutional interpretation that have been propounded and applied by judges is vital to a proper understanding of the subject of judicial approach to interpretation of the Constitution in Australia. As Kirby M explained:

> The Constitutions of the United States of America, (1776 - 1790); Canada (1867), and Australia (1901) are amongst the three most enduing of such documents in the world today. But what do they mean? The question of

---

[109] Sir Anthony Mason, past Justice and Chief Judge of the High Court of Australia. See also Mason A.F. "The interpretation of a Constitution in a Modern Liberal Democracy" in C Sampford and K Preston (eds.) Interpreting Constitutions: Theories, Principles and Institutions (1996) 13 at 14.
[110] Ibid at p. 14.
[111] Ibid at p. 15.
[112] Ibid. The Literalist approach was favoured in Australian Society of Engineers v Adelande Steamship Co. Ltd (The Engineer's case) (1920) 28 CLR 129.
[113] Ibid.
[114] Ibid at p. 30.
[115] Ibid at p. 30.
[116] (1999) 73 ALJR 1016.

constitutional interpretation arises at the very threshold of every cases in which the constitutional text must be elucidated. The text of the Australian Constitution – like that of the United States and Canada is written in language which is brief, sometimes obscure and often ambiguous. As recent shifts in the court's elaboration of the meaning of the Constitution demonstrate, even an assertion that a particular construction of the text is "settled" by many past decisions does not necessarily bolt the door against re-examination of the Constitution if new scrutiny is considered necessary by the majority of the Justices of the High Court. This is why the approach to construction of the Constitution arises at the threshold of all the great constitutional disputes. It is one which has fascinated the Justices themselves. It has attracted a great deal of writing by scholars, both in Australia and overseas. It ought to concern all practitioners and students of the law in a federation, like Australia, with a written Constitution adopted long ago. Citizens know about it. [117]

Justice Kirby is a strong advocate of a "dynamic" approach to constitutional interpretation, whereby the constitutional text is interpreted according to the meaning it has for a contemporary reader, not anchored in or fettered by the meaning the words may have had for the Founding Fathers who drafted them and the above quote reflects Kirby J's approach. However, Kirby J is the only one of the current High Court Justices to adopt an avowedly "dynamic" approach to the interpretative task (although Mason CJ and Deane J flirted with such an approach from time to time). Most of the current Justices, profess to adhere either to the traditional interpretative theory, which may best be described as "textualist", or to "intentionalism" (sometime known as "semantic originalism" or various other names). McHugh J, and possibly Gandron J (although she has not expressly spelled out her theory of constitutional interpretation), now seem to have adopted a theory of interpretation expounded by the American jurisprudential scholar, Ronald Dworkin in his book, *Law's Empire*. Mc Hugh J also seems to approve of an approach recently developed by Australian academic Jeremy Kirk and known as "evolutionary originalism". [118]

Jeremy Kirk explains the need for a consistent theory of constitutional interpretation:

A Constitution cannot be applied without employing some theory of interpretation. An adequate theory – that is, a coherent method or approach – must address two fundamental, connected questions. In what sense are words in the text to be understood? and how is ambiguity or

---

[117] Kirby, M. Constitutional Interpretation and Original Intent – A Form of Ancestor Worship? "Being text of a lecture delivered in September 1999.
[118] Ibid.

uncertainty to be resolved? Resolution of these matters is logically prior to the determination of particular controversies. Of necessity, judges have provided some answers to these fundamental questions. But the issues have only began to attract significant express attention in recent times, particularly in light of developments relating to implied rights. This new – found concern is not further one moves from considering clear and direct stipulations of particular text, the more important one's interpretational approach become. The theory of constitutional interpretation employed affects both one's readiness to recognize implications, and the nature and age of the sources to which reference is made in so doing. [119]

A further reason why an "internally consistent and normatively defensible" theory (to use Jeremy Kirk's words) is needed is fairly obvious fact that most provisions in the Commonwealth Constitution are expressed in rather vague and general terms. As McHugh J put it in *Eastman* v. *The Queen*:

> Our Constitution is constructed in such a way that most of its concepts and purposes are stated at a sufficient level of abstraction or generality to enable it to be infused with the current understanding of those concepts and purposes. This is consistent with the notion that our Constitution was intended to be an enduring document able to apply to emerging circumstances while retaining its essential integrity. The Constitution was addressed to posterity as well as to those living at the time of its enactment. Those who framed and enacted the Constitution knew that the meaning of the document would have to be deduced by later generations as well as their contemporaries. [120]

Undoubtedly, the decisions of a constitutional court like Australia's High court are "political" and equally undoubtedly judges' decisions must be influence at least to some extent by their subjective values and perceptions.

The earliest Constitutional approach to the interpretation of the Constitution in Australia started at the time of Chief Justice Griffith, and Justice Barton and O' Connor. Their approach does not appear to be legalistic, for example, in *D' Emdan* v. *Pedder*,[121] which concerned whether a state law could interfere with a federal agency or instrumentality, Chief Justice Griffith indicated that "in considering the validity of legislation under the Constitution, the substance and not the form of the legislation is to be regarded...[122] In this case, the Chief Justice also indicated the court's approach to interpreting federal grants

---

[119] Ibid.
[120] (2000) HCA 29 (25 May, 2000).
[121] (1904) 1 C.L.R. 91.
[122] Ibid. at p. 108 (Griffith, C.J.).

of legislative power under the Constitution.[123] Where any power or control is expressly granted, there is included in the grant, to the full extent of the capacity of the grantor... every power and every control the denial of which would render the grant itself ineffective.[124] Among the earliest cases outlining the first High Court's approach to constitutional interpretation, these statements are not those of a strict legalistic.

Similarly, in *Municipal Council of Sydney* v. *Commonwealth*,[125] a case decided two months after D' Emden, Justice O' Connor outlined very clearly an approach to constitutional interpretation not confined to the text's express words.[126] In favouring a broad construction of the word "tax" in Section 114 of the Constitution, Justice O' Connor stated:[127]

> But to get at the real meaning (the High Court) must go beyond (the Constitution's words), it must examine the content, consider the Constitution as a whole, and its underlying principles and any circumstances which may throw light upon the object which the Convention had in view, when they embodied it in the Constitution.[128]

D' Emden established two elements of the High Court's conception of the Constitution which would remain central to the court's constitutional vision until 1920.[129] First, the court made it clear that when "considering the respective powers of the Commonwealth and of the States, it is essential to bear in mind that each is, within the ambit of its authority, a sovereign State."[130] Following from this, "the Commonwealth is entitled, within the ambit of its authority, to exercise its legislative and executive powers in absolute freedom, and without any interference or control whatsoever except that prescribed by the Constitution itself.[131] The effect on the States was clear: any legislative attempt to interfere with the federal exercise of constitutional powers was invalid.[132] Secondly, D' Emden emphasized that it was the court's duty to determine the validity of federal and state legislation.[133]

---

[123] Ibid at. pp. 101.102.
[124] Ibid at. p 110.
[125] (1904) 1 CLR 208.
[126] Ibid at. pp. 235-42 (O' Connor, J.).
[127] Ibid at pp. 238-39.
[128] Ibid at p. 239.
[129] D' Emden (1904) I CLR at p. 177 (Griffith, C.J).
[130] Ibid at p.109. See also Municipal Council (1904) l CLR at. p. 231 (Griffith, C.J.)
[131] D' Emden op. cit at pp.110-111.
[132] ibid at. p. 111. This Principle was affirmed in Deakin v. Webb (1904) l CLR p.585 (here in after referred to as Deakin.)
[133] Ibid at p. 117.

D' Emden's holding that a state legislature cannot "fetter, control, or interfere with, the free exercise of the legislative or executive power of the Commonwealth...unless expressly authorized by the Constitution"[134] was not based on any express provision of the Constitution. Rather, the limitation was implied in the Constitution.[135] Even so, the court clearly viewed its methodology as orthodox, considering itself to be acting entirely within the principles of ordinary statutory interpretation that formed part of the English legal canon.

Interestingly, the Judicial Committee of the Privy Council did not agree[136] in *Webb* v. *Outtrim*,[137] the Privy Council considered the question of whether a federal officer, who lived in the State of Victoria and earned and received his salary in Victoria, was liable to pay tax under Victorian income tax legislation.[138] The question required the Privy Council to examine the High Court's D' Emden decision.[139] The Privy Council disapproved of D' Emden, holding that the federal officer was liable to assessment under the state income tax legislation.[140] The Privy Council's reasons are interesting, particularly because what seems to principally aggrieve the Privy Council is the court's reliance on Chief Justice Mashall's opinion in Mc Cuttoch.[141] Moreover, the Privy Council specifically took issue with the High Court's approach to constitutional interpretation outlined in D' Emden.[142] Specifically, their Lordships were "not able to acquiesce" in the High Court's "expansion of the canon of interpretation... to consider the knowledge of those who framed the Constitution and their supposed preferences for this or that model which might have been in their minds."[143] In disapproving of D' Emden, the Privy Council not only gave the High Court Justices a serious rebuke, but delegitimized the High Court's claim that it merely applied conventional English common law methods of statutory interpretation to the Constitution.

The High court responded forcefully to Webb. In *Baxter* v. *Commissioners of Taxation (N.S.W.)*,[144] Chief Justice Griffith (writing also for Justices Barton and O' Cannor) penned what has been described as "the most vitriolic judgment in the Commonwealth Law Reports"[145] Concluding that a Privy Council decision

---

[134] Ibid at p. 111 (Griffith, C.J).
[135] Ibid.
[136] See Webb v. Outtrim (1906) 4 CLR at p. 356 (here in after referred to as Webb).
[137] Ibid.
[138] Ibid at pp. 356- 57.
[139] Ibid at pp. 356-60.
[140] Ibid at p. 361 (The Earl of it Halsbury delivered their Lordships' Judgment).
[141] Ibid.
[142] Ibid at pp. 360- 361.
[143] Ibid at p. 360.
[144] (1907) 4 CLR at p. 1087.
[145] Chief Justice Murray Glesson. The Centenary of the High Court: Lessons from History (Oct 3, 2003) available at http://www.hcourt.gov.an/speeches/cj/cj_3oct.html.

regarding the parameters of the Australian Constitution could not "be put any higher than a decision on foreign law as a question of fact," the joint Justices held the High Court not bound by the Webb.[146]

Ultimately, however, the implied immunity doctrine did not survive, and with its death also came the demise of the most flexible approach to constitutional interpretation it supported. The High Court rejected the implied immunity doctrine, as well as another doctrine developed in the early years of the Court, the "reserved power doctrine", in one of its most famous decisions, *Amalgamated Society of Engineers* v. *Adelande Steamship Co. Ltd. (Engineers' case)*.[147] It is important, however, to first emphasize that the approach taken in D'Emden was not wholly representative of the early Court's approach to constitutional interpretation. Indeed, in other cases, the High court demonstrated its unwillingness to interpret the Constitution more flexibly than conventional methods of statutory interpretation might otherwise allow.[148]

The High Court delivered the Engineers' Case decision in 1920.[149] Chief Justice Knox presided over the court after becoming Chief Justice in 1919.[150] The *Engineer's case* began when the Amalgamated Society of Engineers, a union, lodged a claim under the Commonwealth Conciliation and Arbitration Act (1904). The respondents included the Western Australian Minister of Trading concerns, the State Implement and Engineering Works and the State Sawmills.[151] Consequently, the question that arose regarded whether an award under the federal legislation could bind the state of Western Australia.[152] In making his case for the Union, Robert Menzies, who later became Prime Minister of Australia, challenged the *Railway Servants' case*.[153] The High Court seized this opportunity to reconsider the implied immunity doctrine, holding in a five-to-one decision that the Federal Parliament had the power to enact laws binding the States.[154]

The High Court's rejection of the implied immunity doctrine proved a critical step in the Court's development of its approach to constitutional

---

[146] Baxter (1907) 4 CLR at 1118 (Griffith, C.J, Barton and O' Connor, JJ). Justice Isaacs also held Webb not binding but for different reason.

[147] (1920) 28 CLR 129.

[148] e.g. Tax v. Commonwealth (1904) 1 CLR 329, 333, 338, 340 (Griffith C.J.), 348 (Barton, J) 358 (O'Connor, J), Federated Amalgamated Gov't Ry, and Traim way Serv. Ass'n v. N.S.W. Ry Traffic Employees Ass'n (Railway Servants Case) (1906) 4 CLR 488, 534 (Griffith, C.J, Barton and O'Connor, JJ.).

[149] Engineer's Case (1920) 28 CLR at 129, Six Justices heard the case: Chief Justice Knox, and Justices Isaac, Higgins, Gavan Duffy, Rich, and Starke, Justice Powers did not hear the case.

[150] Engineers' Case (1920) 28 CLR at pp. 131-132 (Knox, C.J, Isaacs, Rich, and Starke, JJ.).

[151] Ibid.

[152] Ibid.

[153] Ibid at pp.132-134. See also Keven Booker Arthur Glass, the Engineers Case in Australian Constitutional landmark 34, 40 (HP. Lee and George Winterton eds 2003).

[154] Ibid. at pp. 129, 140, 171, Justice Gavan Duffy dissented.

interpretation.[155] In rejecting the doctrine, the High Court made it clear that it considered the D'Emden approach erroneous and outlined its view regarding the correct method.[156] For the Engineers' Case Court, a principal difficulty with D'Emden and ilk was the Constitution's interpretation by reference to implications drawn from outside the Constitution's text or any "acknowledged common law constitutional principle.[157] Thus, the joint Justices chided their predecessors for interpreting the Constitution by reference to an implication "formed on a vague, individual conception of the spirit of the compact, which is not the result of interpreting any specific language to be quoted, nor referable to any recognized principle of the common law of the Constitution.[158]

Moreover, an extremely disapproving view was taken of the early High Court's reliance on decisions of the United States Supreme Court in its development of the implied immunities doctrine.[159] For the Joint Justices, two "cardinal features" of the Australian political system – "the common sovereignty of all parts of the British Empire", and the principle of responsible government – fundamentally distinguished the Australian system from that of the United States.[160] Therefore, reliance on America constitutional law when interpreting the Australian Constitution constituted "profound error"[161] Looking beyond the rhetoric, one wonders whether the High Court's resistance to the use of American Case law is really attributable to the more purposive style of Constitutional interpretation exhibited in decisions such as Mc Culloch.[162]

According to the *Engineers' case*, the correct approach to constitutional interpretation was not found in the developing jurisprudence of the United States, but instead by reference to the "settled rules of construction…very distinctly enunciated by the highest tribunals of the Empire."[163] Applying these established rules to the interpretation of the Australian Constitution, the joint Justices emphasized the need to give constitutional words their natural meaning,[164] taking guidance from "the circumstances in which the Constitution was made, with knowledge of the combined fabric of the common law, and the statute law which preceded it…"[165] In determining whether a statute exceeded a grant of power, the joint Justices adopted the approach taken by the Privy Council, namely,

---

[155] See e.g Booker & Glass op. cit at. p.138 at pp 36, 47.
[156] Engineers Case op.cit at pp. 145-146, 148-146, (Knox, CJ, Isaacs, Rich and Starke JJ.).
[157] Ibid at p. 145
[158] Ibid at. p. 145.
[159] Ibid at pp. 145-147.
[160] Ibid at p. 146.
[161] Ibid.
[162] See generally Mc Culloch, 17 U.S (4 Wheat) 316 (1819).
[163] Engineers Case op. cit at p. 148 (Knox, C.J. Isaacs, Rich, and Starke, JJ.).
[164] Ibid at pp 149-152.
[165] Ibid at p. 149.

affirmative grants of power should be limited only by express conditions or restrictions in the granting instrument itself.[166] Focusing upon the text's express words and insisting that constitutional interpretation not drawn upon extra-constitutional matters, the *Engineers' case* has been viewed as casting an unfavourable light on the drawing of constitutional implications generally.[167] Applying "ordinary principles of construction" to the Constitution,[168] the joint Justices construed the constitution's grant of legislative power to the Federal Parliament as plenary but "within prescribed limits..."[169] The joint Justices held that federal legislative power could not be limited by reference to a doctrine which "finds no place" where those "ordinary principles" are applied.[170] Therefore, the *Engineers' case* held that States were subject to application and enacted federal legislation.[171]

The *Engineers' case* represents a seminal moment in the High Court's constitutional jurisprudence.[172] Particularly, its affirmation of the application of traditional principles of statutory construction to constitutional interpretation has had a lasting impact on Australian jurisprudence.[173] Development of the Australian approach to judicial review, however, cannot be fully understood without reference to Australia's pre-eminent jurist, Sir Owen Dixon.

Dixon, a forceful proponent of "strict and complete legalism"[174] during his tenure as Chief Justice, (1952-54), served to consolidate legalism as the Australian High Court's dominant approach to constitutional interpretation.[175] In advocating his brand of legalism, Dixon saw himself as applying the historic judicial method developed over time in the English courts.[176] Because this method reverses "uniformity, consistency, and certainty,"[177] the doctrine of stare decisis was of fundamental importance to Dixon.[178] He was enormously reluctant to depart from precedent, even in significant constitutional cases.[179]

---

[166] Ibid approving of the Queen v Burah, 3 App. Cas 889, 904-095 (U.K).
[167] Booker and Glass, op.cit at p.44.
[168] Engineers' Case op. cit at p.155 (Knox, C.J, Isaacs, Rich and Starke JJ.).
[169] Ibid at. p. 153.
[170] Ibid at. p.155.
[171] Ibid.
[172] Booker & Glass op.cit at p. 36.
[173] Ibid.
[174] Dixon, op. cit at p. 249.
[175] Zine, op. cit at pp. 220, 222
[176] See Dawson & Nicholls op. cit. at p. 545.
[177] Mire house (1833) 1 CL & F 527, 546, 6 ER 1015, 1023 (Eng.).
[178] Dawson & Nicholls op. cit p. 91 at 547-548.
[179] Ibid at pp 548-549.

Relevant to this Article, Dixon chose to apply the traditional common law method to the adjudication of constitutional cases.[180] Dixon thought it "of particular importance that the technique of the common law should be applied to the construction of what he described more than once as a "rigid" Constitution, in order to maintain public confidence in the Court's judgments in areas of political conflict."[181] Thus, as a general proposition, Dixon considered questions arising under the Constitution as not requiring a different judicial method than questions arising under the general law.

An important theme emerges from the decisions previously discussed. From the very earliest High Court decisions to Dixion's enunciation of preferred approach to constitutional interpretation, there existed a clear insistence on the application of ordinary principles of statutory interpretation of the interpretation of the Constitution. Given that "statutes more readily lend themselves to a legalistic approach,"[182] it is unsurprising that legalism became such a dominant force in Australian constitutional interpretation.

However, the High Court's application of statutory interpretation principles to the Constitution's interpretation is problematic, given the obvious differences between them. For example, while constitutions tend to be broadly framed so that they can be judicially adopted over time, statutes generally use more specific language and are usually tailored to deal with a narrow set of issues or circumstances.[183]

The Canadian Constitution

Canada does not have a single constitutional text. Canada's Constitution includes several components, including portions of the unwritten Constitution and common law of Great Britain, as well as two major texts of constitutional import: the Constitution Act of 1867 (as amended) and the Constitution Act of 1982, of which the Charter of Rights and Freedoms is a part.

Prior to 1982, Canada like Great Britain did not have a constitutionally secure "bill of rights" that was immune from ordinary parliamentary amendment.[184] Despite the absence of written constitutional guarantee of rights

---

[180] Ibid at pp. 544- 545.

[181] Ibid at p. 545.

[182] Moson, op. cit at p. 5.

[183] Ibid.

[184] For example, the 1960 "Canadian Bill of Rights" was an ordinary statute susceptible to amendment by Parliament and it applied only to the federal government. It must be noted that an ordinary statute, the freedom of Worship Act, adopted in 1851 under the Act of Union, was for the first time and successfully invoked by Jehovah's Witnesses in the Supreme Court of Canada, in the following cases: Boucher v. the King (1951) 1 SCR 265, Saumur v. the City of Quebec, (1953) 1 SCR 299 Chaput v. Romain (1955) 1 SDR 834.

before 1982, Canada inherited the unwritten English Constitution and common law, which had made a contribution toward protecting civil liberties.

The supreme law in Canada is the Constitution. Canada's Constitution is a combination of both codified and uncodified acts, conventional practices and traditions. The Constitution Act 1867, originally the British North America Act, provides the core of the Canadian Constitution. It describes the structure and workings of government at the federal and provincial levels, among other things. The Constitution Act 1982 includes the Charter of Rights and Freedoms which functions as an entrenched bill of rights, is also an integral part of Canada's Constitution. Because it has a long and storied history as a member of the Commonwealth, Canada's legal system is solidly embedded in the British common law tradition. However, Quebec has its own separate history as a French colony which makes it a special case in many aspects of law, and it retains a unique civil system for handling issues of private law. Both Canadian legal systems are subject to, and protected by the Constitution of Canada.

The Canadian court system is made up of many courts differing in levels of the legal superiority and separated by jurisdiction. Some of the courts are federal in nature while others are provincial or territorial. This intricate inter-wearing of Canada's federal and provincial powers is typical of the Canadian Constitution. Generally speaking, Canada's court system is a four – level hierarchy. Each court is bound by the rulings of the courts above them however, they are generally not bound by their own past rulings or the rulings of other courts at the same level of hierarchy. The Canadian Constitution gives the federal government the exclusive right to legislate criminal law while the Provinces have exclusive control over civil law. The Provinces have jurisdiction over the administration of justice in their territory. Almost all cases, whether criminal or civil, start in provincial courts and may be eventually appealed to higher level courts. The quite small system of federal courts only hear cases concerned with matters which are under exclusive federal control, such as immigration.

In its preamble, the Constitution of Canada speaks of the desire of the Provinces of Canada to be "federally united into one Dominion under the Crown of the United Kingdom of Great Britain and Ireland with a Constitution similar in principle to that of the United Kingdom." Historically, then, the Constitution of Canada like the Constitution of the United States, stems from a compact between a number of different territorial units: the provinces of Lower Canada (Quebec), Upper Canada (Ontario), and the eastern maritime promises of Nova Scotia and New Brunswick, joined together in 1867 to form the new Dominion of Canada, a number of other provinces having been admitted to the union since that time. Jurisdically speaking, however, the origins are rather different. The fundamental instrument in which the Canadian Constitution is embodied, the British North

America Act of 1867 (B.N.A.)[185] is a statute of the United Kingdom Parliament, which calls attention to the fact that though Canada in 1867 became a self-governing Dominion within the then British Empire by virtue of the Act, her status for many purposes internationally was still something less than a full sovereign state. Although by 1931 the highly developed conventions governing the relationship of the United Kingdom to the self-governing Dominions had crystallized into the positive law rules of the statute of Westminster, some vestiges of Canada's former subordinate position still remained.

The B.N.A. Act contains no provision as to its own amendment, constitutional change in Canada had perforce to be achieved by recourse to the original source of the Canadian Constitution, the United Kingdom Parliament. The considerable number of amendments to the Canadian Constitution that have been effected since 1867 have been in the form of Acts of the United Kingdom Parliament. Even today, when all political parties are satisfied as to the desirability of some amending procedure that can be operated by the Canadian people themselves, it is agreed that the exact formula for amendment, a matter of some considerable controversy as yet must finally be embodied in an Act of the United Kingdom Parliament to become effective.[186]

Theories of Interpretation of the Constitution in Canada
The theories of interpretation of the Constitution in Canada include *originalism* or *frozen right theory, the living tree doctrine, progressive interpretation, the dynamic interpretation,* and *deconstruction and critical legal studies.*

Originalism or Frozen Right Theory
It implies that judges should stick to the original meaning of the terms of a Constitution, because that is all that was ratified by the people who are governed by it. This theory is often referred to as the "frozen rights" approach to constitutional interpretation.

The frozen rights theory is not acceptable in Canada for the following reasons:
1. The frozen right theory misconceives the nature of Canadian Constitution and government institutions and history;
2. Supporters of "original meaning" in Canada ignore the lessons of some of the less glorious episodes in the Canadian constitutional history, including the Persons' Case where the courts in Canada embarrassed themselves by holding, in accordance with the "original meaning" of section 32 of the Constitution

---

[185] 36, & 31 Vict, c. 3(1867)
[186] Livingston. The Amending Power of the Canadian Parliament 45, AM. POL. SCT. REV. 437 (1951); Gerim-Lajoie Du pouvoir d'amendment constitutionnel on Canada, 29 CAN. B REV. 1736 (1951).

Act, 1867, that women were not qualified for appointment to the Senate because they were not "qualified persons";

3. The argument about "original meaning" is at bottom an argument about judicial legitimacy;

4.   Lastly the "living tree" approach is considered to be a better alternative to the "original meaning" theory.

The living Tree Doctrine

The living Tree Doctrine is an entirely new approach to constitutional interpretation in Canada that has since become one of the core principles of constitutional law in Canada.

Viscount Sankey invented the "living tree", along with the large – and – liberal approach to constitutional interpretation. In Canada, the living tree doctrine is a doctrine of constitutional interpretation that says that a Constitution is organic and must be read in broad and liberal manner so as to adopt it to the changing times.

This is known as the Doctrine of progressive interpretation. This means that the Constitution cannot be interpreted in the same way as an ordinary statute. Rather, it must be read within the context of society to ensure that it adopts and reflects changes.

The "living tree" method of construing the Constitution was established by the Privy Council in Edwards v. A.G Canada.[187] In that case the Privy Council was asked to interpret S. 24 of the Constitution Act, 1867, which provides (in part) as follows:

> The Governor General shall from time to time, in the Queen's name, by instrument under the great seal of Canada, summon qualified persons to the senate and subject to the provisions of this Act, every person so summoned shall become a member of the senate and a senator.[188]

The question in Edwards was whether the words "qualified persons" in S. 24 included female persons, thus permitting women as well as men to occupy places in the Senate.

Despite historical evidence that the framers of S. 24 had not envisioned women in the senate, the Privy Council in Edwards determined that the section's reference to "qualified persons" shall not be construed in accordance with the framers' expectations. Instead, the construction's provisions must be permitted to evolve in response to changing ideals and shifting social condition. In Lord Sankey's opinion:

---

[187] (1930) AC 124 (PC).
[188] Ibid.

> The British North America Act planted in Canada a living tree capable of growth and expansion within its natural limits. The object of the Act was to grant a Constitution to Canada "Like all written Constitutions it has been subject to development through usage and convention": Canadian Constitutional Studies, Sir Robert Borden (1922). Their Lordships do not conceive it to be the duty of this Board- it is certainly not their desires – to cut down the provisions of the Act by a narrow and technical construction, but rather to give it a large and liberal interpretation.[189]

As a result, the "living tree" approach to interpretation was adopted by the Privy Council as the principal doctrine of constitutional construction.

The living tree approach to interpreting constitutional language has been enthusiastically adopted by Canada's courts. For example in the Provincial Electoral Boundaries case,[190] the Supreme Court of Canada held that "the Charter is engrafted onto the living tree that is the Canadian Constitution" and that the Canadian Constitution "must be capable of growth to meet the future".[191] Similarly the court in Hunter v Southam[192] declared that as a "living tree", the Constitution of Canada "must be capable of growth and development over time to meet new social, political and historical realities often unimagined by its framers." [193] As a result of these and numerous other decisions, it would appear that where the construction of the constitution's language is at issue, the court will employ a "progressive" "dynamic", or "living tree" approach to interpretation.

Progressive Interpretation

According to Peter Hogg,[194] the language of constitutional documents is particularly well suited for progressive interpretation. In his view, the nature and structure of the Constitution demands that the courts adopt a prospective interpretation rather than construing the Constitution's language by reference to the framers' expectations. Hogg P., put it this way:

> The idea underlying the doctrine of progressive interpretation is that the Constitution Act 1867, although undeniably a statute is not a statute like any other: it is a "constituent" or "organic" statute, which has to provide the basis for the entire government of a nation over a long period of time. An inflexible interpretation of rooted in the past, would only serve to withhold necessary powers from the Parliament or Legislatures. It must be

---

[189] Ibid at p. 136.
[190] Reference re Section 94(2) of the Motor Vehicle Act (BC), (1985) 2 SCR 486.
[191] Ibid at p. 180.
[192] (1984) 2 SCR 145.
[193] Ibid at p. 155.
[194] Hogg.

remembered too that the Constitution Act, 1867, like other federal Constitutions, differs from an ordinary statute in that it cannot easily be amended when it becomes out of date, so that its adaptation to changing conditions must fall to a large extent upon the courts.[195]

The Supreme Court of Canada has repeatedly demonstrated its willingness to interpret constitutional language in a progressive manner. For example, in Re BC Motor Vehicle Act,[196] the court was called upon to interpret the meaning of "fundamental justice" in S.7 of the Charter of Rights and Freedoms. More specifically, the court was required to determine whether the principles of fundamental justice were restricted to procedural matters such as the right to a fair hearing or whether those principles extended to embrace substantive matters, permitting the courts to invalidate laws on the ground that the substance or policy of the law was unacceptable.

From an "originalist" perspective, the meaning of "fundamental justice" in S.7 was clear: the framers of S.7 had clearly intended the phrase to have procedural content only. According to Assistant Deputy Minister Strayer, one of the legal officials responsible for the drafting of the language:

It was our belief that the words "fundamental justice" would cover the same thing as what is called procedural due process, that is the meaning of due process in relation to requiring fair procedure. However, it in our view does not out cover the concept of what is called substantive due process, which would impose substantive requirements as to policy of the law in question. This has been most clearly demonstrated in the United States in the area of property, but also in other areas such as the right to life. The term due process has been given the broader concept of meaning both the procedure and substantive. Natural justice or fundamental justice in our view does not go beyond the procedural requirements of fairness. The term "fundamental justice" appears to us to be essentially the same thing as natural justice.[197]

Despite the clear and convincing evidence that the drafters of the Charter intended "fundamental justice" to have procedural content only, the court in BC Motor Vehicle Act gave the phrase a broad, substantive meaning. Speaking for a majority of the court, Lamer J (as he then was) acknowledged the statements set out above, but claimed that this historical understanding of the language used in the Charter was inappropriate. In adopting a decidedly progressive interpretation of S.7, Lamer J claimed that the framers' understanding of the constitutional text

---

[195] Ibid at p. 421.
[196] Reference re Section 94(2) of the Motor Vehicle Act (BC), (1985) 2 SCR 486.
[197] Ibid at pp 404-5.

was neither binding on the court nor particularly convincing. According to Lamer J for the majority, the language of the Charter required a forward looking, progressive interpretation, regardless of what the constitutional drafters had intended. Lamer J held as follows:

> If the newly planted "living tree" which is the Charter is to have the possibility of growth and adjustment over time, care must be taken to ensure that historical materials, such as the minutes of proceedings and evidence of the Special Joint Committee, do not stunt its growth.[198]

By acknowledging the potential for "growth" and "adjustment" in the Constitution's provisions, the court in BC Motor Vehicle Act made it clear that where the Constitution's language is being interpreted, a dynamic form of construction is both permitted and required.[199]

The Dynamic Interpretation

The dynamic interpretation does a better job than originalism in dealing with the dynamic relationship between drafter and interpreter. According to Cote, the drafters of statutory language do not establish the legislation's meaning, because meaning is born of interpretation. Over time, as the law is applied to more and more unforeseen situations, the statute's meaning evolves into something beyond what was envisioned by its drafters. Francis Bennion describes the forces behind this evolutionary process as follows:

> Each generation live under the law it inherits. Constant formal updating is not practicable, so an Act takes on a life of its own. What the original framers intended sinks gradually with history. While their language may endure as law, its current subjects are likely to find that law more and more ill-fitting.[200]

Beyond its obvious descriptive power, dynamism has demonstrated the power to promote justice in difficult cases. Because dynamism explicitly recognizes the "evolutive" nature of language, dynamic interpretation can permit an archaic law to evolve and respond to society's current vision of justice.

Despite the advantages in dynamic interpretation above, dynamic interpretation is unpredictable. The ability of the courts to interpret statutes in

---

[198] Ibid at p. 509.

[199] Despite the court's willingness to use a dynamic form of construction when interpreting the Constitution's provisions, the court has repeatedly voiced its reluctance to stray from the framers' expectations when interpreting the language of "normal" statutes. Recently, however, supporter of dynamism have criticized the court's unwillingness to apply dynamic construction across the board.

[200] Bennion F., Statutory Interpretation, 2nd ed (London: Butterworth's, 1992) 618.

unpredictable ways points to an even greater problem with dynamic interpretation.

Deconstruction Theory

According to Deconstruction theory, words have no essential meanings. Words are seen as constantly shifting variables that impede, rather than promote the possibility of precise communication. Each word carries a wide variety of meanings that may (or may not) depend on context, authorial intention, audience interests, or countless other factors.

Judicial Approach to the Interpretation of the Constitution in Canada

The modern approach to statutory interpretation in Canada requires a textual, contextual and purposive analysis.[201]

Since the meaning of legislation cannot be understood in isolation, in every case it is necessary to consider the consequences of proposed interpretations in the light of the wider social context. This includes examination of the effects on those groups who lack political power and who have required protection under S.15 of the Charter:

> There is only one rule in modern interpretation, namely, courts are obliged to determine the meaning of legislation in its total context... The courts must consider and take into account all relevant and admissible indicators of legislative meaning. After taking these into account, the court must then adopt an interpretation that is appropriate. An appropriate interpretation is one that can be justified in terms of its plausibility, that is, its compliance with the legislative text, its efficacy, that is, its promotion of the legislative purpose; and its acceptability, that is the outcome is reasonable and just.[202]

The common law approach to statutory interpretation applied by the courts in Canada leaves very little scope for a finding that a provision is legally in determinate. The courts strive to find meaning in statutory language, and apply numerous interpretation maxims to avoid absurdity or vagueness. The Supreme Court of Canada has ruled that a broad textual, contextual and purposive approach to statutory interpretation is appropriate.[203] In the case of the Income Tax Act, the detailed and precise drafting style leads primarily to a textual interpretation. Where there remains ambiguity, the context, and ultimately the purpose of the legislation is to be analyzed to arrive at an interpretation that

---

[201] Canada Trustco Mortgage Co. v. Canada, 2005 SCC 54 at para. 10.

[202] Sullivan, ed., Driedger on the Construction of Statutes, 3rd ed. (Toronto: Butterworths, 1994) at 131, as cited in Verdun v. Toronto- Dominion Bank (1996) 3 S.C.R. 550 para 5-7.

[203] Canada Trustco Mortgage Co. v. Canada (2005) 2 S.C.R. 601, 2005 SCC 54.

resolves the dispute. In extreme cases, where the latter process does not point to result, there may be applied a residual presumption in favour of the taxpayer.[204] It is for Parliamentary to amend ambiguous statutory language.

In respect to human rights provisions, the Canadian Constitution laid certain provisions which must be adopted by the courts. These are:

1. The rules of statutory interpretation ought not to be applied;
2. The draftman's intention is irrelevant;[205]
3. A broad, liberal, generous and benevolent construction should be given, not a narrow, pedantic literal or technical interpretation.[206] A Bill of Rights must be broadly construed in favour of the individual rather than in favour of the State;
4. A purposive interpretation should be given, i.e fundamental rights should be interpreted in accordance with the general purpose of having rights, namely the protection of individuals and minorities against an overbearing collectivity.[208] The meaning of a right or freedom should also be ascertained by an analysis of the purpose of the guarantee; it should be understood, in other words, in the light of the interests it is meant to protect. This analysis should be undertaken, and the purpose of the right or freedom sought by reference to the language chosen to articulate the specific right or freedom, to the historical origins of the concept enshrined, and, where applicable, to the meaning and purpose of the other specific rights and freedoms with which it is associated within the text of the Bill of Rights;[208]
5. A contextual approach is preferred to an abstract approach, i.e. the content of a right ought to be determined in the context of the real life situation brought to the court by the litigant and on the basis of empirical data rather than on the basis of some abstraction;[209]
6. A hierarchical approach to rights must be avoided when interpreting a human rights instrument.[210]

---

[204] Johns – Manville Canada Limited v. The Queen (1985) 2 SCR 46 and Placer Dome Canada Ltd V. Ontario (Minister of Finance) 2006 SCJ No. 20; 2006 SCC 20.

[205] Re BC Motor Vehicle, Supreme Court of Canada (1985) 2SCR 486 per Lamer J: " The draftman's intention is not the key. We must not freeze the Charter in time. Its potential for growth must be preserved. See also Edwards .v. The Attorney General of Canada Privy Council on appeal from the Supreme Court of Canada,(1930) AC 124, per Lord Sankey: The Constitution is a "living tree" capable of growth and expansion within its natural limits.

[206] See Law Society of Upper v. Skapinker, Supreme Court of Canada (1984) LSCR 357; R v. Wrong, Supreme Court of Canada (1990) 3 SCR 36.

[208] See Reference re Public Service Employees Relations Act (Alberto), Supreme Curt of Canada (1987) 1 SCR 313.

[208] Rv. Big M Drug Mart Ltd, Supreme Court of Canada (1986) LRC (onst.) 332 at 364.

[209] See Edmonton Journal v. Alberta, Supreme Cort of Canada (1989) 2 SCR 1326; PSAC v. Canada (1987) 1 SCR 424; RWDSU v Saskatchewan, Supreme Court of Canada, (1987) 1 SCR 460.

[210] Dagenais v. Canadian Broadcasting Corporation, Supreme Court of Canada, (1994) 3 SCR 835.

7. When examining the compatibility of legislation with a Bill of Rights, it is the effect of the legislation rather than its purpose or intent that is relevant.

On the issue of freedom of expression in Canada. Section 2(b) of the Charter states that "Every one has the following fundamental freedoms:…freedom of thought, belief, opinion and expression including freedom of the press and other media communication"[211]

The Canadian approach to freedom of expression allows for a wide conception of "expression" within S. 2(b). The Supreme Court of Canada has stated that a wide and inclusionary approach to the interpretation of the Charter's free expression guarantee is to be preferred.[212] Thus, in Irwin Toy, Chief Justice Dickson explained that:

> Expression has both a content and a form, and the two can be inextricably connected. Activity is expressive if it attempts to convey meaning. That meaning is its content.[213]

Not only is there a freedom of expression, there is also a freedom to not express. As Justice Beetz said in *National Bank of Canada* v. *R.C.U.*:

> All freedoms guaranteed by S. 2 of the Charter necessarily imply reciprocal rights… freedom of expression includes the right to not express.[214]

There are of course limits to free speech and free press guarantee, as the Canadian Supreme Court is quite ready to point out.[215] For example, even though the press enjoys core constitutional rights of access and publication, they do not have protection for all operational means and methods the press may choose to adopt. The press does not, for example, enjoy immunity if they run a pedestrian down in pursuit of a new story under the guise of "freedom of the press". Nor is a violent attack on someone (however dramatic the attack may be) considered to be expression. Understanding freedom of expression requires not only understanding its place in the Canadian Constitution, but also, understanding it within the context of society's competing values.

The Supreme Court of Canada was faced with the challenge of interpreting S.3(1) of the Copy Right Act of Canada[216] as contained in the Constitution of

---

[211] The section potentially could cover a wide range of action, from commercial expression to political expression; from journalistic privilege to hate speech to pornography. The jurisprudence of the Supreme Court has largely been an attempt to carve out: first, the purpose of S. 2(b) (what values does it seek to protect, who should be entitled to its protection), and second, the scope of S. 2(b) (what is "expression").

[212] See Ford v Quebec 1988 SCC French and Irwin Toy Ltd v. Quebec (A.G.) 1989 SCC.

[213] Irwin Toy Ltd Ibid.

[214] 1984 SCC.

[215] See CBC v A. G.N.B. 1991 SCC.

[216] R.S.C. 1985. c 42 as am.

Canada. In *Theberge* v. *Galerie d'Art du Petit Champlain*.[217] The case involved a dispute over whether the use of an ink transfer process to remove the ink surface from a paper poster and transfer it to a canvas backing amounted to a reproduction of the artistic work depicted in the poster, or whether, at best, it would be a moral rights infringement. The majority of the court, in a 4-3 decision, ruled that the ink transfer process did not amount to a reproduction. The majority defined reproduction as: "the physical making of something which did not exist before[218] and rejected the idea that there could be "reproduction" without "multiplication"[219]. In the view of the majority, the respondent was "asserting a moral right in the guise of an economic right."[220] The approach of the majority placed a limit on the economic rights of authors vis a vis owners of physical copies of works. Gonthier J., writing for the dissenting justices, rejected this approach, stating:

> ...the primary and essential meaning of the word "reproduce" as it appears in S.3(1) C.A. is "produce a copy of" or "cause to be seen again" or "give a specified quality or result when copied". Accordingly, in order for a work to be reproduced, there is no requirement, whatsoever to establish that there has been an increase in the total number of copies of the work.[221]

More significant, perhaps, than the dispute over the meaning of reproduction in the Act was the statement of the purpose of copyright that was articulated by the majority of the court. Binnie J. wrote:

> The Copyright Act is usually presented as a balance between promoting the public interest in the encouragement and dissemination of works of the arts and intellect and obtaining a just reward for the creator (or, more accurately, to prevent someone other than the creator from appropriating whatever benefits may be generated)... The proper balance among these and other public policy objectives lies not only in recognizing the creator's rights but in giving due weight to their limited nature. In crassly economic terms it would be as inefficient to overcompensate artists and authors for the right of reproduction as it would be self-defeating to undercompensate them.[222]

---

[217] (2002) 2 SCR 336, 2002 SCC 34 online: http://www.canli:org/ca/cas/scc/2002scc 34.html.
[218] Ibid., at para 44.
[219] Ibid., at para 45.
[220] Ibid., at para 74.
[221] Ibid., at para 139.
[222] Ibid., at paras 30 – 31.

There had been no authoritative statement of the purpose of copyright law in Canada. Both the Constitution[223] and the Copyright Act were silent on this point, and past court decisions had either avoided the issue, or offered inconsistent view. More importantly still, the Theberge decision articulated a view of the public domain that had been largely lacking from Canadian copyright law. Binnie J. wrote: "Excessive control by holders of copyrights and other forms of intellectual property may unduly limit the ability of the public domain to incorporate and embellish creative innovation in the long-term interests of society as a whole, or create practical obstacles to proper utilization."[224]

The question is, what approach must judges take in interpreting a Charter or bill of right? The answers which have been given to this question are numerous and varied, but they all seem to fall roughly within one of three categories:

(a) Those who think that judges should be faithful to the text of the Constitution;
(b) Those who believe that the proper object of deference is the intent of the original framers; and
(c) Those who claim that judges should view the Constitution as "living tree" and interpret it in ways which express an ever-changing and developing political morality.[225]

Position (a) above has been variously described as the "literalist", strict constructionist", or "textualist" theory, and it appears to have been this view to which Chief Justice Brian Dickson was expressing his opposition in *R* v. *Big M. Drug Mart*[226] and *Hunter* v. *Southern Inc.*[227]

Position (b) above is often referred to as the "intentionalist", "originalist", or "original intent" approach. It has been criticized by many legal philosophers as being at best misguided, at worst incoherent.[228]

Despite their differences, (a) and (b), the literalist and originalist theories are both frequently viewed as requiring judicial restraint in the interpretation and application of constitutions. Each is thought to require political and moral neutrality on the part of judges, something which is thought to be both possible and essential to the fulfilment of the judicial role within liberal democracies. Anything less than this amounts to the naked usurpation of the legislative

---

[223] Constitution Act, 1867, U.K. 30 & 31 Victoria C,3, S. 91 (23).

[224] Theberge , Ibid. at para 32.

[225] The living tree metaphor was first applied to the BNA Act by Lord Sankey in Edwards v. A-G Canada (1930) AC 124 at 136. According to Lord Sankey, "the B.N.A. Act planted in Canada a living tree capable of growth and expansion within its natural limits". As Peter Hogg notes, "The Supreme Court of Canada has approved the living tree "City of Upper Canada v. Skapinker (1984) 1 SCR 357 at 365.

[226] (1985) 1 SCR 295.

[227] (1984) 2 SCR 14.

[228] For critiques of the originalist position, see D. Lyons, 'Constitutional International and Original Meaning', 26-9; D. Brink, "Legal Theory, Legal Interpretation, and Judicial Review", 105; Law's Empire, 359-63.

function, a function properly fulfilled by elected political representatives. On each of these views, constitutional interpretation is, or at least should be, essentially a value-neutral activity, requiring nothing more than factual enquiry either into the meaning of words, as governed by linguistic conventions, or the historical intentions of a possibly long-dead group of founders. On this view, the existence and content of law are established by non-moral factors and it is to these alone that judges must repair in constitutional cases.

Position (c), by contrast, is commonly conceived to require a more activist, liberal approach. Calling this approach "liberal" can be somewhat misleading, however, if only because a liberal approach to the interpretation of constitutional documents is often associated with a commitment to political liberalism.[229]

In any event, position (c) is commonly thought to require that judges take an active part in ensuring that the Constitution is consonant with current trends in political morality. The metaphor commonly used in Canada is the "living tree". According to the defenders of this approach, reference to political morality is essential to determining what the Constitution really means within a contemporary context. To use Dworkin's terminology, the Constitution defines the concepts in terms of which questions of fundamental legal rights are to be argued. It is up to each generation to provide the best (or at least its own) constructive interpretation of those concepts. Judges takes a leading role in reaching such understandings.[230]

According to critics of (c), on the other hand, the latter permits active meddling in the political process by unelected judges. It allows judges to subvert the real Constitution – the real law-to be discovered, not in political morality, but within the "four corners" of the documents, or alternatively, the intention of the framers. It permits judges unjustifiably to pursue their own, possibly idiosyncratic, visions of political morality at the expense of the law enshrines in a Constitution properly adopted by appropriate political means.[231]

The three approaches discussed above, represent the only way to show fidelity to the Constitution.

---

[229] The American Court was notorious for employing a liberal approach to undermine the politically liberal policies of the Roosevelt administration. An example of a liberal approach to interpreting the Bill of Rights which led to the suppression of liberal legislation in Lochner v. New York 198 US 45 (1905) where the US Supreme Court struck down a State law forbidding employment in a bakery for more than sixty hours per week or ten hours per day. The court held that this statute deprived the employer of his liberty of contract without "due process of law" a violation of the fourteenth amendment.

[230] For Dworkin's view of constitutional interpretation, see Taking Rights Seriously, 106-7, 131-49 and Law's Empire, 355. See Brink, "Legal Theory, Legal Interpretation, and Judicial Review" and Lyons "Constitutional Interpretation, History and the Death Penalty: A Book Review', 1372-98.

[231] For a critique of the Canadian Charter and the licence it gives judges to decide legal issues on grounds of political morality, see Patrick Brode, The Charter of Wrongs: Canada's Retreat form Democracy, passim.

The Indian Constitution

The Constitution of India was passed by the Constituent Assembly of India[232] on November 26, 1949, and came into effect on January 26, 1950.[233] The Constitution of India is the longest written Constitution of any independent nation in the world, containing 444 Articles and 10 schedules (later 12), as well a numerous amendments.

The Constitution of India lays down the basic structure of government under which the people are to be governed. It establishes the main organ of government – the executive, the legislature and the judiciary. The Constitution not only defines the powers of each organ, but also demarcates their responsibilities. It regulates the relationship between the different organs and between the government and the people.[234]

The rules of interpretation of the Constitution must be used with care in relation to constitutional documents, because a Constitution is drafted in broad and ample style and lays down principles of width and generality.[235] A Constitution is made for generation to come.[236]

Bhagwati J. in People and Union for Democratic Rights v. Union of India[237] said that:

> The Constitution makers have given us one of the most remarkable documents in history for ushering in a new socio-economic order, and the Constitution that they have forged for us has a social purpose and a mission and therefore every word or phrase in the Constitution must be interpreted in a manner which would advance the socio-economic objectives of the Constitution.[238]

Doctrines/Theories of Interpretation of the Constitution in India

The Doctrines (theories) of interpretation of India include the Basic Features Doctrine, Doctrine of Pith and Substance, Doctrine of Colourable Legislation, Doctrine of Severability, Doctrine of Eclipse and Judicial Activism.

---

[232] The people of India elected the members of the Provincial Assemblies, who in turn elected the members of the Constituent Assembly. The Constituent Assembly had members belonging to different communities and regions of India. It also had members representing different political persuasions.

[233] India celebrates January 26 each year as Republic Day.

[234] The Constitution is superior to all other laws of the country. Every law enacted by the government has to be in conformity with the Constitution. The Constitution lays down the national goals of India- Democracy, Socialism, Secularism and National Integration. It also spells out the rights and duties of citizens.

[235] Minister of Home Affair v. Fisher (1979) 3 ALL ER 21, p. 25, per Lord Wilberforce.

[236] "A Constitution is framed for ages to come, and is designed to approach immorality as nearly as human institutions can approach it": Cohens v. Virginia, 19 US (6 Wheat) 264, p. 387, per Marshal CJ.

[237] AIR 1982 SC 1473, p. 1490.

[238] Ibid.

Basic Features Doctrine

The Basic Feature Doctrine is the judge made principle that certain features of the Constitution of India are beyond the limit of the powers of amendment of the Indian Parliament. The doctrine reflects judicial concern at the perceived threat to the liberal constitutional order posed by the Indian National Congress, in particular under Gandhi.

The basic feature doctrine applies only to the constitutionality of amendments and not to ordinary Acts of Parliament, which must conform to the entirety of the Constitution and not just to its basic structure.

In *Keshavananda Bharati* v. *State of Kerala*,[239] the Supreme Court of India has suggested an approach to constitutional interpretation on the basis of a theory which has come to be known in Indian jurisprudence as the Basic Features Doctrine.[240] The doctrine proposed that the Indian Constitution encompassed certain basic and immutable features, if those basic features of the Constitution were transgressed by Parliament in its exercise of amending powers,[241] the Supreme Court would hold the Acts of Parliament invalid by invoking its constitutional jurisdiction.

The origin of this theory lies in a dissenting opinion of Chief Justice Kennedy of the *Irish Supreme Court in State (Ryan)* v. *Lennon*,[242] where his Honour proposed that certain basic principles or features in a Constitution were fundamental, immutable and outside the amending powers of Parliament.[243]

The problem with the Basic Features Doctrine is that the categories, "supremacy of the Constitution", "separation of powers", or the "dignity and

---

[239] (1973) A.I.R (SC) 1461; (1973) 4 S.C.C 225; (1973) SCR Supp. 1.

[240] The theory has generated some interest in several courts in South and South east Asia. See for example, Darwesb M. Arbey v. Federation of Pakistan, (1980) P.L.D. (Lah.) 206; Hamidul Hug Chowdbury v. Bangladesh, (1981) 33 DLR 381. Arguments based on the Basic Features Doctrine were rejected by the Malaysian Court in a number of decisions. See Loob Kooi Choon v. Government of Malaysia, (1977) 2 M.L.J. 187, Phang Chin Hock v. Public Prosecutor (1980) 1 M.L.J. 70, Mark Koding v. Public Prosecutor (1982) 2 M.L.J. 120. In the context of Malaysia, a judicial interpretation based on the Basic Features Doctrine has been suggested by A.J. Hiokling, Death of a Doctrine? Phang Chin Hock v. Public Prosecutor (1979) 21 Malaya Law Review 365 and by H.P. Lee, Emergency Powers in Malaysia, in F.A. Trindale and H.P Lee (eds.) The Constitution of Malaysia: Further Perspectives and Developments, Singapore, Oxford University Press, 1986, 135-156. For a contrary view on the usefulness of the Doctrine, see J. Hatchard, The Constitution of Zimbabwe: Towards a Model for Africa? (1991) 35 Journal of African Law 79, at pp. 96-97: "...The doctrine is extremely nebulous as it requires the judges themselves to divine what are the essential features of the Constitution and there is by no means complete agreement on this issue". For an elaborate study on the Basic Features Doctrine expounded in Keshavananda Bharati, see R. Dhavan, The Supreme Court of India and Parliamentary Sovereignty, Delhi, Sterling Publishers Ltd., 1976. See also D. Morgan, The Indian Essential Features Case (1981) International and Comparative Law Quarterly 307.

[241] Constitution of India, Article 368.

[242] (1935) 1. R 170.

[243] Ibid., at 209. Dr. Bonbam's Case, (1610) Coke's Reports 114., at 118, where Coke C.J. said "when an Act of Parliament is against common right or reason, or repugnant, or impossible to be performed, the common law will control and adjudge such act to be void.

freedom of the individual", by themselves offer no guidance to constitutional interpretation.

Doctrine of Pith and Substance

Pith means "true nature" or "essence" and substance means the essential nature underlying a phenomenon. Thus, the doctrine pith and substance relates to finding out the true nature of a statute. This doctrine is widely used when deciding whether a state is within its rights to create a statute that involves a subject mentioned in Union List of the Constitution. The basic idea behind this principle is that an act or a provision created by the State is valid if the true nature of the act or the provision is about a subject that falls in the state list.

The test of pith and substance is generally and more appropriately applied when a dispute arises as to the legislative competence of the legislature, and it has to be resolved by reference to the entries to which the impugned legislation is relatable. When there is a conflict between two entries in the legislative lists, and legislation by reference to one entry would be competent but not by reference to the other. The doctrine of pith and substance is invoked for the purpose of determining the true nature and character of the legislation in question.

In *Sajjan Singh* v. *State of Rajasthan*,[244] the court said:

"in construing both the parts of Articles 368, the rule of harmonious construction requires that if the direct effect of the amendment of fundamental rights is to make a substantial inroad on the High Courts' powers under Article 226, it indirect, incidental, or is otherwise of an insignificant order, it may be that the proviso will not apply. The proviso would apply where the amendment in question seek to make any change, inter alia, in Article 226, and the question in such a case would be: does the amendment seek to make a change in the provisions of Article 226? The answer to this question would depend upon the effect of the amendment made in the fundamental rights. In dealing with constitutional questions of this character, courts generally adopt a test which is described as the pith and substance test. It is not necessary to multiply authorities in support of the proposition that in considering the constitutional validity of the impugned Act, it would be relevant to inquire what the pith and substance of the impugned Act is.[245]

On facts, the impugned Act does not purport to change the provisions of Article 226 and it cannot be said even to have the effect directly or in any appreciable measure. If the effect of the amendment made in the fundamental

---

[244] AIR 1965 SC 845.
[245] See also India Cement v. State of T.N. (1990) 1 SCC 12 and Synthetics and Chemical Ltd. v. State of U.P (1990) 1 SCC 109.

rights on Article 226 is direct and not incidental and is of a vary significant order, different considerations may perhaps arise. But in the present case, there is no occasion to entertain or weigh the said considerations.

In *State of Gujarat* v. *Shantilal Mangaldas* the court opined thus:

> The doctrine of pith and substance is applicable in determining whether a statute is within the competence of the legislative body, especially in a federal set-up, where there is division of legislative powers; it is wholly irrelevant in determining whether the statute infringes any fundamental right.[246]

In *Hoechst Pharmaceuticals Ltd.* v. *State of Bihar*,[247] the appellant companies were engaged in the manufacture and sale of various medicines and life-saving drugs throughout India including the State of Bihar. They had their branch or sales depot at Patna (Bihar) registered as a dealer under Section 14 of the Act. Almost 94 per cent of the medicines and drugs sold by them were at controlled prices exclusive of local taxes under the Drugs (Prices Control) Order, 1979 issued by the Central Government under Section 3(1) of the Essential Commodities Act. The price-lists of the appellants showed that one of the terms of their contract was that sales tax and local taxes would be charged wherever applicable. The Bihar Finance Act was reserved for the assent of the President and received his assent on April 20, 1981.

By two separate notifications dated January 15, 1981 the State Government of Bihar in exercise of the power under Section 5(1) of the Act appointed January 15, 1981 to be the date from which surcharge under Section 5 would be leviable and fixed the rate of surcharge at 10 per centum of the total amount of the tax payable by a dealer whose gross turnover during the year exceeded RS 5 lakhs, in addition to the tax payable by him. The appellant challenged the constitutional validity of the levy of surcharge under Section 5(1) as declared by the said notification and Section 5(3) which prohibits such dealers from collecting the amount of surcharge payable by them from the purchasers. Upholding the constitutional validity of the Act the court said:

> For judging the constitutional validity of Section 5(3) of the Act, one must determine whether in its pith and substance it is a law relatable Entry 54 of List 11 and not whether there is repugnancy between Section 5(3) of the Act and Paragraph 21 of the Drugs (Price Control) Order made under Section 3(1) of the Essential Commodities Act. So where in pith and substance the Bihar Finance Act falls under Entry 54 of List 11, there is no conflict with Para 21 of the Order made under Section 3 of the Essential

---

246 AIR 1969 SC 634.
247 (1983) 4 SCC 45.

Commodities Act which relates to Entry 33 of List 111, even if there is any incidental encroachment by the State law into the subject covered by the law made by Parliament. Under Article 246 in respect of any matter falling within List I, Parliament has exclusive and predominant power of legislation. If there is a conflict between an entry in List I and entry in List II which is not capable of reconciliation, the power of Parliament to legislate with respect to a matter enumerated in List II must supersede *pro tanto* to exercise of power of the State legislature. Both Parliament and the State legislatures have concurrent powers of legislation with respect to any of the matters enumerated in List III.248

Doctrine of Colourable Legislation

The Doctrine of Colourable Legislation is based on the maxim that what cannot be done directly cannot also be done indirectly. It is only when a legislature having no power to legislate frames a legislation in a way that it is camouflaging the same as to make it appear to fall within its competence, the legislation thus enacted may be regarded as colourable legislation.

The Seventh Schedule of the Constitution of India distributes legislative powers between the Central and State legislatures. If Parliament enacts a law under any of the entries in List II of the Seventh Schedule, that law will be declared invalid for violating the constitutional limits. Similarly, if any of the State legislature enacts a law falling under any of the entries in List I of the Seventh Schedule, such a law is not validly enacted due to want of legislative competence. If the legislative incompetence is apparent, then no interpretative solution is required. On the other hand, if the law, on the fact of it looks to be enacted by a competent legislature, but on an examination of the pith and substance of the legislation, it transpires that the legislature is not competent to enact the law, such a law is named as colourable legislation. Similarly, a law which is valid prima facie, may violate any of the fundamental rights. Such law is also hit by the doctrine of colourable legislation. The classical exposition of the doctrine of colourable legislation was stated by the Supreme Court of India in *K.C. Gajapati Navain Deo* v. *State of Orissa* where the court said:

> if the Constitution of a State distributes the legislative powers amongst different bodies, which have to act within their respective spheres marked by a specific legislative entries, or if there are limitations on the legislative authority in the shape of fundamental rights, questions do arise as to whether the legislature in a particular case has or has not, in respect to the subject-matter of a statute or in the method of enacting it, transgressed the limits of its constitutional powers. Such transgression may be patent,

---

248 Ibid.

manifest or direct, but it may also be disguised, covert, and indirect and it is to this latter class of cases that the expression colourable legislation has been applied in certain judicial pronouncements.[249]

In *All India Bank Employee's Association* v. *National Industrial Tribunal*, the court said:

> Objections based on colourable legislation have relevance only in situations when the power of the legislature is restricted to particular topics, and an attempt is made to escape legal fetters imposed on its powers by resorting to forms of legislation calculated to mask the real subject-matter. Whether less than what was done might have been enough, whether more drastic provision was made than occasion demanded, whether the same purposes could have been achieved by provisions differently framed or by other means, these are wholly irrelevant considerations for testing the validity of the law. They do not touch or concern the ambit of the power but only the manner of its exercise, and once the provisions of Part III of the Constitution are out of the way, the validity of the legislation is not open to challenge.[250]

Similarly, in *B.R. Shankaranarayana* v. *State of Mysore*, the court said:

> The whole doctrine of colourable legislation resolves itself into the question of competency of a particular legislature to enact a particular law. If the legislature is competent to pass the particular law, the motives which impel it to pass the law are early irrelevant. It is open to the court to scrutinise the law to ascertain whether the legislature, by device, purports to made a law which, though in form appears to be within its sphere, in effect and substance reaches beyond it.[251]

The Doctrine of Severability

The Doctrine of Severability is that if the offending provision of an Act which is contrary to a fundamental right or unconstitutional is severable from the rest of the Act, only the offending provision would be declared void and not the whole Act. So the court must find out whether the offending part can be separated from the rest of the Act.

The Doctrine is applicable to legislation which is partly *utra vires* – that is beyond the legislative competence of the legislature.

In *Kihoto Hollohon* v. *Zachillnu*,[252] the constitutional validity of the Tenth Schedule to the Constitution which was inserted by the Constitution (Fifty-

---

[249] AIR 1953 SC 375.
[250] AIR 1962 SC 171.
[251] AIR 1966 SC 1571.
[252] 1992 Supp (2) SCC 651.

Second Amendment) Act, 1985 was challenged inter alia, on the ground that paragraph 7 which excluded the jurisdiction of High Courts under Article 226 and Supreme Court under Article 136 requires ratification under the proviso to Article 368(2) of the Constitution. All the five judges unanimously agreed that paragraph 7 of the Tenth Schedule required ratification and in the absence of ratification, paragraph 7 becomes unconstitutional by violating Article 368(2) proviso. But the majority held that paragraph 7 can be severed by applying the doctrine of severability and upheld the rest of the Tenth Schedule, Venkatatachahah J. observed thus:

> The test of severability requires the Court to ascertain whether the legislature would at all have enacted the law if the severed part was not the part of the law and whether after severance what survives can stand independently and is workable. If the provisions of the Tenth Schedule are considered in the background of the legislative history, namely, the report of the "Committee on Defections" as well as the earlier Bills which were moved to curb the evil of defection it would be evident that the main purpose underlying the constitutional amendment and introduction of the Tenth schedule is to curb the evil of defection which was causing immense mischief in our body politic.

> The ouster of jurisdiction of courts under paragraph 7 was incidental to and to lend strength to the main purpose which was to curb the evil of defection. It cannot be said that the constituent body would not have enacted the other provisions in the Tenth Schedule if it had known that paragraph 7 was not valid. Nor can it be said that the rest of the provisions of the Tenth Schedule cannot stand on their own even if paragraph 7 is found to be unconstitutional. The provisions of paragraph 7 can, therefore, be held to be severable from the rest of the provisions.[253]

Doctrine of Eclipse

The Doctrine of Eclipse is applied in relation to a pre-constitutional law (i.e. a law enacted before 26 January, 1950) which was valid when it was enacted. Subsequently when the Constitution came into force a shadow falls on it because it is inconsistent with the Constitution. The Act is eclipsed. When the shadow is removed the pre-constitutional law becomes fully applicable and is free from infirmity.

The doctrine of eclipse can be invoked only in the case of a law valid when made, but a shadow is cast on it by supervening constitutional inconsistency.

In *Deep Chand* v. *State of UP.*, the court said:

---

[253] Ibid.

The U.P Legislature passed the U.P Act on April 24, 1955, whereunder the State Government was authorised to frame a scheme of nationalization of motor transport. After following the procedure prescribed therein, the State Government finally published the scheme on June 23, 1956. The Constitution (Fourth Amendment) Act, 1955, received the assent of the President on April 27, 1955, the State Government framed the scheme after the passing of the Constitution Amendment, but the Act was invalid at the time it was passed. Though as a result of the amendment clause (2) of Article 31 had been amended, and clause (2A) had been inserted the validity of the scheme could not be tested on the basis of the amendment but only on the basis of the relevant Articles as they existed prior to the amendment.[254]

The doctrine also applies to rules. In *Kihoto Hollohan* v. *Zachillhu* the court opined thus:

In considering the validity of a constitutional amendment the changing and the changed circumstances that compelled the amendment are important criteria. The observations of the U.S. Supreme Court in Maxwell v. Dow 176 US 581; 44 L Ed. 597 (1899) are worthy of note: (L Ed p. 605) ..."to read its language in connection with the known condition of affairs out of which the occasion for its adoption may have arison, and then to construe it, if there be there in any doubtful expressions, in a way so far as is reasonably possible, to forward the known purpose or object for which the amendment was adopted.[255]

Similarly, in Supreme Court Advocates-on-Record *Assn.* v. *UOI* the court said:

A Constitution is an ever-evolving organic document which cannot be read in a narrow, pedantic or syllogistic way but must receive a broad interpretation. Constitution being a growing document its provisions can never remain static and the court's endeavour should be to interpret its phraseology broadly so that it may be able to meet the requirements of an ever-changing society. But while it may be permissible to give an enlarged or extended meaning to the phraseology used by the Constitution-makers, while it may be permissible to mould the provisions to serve the needs of the society, while it may even be permissible in certain extreme situations to stretch the meaning and, if necessary, bend it forward, it would certainly

---

[254] AIR 1959 SC 648.
[255] AIR 1962 SC 1517.

be impermissible to break it or, in the guise of interpretation, to replace the provisions or rewrite them.[256]

Judicial Activism

Judicial Activism is the process of making law by judges. It means an active interpretation of existing legislation by a judge made with a view to enhance the utility of that legislation for social betterment.

The first monumental judgment in India on judicial activism is *Golak Nath and Others* v. *State of Punjab and Another*[257] where the Supreme Court of India enunciated judicial principle of "prospective overruling", giving a wider beneficial interpretation to the constitutional mandate contained in Article 13 of the Constitution. Article 13 mandates that any legislation which conflicts with the fundamental rights guaranteed by the Constitution of India would be void to the extent of conflict.

In *Minerva Mills Ltd* v. *Union of India*,[258] the Supreme Court of India held that in cases of extreme urgency and public importance it may be necessary for an authority, judicial or quasi-judicial or executive, to act quasi judicially to make immediate orders in which circumstances it may not be possible to implement the maxim *audi alteram partem* in its true spirit. It was held that such order would be valid if followed by a post order hearing or post decision hearing. By this judgment the Supreme Court envisaged the quasi-judicial or judicial authorities to be so fair, fearless and confident as to change their earlier decision on patient and impartial hearing after the decision is rendered. It has given yet another dimension to the age old legal requirement of *audi alteram partem*.

Similarly in *ADM Jabalpur* v. *Shirkant Shukla*[259] where Article 21 which provides that no person shall be deprived of his life or personal liberty except according to procedure established by law. The majority of Bench held that in cases of emergency as were existing between 1975 and 1977, a procedure can be established by law, following which even human life can be taken away.

On the issue of personal rights and fundamental rights the Supreme Court adopted the theory of judicial activism. In *Mrs. Maneka Gandhi* v. *Union of India and Another*,[260] the legislation governing grant of passport was interpreted in a manner so as to enhance the rights of personal freedom and personal liberty.

---

[256] (1993) 4 SCC 441 In India Sawliney v. UOI the court said "No one under the guise of interpreting the Constitution can cause irreversible injustice and irredeemable inequalities to any section of the people or can protect those unethically claiming unquestionable dynastic monopoly over the Constitutional benefits.
[257] AIR 1967 SC 1643.
[258] AIR 1986 SC 2030.
[259] AIR 1976 SC 1207.
[260] AIR 1978 SC 579.

In the *Supreme Court Bar Association* v. *Union of India and Another*,[261] this judgment was delivered by a Bench of the Supreme Court of India on the application of the Supreme Court Bar Association seeking review of the order pronounced by the Supreme Court of India in the matter of V.C. Mishra,[262] former chairman of the Bar Council of India punishing him for contempt of court. The Supreme Court Bar Association claimed that Article 142 envisages that the Supreme Court order to do complete justice can pass any order laying stress on the aspect of doing complete justice in any matter. The Solicitor-General argued that the court cannot create jurisdiction nor create punishment which is not permitted by law. The Supreme Court accepted these contentions, issued a notice of caution to the effect that courts should be sceptical about taking over power of other statutory organs.

Judicial Approach to the Interpretation of the Constitution in India

In Special Reference No. 1 of 2002[263] it was observed that liberal and visional interpretation is necessary to interpret the provisions of the Constitution of India. The reasoning given was that the old articles of the *supreme lex* meet new challenges of life, the old legal pillars suffer new stresses. So the court has to adopt the law and develop its latent capabilities if novel situations are encountered. It was also held that the meaning of the words in the Constitution should be understood having regard to their line of growth and change of concepts.

The courts in India regard the Constitution as sui generis, thus its interpretation is quite different from the way statutes are been interpreted. In *Akhil Bharatiya Soshit Karamchain Sangh (Rhy.)* v. *UOI* the court observed thus:

> ...And so, when the constitutional instrument to be expounded is a Constitution like the Indian Constitution, the expositors are to concern themselves not with words and mere words only, but, as much, with the philosophy or "the spirit and the sense" of the Constitution... (it becomes) the duty of the court to apply the Directive Principles in interpreting the Constitution and the laws...[264]

For the purpose of the construction of the Constitution the courts in India obviously take recourse to various internal and external aids. "Internal aids" mean those materials which are available in the Constitution itself, though they may not be part of enactment. These internal aids include, long title, preamble, headings, marginal notes, illustrations, punctuation, proviso, schedule, transitory provisions, etc. When internal aids are not adequate, court has to take recourse to

---

[261] AIR 1998 SC 1845.
[262] In re: Vinay Chandra Mishra (the alleged contemnor) AIR 1995 SC 2348.
[263] (2002) 8 SCC 237.
[264] (1981) 1 SCC 246.

external aids. It may be parliamentary material, historical background, reports of a committee or a commission, official statement, dictionary meanings, foreign decisions etc.

The Supreme Court of India often take recourse to parliamentary material like debates in Constituent Assembly, speeches of the movers of the Bill, Reports of Committee or Commission, Statement of Objects and Reasons of the Bill, etc.

In *Fagu Shaw, etc.* v. *The State of West Bengal*[265] Bhagwati J observed thus:

> Since the purpose of interpretation is to ascertain the real meaning of a constitutional provision, it is evident that nothing that is logically relevant to this process should be excluded from consideration. It was at one time thought that the speeches made by the members of the Constituent Assembly in the course of the debates of the Draft Constitution were wholly inadmissible as extraneous aids to the interpretation of a constitutional provisions, but of late there has been a shift in this position and following the recent trends in juristic thought in some of the Western countries and the United States, the rule of exclusion rigidly followed in Anglo American jurisprudence has been considerably diluted...We may therefore legitimately refer to the Constituent Assembly debates for the purpose of ascertaining what was the object which the Constitution makers had in view and what was the purpose which they intended to achieve when they enacted clauses (4) and (7) in their present form[266].

Also in *S.R. Chandhuri* v. *State of Punjab and Others*,[267] the Supreme Court of India has stated that it is a settled position that debates in the Constituent Assembly may be relied upon as an aid to interpret a Constitutional provision because it is the function of the court to find out the intention of the framers of the Constitution.

For the purpose of interpretation of the Constitution, the courts in India often refer to decisions of foreign courts which follow the same system of jurisprudence as in India. For instance while interpreting provisions relating to fundamental rights contained in the Indian Constitution, the Supreme Court of India took much assistance form American precedents.

Apart from the external aids, the courts in India also take recourse to other material. For example, whenever necessary, court can look into international conventions.[268] In *Visakha* v. *State of Rajasthan*,[269] the Supreme Court of India

---

[265] AIR 1974 SC 613.
[266] Ibid para 45.
[267] (2001) 7 SCC 126.
[268] P.N. Krishanlal v. Govt. of Kerala (1995) Sup. 2 SCC 187.
[269] AIR 1997 SC 3011.

took recourse to international convention for the purpose of construction of domestic law. The court observed:

> In the absence of domestic law occupying the field to formulate effective measures to check the civil of sexual harassment of working women at all work places, the contents of International Conventions and norms are significant for the purpose of interpretation of the guarantee of gender equality, right to work with human dignity in Articles 14, 15, 19(1) (g) and 21 of the Constitution and the safeguards against sexual harassment implicit therein. Any international convention not inconsistent with the fundamental rights and in harmony with its spirit must be read into those provisions to enlarge the meaning and content thereof, to promote the object of the Constitutional guarantee.[270]

The Supreme Court of India has tried to give effect to human rights norms embodied in the two international covenants. The Covenant on Civil and Political Rights[271] and the principles of freedom from arbitrary arrest and detention.[272] These human rights norms have been incorporated in the domestic law of India by a process of judicial interpretation. The Indian Constitution has Article 21 which says that "No person shall be deprived of his life or personal liberty except by procedure established by law". The view was held by the Supreme Court of India for a long time that this Article merely embodied the Dicyian concept of the rule of law, namely, that no one can be deprived of his life or personal liberty by the Executive without the authority of law.

It was enough so long as there was some law authorising such deprivation and it did not matter what was the nature or character of such law. But the decision in *Maneka Gandi's case*[273] which marks a watershed in the history of Constitutional law in India, the Supreme Court of India held that it is not sufficient merely to have a law in order to authorise constitutional deprivation of life and personal liberty but such law must prescribe a procedure and such procedure must be reasonable, fair and just. The Supreme Court of India thus by a process of judicial interpretation brought in the procedural due process concept of the American Constitution, though the original intent of framers of the Constitution was to exclude the due process clause. The Supreme Court of India

---

[270] Ibid. para 7.
[271] Provides that persons awaiting trial should be released subject to guarantees to appear for trial and Article 28 of the Principles of Equality in the Administration of justice lays down that 'national laws conceiving provisional release from custody pending or during trial shall be so framed as to eliminate any requirement of pecuniary guarantees'.
[272] Article 16 Clause 2 of the Principles of Freedom from Arbitrary Arrest and Detention provides that "to ensure that no person shall be denied the possibility of obtaining provisional release on account of lack of means, other forms of provisional release than upon principal security shall be provided".
[273] Maneka Gandi v. Union of India AIR 1978 SC 597.

then proceeded to hold that insistence on monetary bail in case of a poor accused should be inconsistent with reasonable, fair and just procedure and it would be violative of the constitutional guarantee under Article 21.

The view was taken for the first time that more liberal norms consistent with human rights should be adopted, on which accused persons may be allowed to remain at liberty pending trail, it was observed by the Supreme Court that the risk of monetary loss is not only deterrent against fleeing from justice but there are other factors which act as equal deterrents against fleeing. The entire law of bail was humanised by judicial interpretation of Article 21 and the Supreme Court of India held that a new insight should inform the judicial approach in the matter of pre-trial release if the court is satisfied after taking into account, on the basis of information placed before it, that the accused has his roots in the community and is not likely to abscond, it need not insist on monetary bail and may safely release the accused on his personal bond. The human rights norm set out in the international instruments was thus translated into national practice.

On the right to personal liberty, Article 21 of the Constitution of India reads as follows: "No person shall be deprived of his life or personal liberty except according to procedure established by law." The interpretation of this article in the early years of the Supreme Court of India was that "personal liberty" could be curtailed as long as there was a legal prescription for the same. In *A.K. Gapalan* v. *State of Madras*,[274] the Supreme Court had ruled that "preventive detention" by state agencies was permissible as long as it was provided for under a governmental measure (e.g. legislation or an ordinance) and the Court could not inquire into the fairness of such a measure. It was held that the words "procedure established by law" were different from the "substantive due process" guarantee provided under the 14th amendment to the US Constitution. It was also reasoned that the framers of the Indian Constitution consciously preferred the former expression over the latter.

This narrows construction of Article 21 prevailed for several years until it was changed in *Maneka Gandhi case.*[275] In that decision, it was held that governmental restraints on "personal liberty" should be collectively tested against the guarantees of fairness, non-arbitrariness and reasonableness that were prescribed under Articles 14, 19, 21 of the Constitution. The Court developed a theory of "inter-relationship of rights" to hold that governmental action which curtailed either of those rights should meet the designated threshold for restraints on all of them. In this manner, the courts incorporated the guarantee of

---

[274] AIR 1950 SC 27.
[275] Maneka Gandhi v. Union of India, AIR 1978 SC 597.

"substantive due process" into the language of Article 21.[276] This was followed by a series of decisions, where the conceptions of "life" and "personal liberty" were interpreted liberally to include rights which had not been expressly enumerated in Part III.

In the words of Justice Bhagwati

> we think that the right to life includes the right to live with human dignity and all that goes along with it, namely the bare necessities of life such as adequate nutrition, clothing and shelter over the head and facilities for reading, writing and expressing oneself in diverse forms.[277]

Notably, over the decades, the Supreme Court of India has affirmed that both the Fundamental Rights and Directive Principles must be interpreted harmoniously. It was observed in *Kesavananda Bharati case*, that the directive principles and the fundamental rights supplement each other and aim at the same goal of bringing about a social revolution and the establishment of a welfare State, the objectives which are also enumerated in the preamble to the Constitution. Furthermore, in *Unni Krishnan, J.P.* v. *State of Andhra Pradesh*, Justice Jeevan Reddy declared:

> The provisions of Parts III and IV are supplementary and complementary to each other and not exclusionary of each other and that the fundamental rights are but a means to achieve the goal indicated in Part IV.[278]

This approach of harmonizing the fundamental rights and directive principles has been successful to a considerable extent. As indicated earlier, the Supreme Court has interpreted the "protection of life and personal liberty" as one which contemplates socio-economic entitlements. For instance, in *Olga Tellis* v. *Bombay Municipal Corporation*,[279] a journalist had filed a petition on behalf of hundreds of pavement-dwellers who were being displaced due to construction activity by the respondent corporation. The court recognised the "right to livelihood and housing" of the pavement-dwellers and issued an injunction to halt their eviction.

In *Paraman and Katara* v. *Union of India*,[280] the Court held that no medical authority could refuse to provide immediate medical attention to a patient in need in an emergency case. The public interest litigation had arisen because many

---

[276] See. T.R. Andhyarujina, "The Evolution of Due Process of Law by the Supreme Court" in B.N. Kirpal et. al (eds), Supreme But Not Infallible – Essays in Honour of the Supreme Court of India (OUP, 2000) at pp. 193-213.

[277] Observations Francis Coralie v. Union Territory of Delhi, (1981) 1 SCC 688.

[278] (1993) 1 SCC 645.

[279] AIR 1985 SC 2039.

[280] AIR 1989 SC 2039.

hospitals were refusing to admit patients in medico-legal case. Hence, the Supreme Court ruled that access to healthcare, is a justiciable right. In another prominent Public Interest Litigation, the Supreme Court ordered the relocation of hazardous industries located near residential areas in New Delhi. In the process, it spelt out the citizens' "right to clean environment" which was in turn derived from the protection of life and liberty enumerated in Article 21.[281]

The court has also recognised access to free education as a justiciable right. In *J.P. Unnikrishnan* v. *State of Andhra Pradesh*,[282] this decision prompted a constitutional amendment which inserted Article 21-A with the constitutional text, thereby guaranteeing the right to elementary education for children aged between 6-14 years. The Courts have also pointed to Directive principles in interpreting the prohibitions against forced labour and child labour. The enforcement of these rights leaves a lot to be desired, but be symbolic value of their constitutional status should not be underestimated.

There is no express provision in the Constitution for grant of compensation for violation of a fundamental right in life and personal liberty. But the judiciary has evolved a right to compensation in cases of illegal deprivation of personal liberty. *Rudal Shah* v. *State of Bihar*[283] is an instance of breakthrough in human rights jurisprudence. The court granted monetary compensation of Rs. 35,000 against the Bihar Government for keeping a person in illegal detention for 14 days even after his acquittal. The court departed from the traditional approach, ignored the technicalities while granting compensation.

In *Bhim Singh* v. *State of Jammu and Kashimir*,[284] a member of the Legislative Assembly of Jammu and Kashimir was arrested by the police mala fide and he was not produced before the Magistrate within the required time. Holding that his fundamental rights under Articles 21 and 22(1) were violated, the Court observed that when there is mala fide arrest, the invasion of constitutional or legal right is not washed away by his being set free and in "appropriate cases" the court has jurisdiction to compensate victim by awarding suitable monetary compensation. The court awarded Rs. 50,000 as monetary compensation by way of exemplary costs to the petitioner to compensate him.

The Universal Declaration of Human Rights is binding upon India, The Universal Declaration of Human Rights, which the United Nation Organization, adopted on 10th December, 1948 enumerates various civil and political rights. Many of these rights were incorporated in the Indian Constitution under the headings Fundamental Rights and Directives Principles of the State Policy in

---

[281] M.C. Mehta v. Union of India (1996) 4 SCC 750.
[282] (1993) 1 SCC 645.
[283] AIR 1983 SC 1086.
[284] (1985) 4 SCC 677.

Chapters III and IV respectively and these rights have great influence on some of the decisions of the courts in India.

In the landmark case of *Kesavananda Bharati Sripadagalvaru* v. *State of Kerala*,[285] with the text of the judgment running in hundreds, an important aspect of human rights was involved. The Court took into consideration, that while the Indian Constituent Assembly on December 10, 1948, the General Assembly of the United Nations adopted a Universal Declaration of Human Rights and though the Declaration was not to be a binding instrument but it is an authority to showed how India understood the nature of human rights.

In *Prem Shankar Shukla* v. *Delhi Administration*,[286] a telegram was sent to the court protesting against the humiliation and torture of being held in irons in public, back and forth, when, as under trials kept in custody in the Tihar Jail, i.e. being kept in handcuffs was contended by the petitioner. The practice had persisted despite the courts direction not to use irons on him. The court held that the blurred area of "detention jurisprudence" where considerations of prevention of escape and a personhood of prisoner came into conflict, the court laid that even after discussing the relevant statutory provisions and constitutional requirements, court was to remember Article 5[287] of the United Declaration of Human Rights, 1948, all persons deprived of their liberty shall be treated with humanity and with respect for the inherent dignity of the human person. J. Krishna Lyer categorically stated that in interpreting the constitutional and statutory provisions the court must not forget the core principle found in Article 5 of the Universal Declaration of Human Rights, 1948. The court held that the ambit of personal liberty protected by Article 21 is wide and comprehensive. It embraces both substantive rights to personal liberty and the procedure provided for their deprivation and the handcuffing was a violation of right to live with dignity, unless restricted in the interest and security of the State.

In *Francis Corelie Mullin* v. *Administrator, Union Territory of Delhi*,[288] the question before the court was whether the right to life was limited only to protection of limb or faculty or it went further and embraced something more. The court specifically laid that "the right to life includes the right to live with human dignity and all that goes along with it, namely, the bare necessaries of life such as adequate nutrition, clothing and shelter and facilities for reading, writing and expressing oneself in diverse forms, freely moving about and mixing and commingling with fellow human beings." For the broad interpretation of the right, the court referred to the right to protection against torture or cruel, in

---

[285] AIR 1973 SC 1461.
[286] AIR 1980 SC 1535.
[287] Art 5. No one shall be subject to torture or to cruel, inhuman or degrading treatment or punishment.
[288] AIR 1981 SC 746.

human or degrading treatment, enunciated in Article 5 of the Universal Declaration of Human Rights. The right extended to prisoners where as part of the right to live with human dignity, they would be entitled to have interviews with the members of his family and friends and no prison regulation or procedure laid down by prison regulation regulating the right to have interviews with the numbers of the family and friends can be upheld as constitutionally valid under Articles 14 and 21, unless it is reasonable, fair and just.

However, the Courts in Indian would refrain from adopting the Universal Declaration on Human Rights where its effects would be to protect a criminal.

In *Satwant Singh Sawhney* v. *Ass. Passport Officer, Government of India*,[289] the Supreme Court held that in the light of the Universal Declaration stating "Everyone has the right to leave any country including his own", the right was available only to normal citizens, i.e. it was not available and not applicable to criminals avoiding penalties or political agitators etc., likely to create international tension or to persons who may disgrace the government of India.

---

[289] AIR 1967 SC 1836.

Judicial Approach to the Interpretation of the Constitution in Nigeria

The Nigerian Constitution

Nigeria is a federation comprising the Federal Government and as at today, thirty-six States and the Federal Capital Territory. Apart from the period of military regimes and Chief Shonekan led interregnum during which a somewhat military system of administration was practised because of the command structure of the military, Nigeria has always been a federation even before it became an independent country by the Nigeria (Constitution) Order in Council, 1960, that gave birth to the Federal Constitution of 1960 under a parliamentary system where each of the Regions (then three) had its own Constitution. The Republican Constitution of 1963 retained this pattern, the Regions having increased to four, it was the 1979 Constitution which introduced a presidential system. Since then, more States have been created, also by the Military Government, whereof under the 1999 Constitution there are now thirty- six States.

Principles of Interpretation of the Constitution in Nigeria

The guiding principles of interpretation of the Constitution in Nigeria are as follows:

1. The language of the Constitution must be given its plain meaning;
2. The provisions of the Constitution must be read together as a whole;
3. Words of the Constitution must be given broader interpretation;
4. The provisions of the Constitution should not be interpreted to have a retrospective.[1]

Language of the Constitution must be given its plain meaning

The Constitution cannot be strictly interpreted like an Act of the National Assembly or a law of the State Assembly. The Constitution must be construed without ambiguity because it is the fountain of all laws. The Constitution must be

---

[1] See Tribune v. IMB Securities (2001) 8 NWLR (pt. 740) 192, Global Excellence Communication Limited and others v. Mr. Donald Duke Suit No. SC 313/2006 delivered on 13th July, 2007. Attorney – General of Bendel State v. Attorney General of the Federation and Others (1981) 9 SC 1 at pp. 78-79.

literally interpreted so that every section therein will have meaning. Thus, when the Constitution is clear as to its intendment on any subject, the courts in giving construction thereto, are not at liberty to search its meaning beyond it. Any power given by the Constitution cannot therefore be taken away by any Act of the National Assembly or law of a State or a subsidiary legislation.[2]

The Constitution is not to be construed with any ambiguity or mistake by its framers, it must not be subordinated to any other law and in construction must not be subjected to indignity of deletion of any section or part thereof.[3]

The court should always resist attempts by parties to insert into the provisions of the Constitution words that are not contained therein. Thus a party should not be allowed to import into the statutory provisions words that are not contained or used therein in order to achieve or suit his purpose. In *Garji* v. *Garji*[4] the court rejected the move of the respondent to equate the term "Wakf" used in section 277 (2) (c) of the 1999 Constitution with the word "trust" Adamu, JCA opined thus:

> By importing into the provision under review the word "trust" which is not used or mentioned in the said provision, the respondent has misconceived the point and has thereby changed the true meaning of the provision and the intention of the legislature to suit his purpose.[5]

The provisions of the Constitution must be read together as a whole

In interpreting the provisions of the Constitution, all the provisions must be read together and not disjointly.[6] Any narrow interpretation of its provisions will to violence to it and will fail to achieve the goals set by the Constitution.[7]

The provisions of the Constitution are to be read together, when one deals with a matter of construction of the Constitution. This is age long and has become elementary. The provisions are not meant to be put into compartments. To do this will defeat the whole purpose of the construction of the Constitution.[8]

The provisions of the Constitution must be interpreted wholly and not in piece meal. As Nnamani, JSC in *Attorney-General of Bendel State* v. *Attorney-General of the Federation and 22 Ors* observed:

---

[2] Nkwocha v. Governor of Anambra State (1984) I SCNLR 634, Lemboye v. Ogunbiyi (1990) 6 NWLR (pt. 155) p. 210, Adisa v. Oyinwola (2000) FWLR (pt 8) 1349; (2000) 10 NWLR (pt. 674) 116.

[3] FRN v. Osahon (2006) ALL FWLR p. 1975 at p. 2002

[4] (2007) ALL FWLR (pt. 346) p. 494 at pp. 508 – 509.

[5] Ibid.

[6] Kalu v. Odili (1992) 5 NWLR (pt. 240) 130 at p. 156.

[7] AG Ondo State v. AG of the Federation & 3 Ors (2002) FWLR (pt. 111) 1973 at p. 2070 Nafiu Rabiu v. State (1990) 8 – 9 SC 130, (1982) 2 NCLR 117 Agua Ltd. v. Ondo State Sports Council (1985) 4NWLR (pt. 91) 622, Tuku`r v. Government of Gongola State (1989) 4NWLR (pt.117), Ishola v. Ajiboye (1994) 6NWLR (pt. 117).

[8] *Attorney-General Bendel State* v. *Attorney-General of the Federation and 22 Ors* (1981) 1 ALLNLR p. 85 at p. 228.

The constitutional provisions cannot be interpreted in watertight compartment but as a whole. I do not therefore see how we can extract section 58 (3) and ignore subsections 1, 2 and 3. In the circumstances, the Joint Conference Committee on Revenue Allocation having resolved the difference, albeit by majority votes, ought to have sent its report to both Houses of the National Assembly for their resolution before the bill proceeded to the President for their resolution before the bill proceeded to the President for his assent. The Committee in "resolving the differences between both House" was no more than a mediator or conciliator, a vehicle through which a formula or some compromise agreement may be worked out. To interpret it otherwise would be to do violent injustice to the terms and intendment of section 54 (1) and (2) of the Constitution.[9]

In *Senator Adesanya* v. *President of Nigeria,*[10] Fatai Williams CJN quoted the dictum of Barwick, CJ in *Attorney General* v. *Commonwealth of Australia...*[11] thus:

The only true guide and the only course which can produce stability in constitutional law is to read the language of the Constitution itself, no doubt generously and not pedantically but as a whole.

Also Fatai Williams, CJN in *Nafiu Rabiu* v. *the State* said:

I only need to add that I am also strongly of the view that when interpreting the provisions of our 1979 Constitution, not only should the Courts look at the Constitution as a whole, but should also construe its provisions in such a way as to justify the hopes and aspirations of those who have made the strenuous effort to provide us with a Constitution for the purpose of promoting persons in our country on this principle of Freedom, Equality and Justice, and for the purpose of consolidating the unity of our people.[12]

Words of the Constitution must be given broader interpretation

The court should when interpreting the provisions of the Constitution, bear in mind that the function of the Constitution is to establish a framework and principles of government, broad and in general terms, intended to apply to the varying conditions which the development of a plural and dynamic society must involve. Therefore, mere technical rules of interpretation are to some extent

---

[9] Ibid.
[10] (1981) 2 NCLR 358 at 374.
[11] (1975) 135 CLR, p.1 at p.17.
[12] Ibid.

inadmissible in a way as to defeat the principles of government enshrined in the Constitution. Thus, where the question is whether the Constitution has used an expression in a wider or in the narrow sense, the court should, whenever possible and in response to the demand of justice, lean to the broader interpretation, unless there is something in the text or in the rest of the Constitution to indicate that the narrow interpretation will best carry out the object and purpose of the Constitution.[13]

The proper approach to the interpretation of clear words of a statute is to follow them in their simple, grammatical and ordinary meaning rather than look further because that is what *prima facie* gives them their most reliable meaning. This is also true of construction of constitutional provisions if they are clear and unambiguous even when it is necessary to given them a liberal or broad interpretation.

Where the Constitution has used an expression in a broader or narrow sense, the court should lean to the broader interpretation, unless there is something in the text or in the rest of the Constitution to indicate that the narrower interpretation will best carry out the objects and purposes of the Constitution.

In *Nafiu Rabiu* v. *The State* [14] Udo Udoma JSC cited with approval what was said by the Privy Council in *Attorney-General for the Province of Canada* v. *Attorney-General for the Dominion of Canada*[15]

Thus:

> In the interpretation of a complete self-governing Constitution upon a written organic instrument ...if the text is explicit the text is conclusive, alike in what it directs and what it forbids. When the text is ambiguous...recourse must be heard to the context and scheme of the Constitution.[16]

In *Attorney-General, Ondo State* v. *Attorney-General of the Federation and 36 Others*, Uwaifo JSC said:

> I am of the view that a situation whereby section 15(5) which seeks for the abolition of corrupt practices and abuse of power has been incorporated into the Exclusive Legislative List by item 60(a), deserves to be given a very liberal interpretation so as to achieve the purpose of the Constitution in that regard and support the enactment to back it up. I think the intention is to given effect to the state policy on corruption and abuse of power

---

[13] Ehuwa v. Ondo State INEC (2007) ALL FWLR (pt. 351) p. 1415 at pp 1448 – 1449, Fawehinmi v. I.G. of Police & Ors (2002) FWLR (pt. 108) 1355, (2007) 7 NWLR (pt. 76) 606 at p. 678.

[14] (1980) 12 NSCC 291 at 300 – 301.

[15] (2003) 10 NWLR (pt. 828) 307.

[16] See also Director SSS v. Agbokoba (1999) 3 SC at p. 77

underlying the provisions of section 15(5) can be sufficiently made manifest by viewing the introduction of it through item 60(a) as a call on the National Assembly to legislate on that aspect of the Directive Principles to give legal backing to that policy as rightly suggested and reasoned by the learned author Basu in his commentary on the Constitution of India.[17]

The provisions of the Constitution should not be interpreted to have retrospective effect

Unless there are express words to the contrary, the provisions of the Constitution cannot be interpreted retrospectively. As *Obaseki in Afolabi* v. *Governor of Oyo State.* [18] Observed:

> This is necessary because every law when takes away or impairs any vested right acquired under existing laws or creates a new obligation or imposes a new duty or attaches a new disability in respect of transaction or consideration already past, is deemed to be retrospective (Allen vs. Gold Reets of West Africa (1900) 1 Ch. 656, 673). It is a fundamental rule of our laws in Nigeria that no statute shall be construed so as to have retrospective operation unless its language is such as to require such a construction (see Lauvi v. Renad (1892)3 Ch. 403, 421)...to determine the intendment of the makers of the Constitution, the Constitution must be read as a whole. Provisions of the Constitution should not be read in isolation.... to correctly interpret the provisions of section 182 (1) (b) of the 1999 Constitution, we must consider other related provisions of the Constitution including the definition section. Taking with consideration the provisions of sections 318 and 320 of the 1999 Constitution it will be seen that section 182(1) (b) is prospective and I so hold.

In *Attorney-General of the Federation* v. *All Nigerian Peoples Party*[19] the question was whether the nomination of the 2nd respondent Prince Abubakar Audu as the Governor of Kogi State for the 3rd term in office is in consonance with the provision of section 182(1) (b) of the 1999 Constitution which provides thus:

> No person shall be qualified for election to the office of Governor of a State if...(b) he has been elected to such office at any two previous elections.

The 1999 Constitution became operative with effect from 29th May, 1999 and the 2nd respondent first term in office under military government was in 1991. The Supreme Court held that the provision of the 1999 Constitution which

---

[17] (2002) FWLR 1972 at p. 2137.
[18] (1985) 2 NWLR (pt. 9) 734.
[19] (2003) FWLR (pt. 167) p. 839..

came into effect on 29th May, 1999 cannot be interpreted retrospectively as to cover the 2nd respondent term of office in 1991 more so that the election of 1991 was conducted under the military regime and that the 1999 Constitution was for democratic government. Furthermore the 2nd respondent only spent two years in office before he was removed undemocratically and that the 1999 Constitution envisaged two terms in office of four years each, i.e. eight years together. Oguntade JCA said:

> ...And finally on the point, to construe section 182(1)(b) retrospectively as appellant would want us to do will create absurdity. Quite apart from the fact that the said election will have different meaning in relation to the states in the federation depending on when a particular state was created, it will also operate oppressively on the 2nd respondent who served as a governor in 1991 and others in that category Section 182(1) (b) is not a punitive provision. It has recurred in all our Constitutions. Why would it allow the service of the 2nd respondent as a Governor to terminate after a total number of six years while the same Constitution allows others to serve a total of eight years? The result of what I have said is that section 182(1) (b) of the 1999 Constitution ought to be construed only prospectively and not retrospectively.[20]

Judicial Approach to the Interpretation of the Constitution in Nigeria

The Supreme Court has ruled that the Constitution of the Federal Republic of Nigeria should not be given slavish interpretation. In *Adegbenro* v. *Akintola*, [21] the case arose over the political crisis in Western Nigeria that led to the removal of Chief Akintola by the Governor in 1961 purportedly under the constitutional power to do so if it appears to him that the premier no longer commands the support of a majority of the members of the House of Assembly. Acting on the basis of a letter signed by 66 of the 124 Assembly members, the Governor removed Akintola and replaced him with Chief Adegbenro. The Federal Supreme Court held that the removal was unconstitutional since it was carried out after a vote on the floor of the House as required by a convention of the British Constitution. However, the Privy Council disagreed and held that it could not find any indications either in the general scheme or in other specific provisions of the Constitution of Western Nigeria which would enable them to say that the Governor was legally precluded from forming his opinion upon the basis of anything but votes formally given on the floor of the House. Delivering the judgment of the Court, Viscount Radclife said:

---

[20] Ibid at p. 886.
[21] 1963 AC 614

> It is true that the Western Nigerian Constitution...embody much of the constitutional practice and principle of the United Kingdom. But...the Constitution of Western Nigeria is now contained in a written instrument in which it has been sought to formulate with precision the powers and duties of the various agencies that it holds in balance. That instrument now stands in its own right; and, while it may well be useful on occasion to draw on British practice or doctrine in interpreting a doubtful phrase whose origin can be traced...it is in the end the wording of the Constitution itself that is to be interpreted and applied, and this wording can never be overridden by the extraneous principles of other Constitutions which are not explicitly incorporated in the formulae that have been chosen the framer of this Constitution.[22]

In the interpretation, application and enforcement of either category of fundamental right, the broader interpretation is the rule. By a very impressive pedigree of case law, it is finally settled that in the interpretation of the constitutional provisions pertaining to fundamental rights and liberties, a very broad and literal interpretation should be applied so as to give effect to the constitutional purpose of securing, entrenching and effecting the protection of individual rights and liberties. For instance where the law talks about a trial within two months from the date of arrest or detention, what period is the law talking about? Is it stipulating that prosecution must be commenced within two months of arrest or that it must be concluded within two months?

It has been conclusively interpreted and decided by the Nigerian court that when an act is required to be done "within" a specified period of time, the act must be done and completed before the expiry of the stated period of time. The word *"within"* when used relative to time means before the expiration of specified time.

Where any person is arrested or detained for the purpose of bringing him before a court upon reasonable suspicious of his having committed a criminal offence, and where his trial is not completed within a period of two months from the date of his arrest or detention he becomes immediately entitled to bail. Even where the accused person may ordinarily be disentitled to bail, a failure of the prosecution to conclude the trial within two months immediately creates an unimpeachable right to bail for the accused. This right to bail, though created by default, stands on as strong a position as any other constitutional right. This right is not enjoyed at the goodwill of either the prosecution or the court. It is enjoyed at the goodwill of the Constitution and may not be circumscribed or abridged by the court. The court may elect to grant the bail unconditionally. Where the court

---

[22] Ibid.

elects to impose some condition to the bail, the conditions must be such as are solely reasonably necessary to ensure he appears for trial at a later date.

On the proper interpretation of Section 308 of the Constitution of the Federal Republic of Nigeria which conferred absolute immunity on the President. Governor/Deputy Governor from civil and criminal prosecution against them while in office was under a serious challenge on the fact as to whether the President, Governor/Deputy Governor can correspondingly institute civil or criminal proceedings against any other person while in office. The wide spread speculation is that since they are immunized from civil and criminal prosecutions on the ground of social justice, equity and morality they cannot institute similar actions.

Section 308 of the 1999 Constitution provides thus:

308(1) Notwithstanding anything to the contrary in this Constitution, but subject to subsection (2) of this section -

(a) no civil or criminal proceedings shall be instituted or continued against a person to whom this section applies during his period of office;

(b) a person to whom this section applies shall not be arrested or imprisoned during that period either in pursuance of the process of any court or otherwise; and

(c) no process of any court requiring or compelling the appearance of a person to whom this section applies, shall be applied for or issued:

Provided that in ascertaining whether any period of limitation has expired for the purposes of any proceedings against a person to whom this section applies, no account shall be taken of his period of office.

2. The provision of subsection (1) of this section shall not apply to civil proceedings against a person to whom this section applies in his official capacity or to civil or criminal proceedings in which such a person is only a nominal party.

3. This section applies to a person holding the office of President or Vice President, Governor or Deputy Governor, and the reference in this section to "period of office" is a reference to the period during which the person holding such office is required to perform the functions of the office.

In *Tinubu* v. *IMB Securities*,[23] on 26th November, 1992 at the High Court of Lagos, the respondent sued Tinubu along with others claiming the sum of ₦2.5million granted to 1st defendant on facilities. As at December 1999, the matter was at the Court of Appeal on interlocutory appeal when Tinubu was elected Governor of Lagos State, and consequently, an application to adjourn the proceedings sine die until such a time as the appellant would cease to hold office as Governor of Lagos State. Learned counsel to Tinubu contended that the civil proceedings in issue, in so far as it concern the claim against the appellant (Tinubu) could no longer be continued, having regard to Section 308 (1)(a) of the Constitution of the Federal Republic of Nigeria, 1999. The Court of Appeal granted the respondent application and adjourned the matter sine die. On appeal to the Supreme Court, Karibi-White JSC stated as follows:

> The interpretation of the Constitution should be guided by the facts of the case. Appellant in the instant case was the defendant. The provision of Section 308 speaks of a civil or criminal proceedings instituted or continued against a person to whom the section applies during his period of office. The provision goes to preclude arrest or imprisonment, and issuance of process requiring or compelling appearance of some person. There is no suggestion that such person can institute actions against other persons, who cannot apply for process against them. The provision of Section 308 is a policy legislation designed to confer immunity from civil or criminal process on the public officer named in Section 308 (3) and to insulate them from harassment in their personal matters incurred before their election. It follow from such immunity that such persons will not be involved in ordinary transactions that will necessitate resorting to the institution of civil suit or criminal actions. The text of Section 308 is explicit and conclusive. The liberal approach to the interpretation of our Constitution counselled in Nafiu Rabiu v. The State (1988) 12 NSCC 291, does not encourage reading the provisions to neutralize the public policy protected by the provision...[24]

It is very clear that Section 308(1) of the 1999 Constitution confers on the President, Vice President, Governor or Deputy Governor absolute immunity against the institution of civil or criminal proceedings or the continuation of such civil and criminal proceedings against the President or Vice-President, Governor or Deputy Governor as long as they remain in office as such. It follows therefore that where an action or proceeding had been instituted prior to the person assuming the relevant office, such action or proceeding cannot be continued against the occupant of the relevant office during his tenure in the said office. By

---

[23] (2001) 8 NWLR (pt. 740) 192.
[24] Ibid.

the provision of subsection 2 of Section 308, it is also clear that immunity conferred on the persons occupying the offices mentioned under Section 308 of the 1999 Constitution does not extend to cases or actions instituted against the said persons in which persons are nominal parties and in their official capacities such as the President, Vice-President, Governor or Deputy Governor.

But on the power of the President, Vice President, Governor or Deputy Governor to institute actions against persons while in office is well articulated in Global Excellence Communication Limited and Others v. Mr. Donald Duke.[25] The respondent is the Governor of Cross River State of Nigeria and that he instituted suit No. HC/261/2004 at the High Court of Cross River State Calabar, against the appellants while holding that office, that the action so instituted is in the personal capacity of the said respondent arising from an alleged libel against the person and/or character of the respondent. It is not disputed that Section 308 (1) of the 1999 Constitution grants absolute immunity to the respondent against the institution or continuation of any civil or criminal action against the respondent in any court in Nigeria. The bone of contention however relates to the issue as to whether the respondent, having regards to the absolute immunity conferred on him by the said Section 308(1) of the 1999 Constitution has the right or liberty to institute or continue any civil action against any person(s) during his tenure of office as Governor of Cross River State. In other words, does the immunity against institution or continuation of civil or criminal proceedings include a corresponding disability to institute or continue any proceedings by the Governor against any person(s) in any court in Nigeria. Relying on the dictum of Ayoola JSC in *Tinubu* v. *I.M.B Securities Plc.* where the following view was expressed:

> Thirdly, I am unable to construe a provision of the Constitution that granted an immunity such as Section 308(1) as also constituting a disability on the person granted immunity when there is no provision to that effect, either expressly or by necessary implication in the enactment. If the makers of the Constitution had wanted to prohibit a person holding offices stated in Section 308 from instituting or continuing action instituted against any other person during his period of office, nothing would have been easier than to provide expressly that no civil or criminal proceeding shall be instituted against any person by a person to whom this section applies during his period of office and "no civil or criminal proceedings shall be instituted or continued against a person during his period in office" or in

---

[25] Delivered on 13th July, 2007 SC 313/2006.

like terms. The makers of the Constitution in their wisdom did not so provide.[26]

Niki Tobi JSC dismissed the appeal and hold that the Governor of River State in view of the provision of Section 308(1) of the 1999 Constitution has the legal capacity to institute the action against the respondent in his personal capacity as the Governor of River State.

The Courts in Nigeria has subjected Section 308 of the Constitution of the Federal Republic of Nigeria to an intense microscopic scrutiny. In *Tinubu* v. *IMB Securities Plc.* [27] The Supreme Court held that no civil or criminal proceedings can be initiated or brought against the holder of any of the offences mentioned under Section 308(3) of the Constitution during his tenure. The court followed the decision in *Alamieyeseigha* v. *Yeiwa*[28] to hold that Section 308 which confers on the appellant absolute immunity from civil and criminal proceedings cannot be invoked to deny him the right to fair hearing when an order sought directly affects him. In *Media Tech (Nig.) Ltd.* v. *Lam Adesina*[29] the Supreme Court of Nigeria held that the Respondent is shielded from being prosecuted civilly or criminally while still occupying the office of Governor but that the Respondent as Governor, would institute action against any other person or persons in his personal capacity. In *I.C.S. (Nig.) Ltd* v. *Balton B. V.* [30] it was held that once one of the parties to the suit belongs to the category of office holders named in Section 308(3), the suit must be struck out. In *Umanah* v. *Attah,* [31] it was held that any charge or indictment against the 1st Respondent while he was the Governor of a State, before or by the Code of Conduct Tribunal, would have been rendered null and void under the provisions of Section 308 of the 1999 Constitution. [32] Similarly in *Attorney-General of the Federation and Others* v. *Alhaji Atiku Abubakar*[32] the Supreme Court held that the respondent is not entitled to be tried by the Code of Conduct tribunal for an offence under Section 308 of the Constitution while in office as the Vice President of the Federal Republic of Nigeria. The court also held that the respondent Alhaji Atiku Abubakar could institute an action against any person in his personal capacity. The court said:

---

[26] Ibid.

[27] (2001) 16 NWLR (pt. 740) p. 670.

[28] (2002) 7 NWLR (pt. 767) p. 581 at pp. 601- 957.

[29] (2005) 1 NWLR (pt. 908) p. 461 at 475.

[30] (2003) 8 NWLR (pt. 822) p. 223

[31] (2004) 7 NWLR (pt. 871) p. 63.

[32] See also Ejudra v. Idris (2006) 4 NWLR (pt. 971) p. 538, Alamieyseigha v. Federal Republic of Nigeria (2006) 16 NWLR (pt. 1004) p. 1, Gani Fawehinmi v. Inspector-General of Police & Ors. (2002) 7 NWLR (pt. 766) p. 683.

[32] Appeal No CA/A/21/07 delivered on 5th April, 2007 at Abuja.

One of the basic principles of interpretation of all Constitutions and statutes is that the lawmaker will not be presumed to have given a right in one section and take it in another. In the instant case, it will not be presumed that the makers of the 1999 Constitution intended the immunity provided to certain categories of Public Officers in Section 308 of the Constitution during the tenure of their office to be taken away by the Code of Conduct Bureau created under Section 153 of the Constitution.[33]

The situation of the ill-health of the former President of the Federal Republic of Nigeria, Umaru Musa Yar'Adua call for the interpretation of Section 145 of the 1999 Constitution which provides thus;

Whenever the President transmits to the Senate and the Speaker of the House of Representative a written declaration that he is proceeding on vacation or that he is otherwise unable to discharge the function of his office, until he transmits to them a written declaration to the contrary, such functions shall be discharged by the Vice President as Acting President.[34]

The operative word here is "a written declaration". The mode and manner the President make such a declaration is the subject of judicial interpretation in *Kayode Ajulo* v. *The President of the Senate, Speaker of the House of Representatives and the Attorney-General of the Federation.* [35] On 18th January 2010 at the Federal High Court, the plaintiff instituted an action to claim inter alia the court's declaration that by the combined effect of the authorized and un-contradicted public declaration made by the President Umaru Musa Yar'Adua, on January 12, 2009 voiced thus;

At the moment, I am undergoing treatment, and I'm getting better from the treatment. I hope that very soon there will be tremendous progress, which will allow me to get back home... As soon as my doctors discharge me, I will return to Nigeria to resume my duties...I wish, at this stage, to thank all Nigerians for their prayers for my good health, and for their prayers for the nation.[36]

It is the contention of the plaintiff that the declaration was transmitted by a credible medium and subsequently transcribed and published by virtually all Nigeria print media,[37] and was received and read by all including the President of

---

[33] Ibid.
[34] Constitution of the Federal Republic of Nigeria, 1999.
[35] Suit No. FHC/ABJ/CS/28/10
[36] BBC News of 12th January, 201
[37] It was reported in Thisday, Punch, Guardian, The Nation, Sun, Vanguard Newspapers and other National and International Newspapers.

the Senate, Speaker of the House of Representative at both chambers of the National Assembly. President Yar'Adua has duly informed the President of the Senate, Speaker of the House of Representative of his inability to perform the functions of his office and proceeded on vocation owing to his ill-health and had therefore complied with the provision of Section 145 of the 1999 Constitution. The plaintiff also prays for consequential order of the court directing the National Assembly to recognize and allow the Vice-President to begin, without any further delay, the performance of his duties of the President of the Federal Republic of Nigeria in his own right as Acting President.

No sooner had the defendants were served with the court processes on 2nd of February, 2010 that on the National Assembly in their deliberation on 9th February 2010 passed a separate resolutions to yield in tadem to the immutable reliefs sought in the matter and declared the Vice-President as the Acting President. The Senate resolution read thus:

> Viewed from an ordinary reading of Section 145, we came to the conclusion that the President, through his declaration transmitted worldwide on the British Broadcasting Corporation, has furnished this parliament with irrefutable proof that he is on medical vacation in the United Kingdom of Saudi-Arabia and has therefore complied with the provision of Section 145 of the 1999 Constitution.[38]

The literal interpretation of section 145 of the 1999 Constitution is that when the President had realized the fact that he has to vacate his office for any reason and reasoned that his vacation may cause a vacuum in his office and/or the President holds a conviction of his inability to discharge the functions of his office, one of the options therefore available for the President is what Section 145 has revealed.

The manner the President is expected to make the declaration within the contemplation of Section 145 of the 1999 Constitution by broadcasting same on the BBC Network news has been given judicial interpretation by Uwais CJN in A.G. Lagos v. A.G. Federation thus:

> Be that as it may, it should be borne in mind that we are in this case concerned with the interpretation of the Constitution. The inconsistency and confusion notwithstanding, this court has since laid down that in interpreting the Constitution we should avoid technicality.[39]

---

[38] Senate Resolution of 9th February, 2010 in Abuja, Nigeria
[39] (2004) 18 NWLR (pt. 904) at pp. 75-76. para F-C. Infra, the procedure for proclamation of state of emergency and resignation as provided in Sections 305 and 306 of the Constitution respectively, where the procedures, manners and formats in which the President should make a proclamation of state of

The function of the Constitution is to establish a framework and principle of government, broad and general in terms, is to be to applied to the varying conditions of the provisions of the Constitution, as observed by Onnoghen JSC in *Rt. Hon. Michael Balonwu* v. *Governor of Anambra* thus:

> it is therefore proper to hold that the intention of the legislature is to ensure continuation of government action in order to avoid a vacuum.[40]

The word "whenever" in Section 145 of the Constitution implies "from time to time" in that within the tenure of four years or eight years, as the case may be, the President will be expected to be unavailable to discharge the functions of his office on several occasions. On such occasions, he is expected to "transmit a written declaration" to the President of the Senate and the Speaker of the House of Representatives that he is proceeding on vacation or that he is otherwise unable to discharge the functions of his office.

Compliance with the provision of Section 145 of the Constitution could be carried out in two ways:

(a) The President has discretion to prepare a written document with the content that he would be proceeding on vocation and such document should be directed purposely to the President of the Senate and the Speaker of the House of Representatives; or

(b) In any case where the President has failed to follow the first path, especially where it is glaring that the President is ill and cannot be said to be medically fit to prepare a written document, then once the President has expressed in his own words the intention of his going on vacation and such is published in public document communicated to the whole world including the President of the Senate and the Speaker of the House of Representatives, the acknowledgement of same has generated a compliance with Section 145 of the Constitution.

It is important to note from the above propositions that the first interpretation is literal and strict while the later is liberal.

The fact that the President has expressed intention that he is seriously ill, and will only resume his duty once his doctors discharge him, is sufficient to declare that the President is medically incapacitated to the extent that he cannot even write any document as provided in Section 145, but once he granted an oral interview with the BBC Network which was broadcasted and transmitted by almost all the Newspapers in Nigeria, the intention of the President could be said to have been impliedly reduced into writing as required by Section 145. More so

---

emergency and office holders under the Constitution should declare their resignations respectively were specifically provided.

[40] Suit No. SC/233/2008 (unreported) delivered on 4th December, 2009.

that the interview granted by the President on the BBC Network was thoroughly debated by the two chambers of the legislature presided over by the leaders of the chambers, the President of the Senate and the Speaker of the House of Representatives is sufficient to show that the two chambers had knowledge of the President's intention.

The Constitution is *sui generis* and calls for a generous interpretation. As Udo Udoma in *Nafiu Rabiu* v. *The State* put it: [41]

> ...the approach of this court to the construction of the Constitution should be, and it has been, one of liberalism, probably a variation on the theme of the general maxim *ut res magis valeat guam pereat*. I do not conceive it to be the duty of this court so to construe any of the provisions of the Constitution as to defeat the obvious ends the Constitution was designed to serve whether another construction equally in accord and consistent with the words and sense of such provisions will serve to enforce and protect such ends...I have not argued that the meaning of the word or phrase change, but the changing circumstances illustrate and illuminate the full import of that meaning. [42]

---

[41] (1981) 2 NCLR 293. See also James v. Commonwealth (1936) 55 CLRI 43 Lord Wiberforce in *Minister of Home Affairs* v. *Fisher* (1980) AC 319 described the constitutional instrument as sui generis and calls for a generous interpretation avoiding what he called "the authority of tabulated legalism".
[42] Ibid.

Chapter 5

Analysis

The judicial approach to the interpretation of the Constitution in Australia, Canada, India and Nigeria have common features in common while at the time differ in some aspects.

Similarities

(a) Australia and Canada

One of the principles often adopted by the Australian and Canadian courts in the interpretation of the human rights provisions in the Constitutions of both countries is that the draftman's intention is irrelevant. For example in Re BC Motor Vehicle[1] Per Lamer of the Supreme Court of Canada said "the draftman's intention is not the key, we must not freeze the Charter in time. Its potential for growth must be presumed" Also *Edwards* v. *The Attorney-General of Canada*, the Privy Council on appeal from the Supreme Court of Canada[2] Per Lord Sankey remarked that "The Constitution is 'a living tree capable of growth and expansion within its natural limits."

In Australia, the High Court of Australia in *Theophanous* v. *Herald and Weekly Times Limited*, Deane J. said:

> The intention of the Constitution's framers was irrelevant since a Constitution was a living force representing the will of contemporary Australians social changes since 1901 (such as universal adult franchise, compulsory voting, mass communication, general education and appreciation of the intrinsic equality of all human beings) enhanced the need for unrestricted access to political information.[3]

The Constitution of Canada (1867) and Australia (1901) are among the most enduring of such documents in the world today. The text of the Australian Constitution like that of Canada is, written in language which is brief, sometimes obscure and usually ambiguous.

---

[1] (1985) 2 SCR 486.
[2] (1930) A.C. 124.
[3] (1994) 3LRC 369.

In Canada, it is well established that the language of the Constitution Act 1867 is not to be frozen in the sense in which it would have been understood in 1867. Rather, the language is to be given a "progressive interpretation" so that it is continuously adopted to new conditions and new ideas. The principles of progressive interpretation may be compared with originalism which focuses on the original understanding of a constitutional text.

In Australia, legal reasoning as the only proper approach for a court of law received great emphasis in the much celebrated decision of the High Court of Australia in the *Engineers' case*.[4] In recent years, however, there have been indications of a change in attitude and approach – a greater awareness by some judges of the role of the court and its relation to social and political change.

(b) Canada and India

A contextual approach is preferred to an abstract approach in interpreting the human rights provisions of the Constitutions of India and Canada. The context of a right ought to be determined in the context of the real life situation brought to the court by the litigant and on the basis of empirical data rather than on the basis of some abstraction.[5]

A broad, liberal, generous and benevolent Constitution is being given, not narrow, pedantic, literal or technical interpretation by the courts in interpreting the human rights provisions of the Constitutions of India[6] and Canada.[7]

(c) India and Nigeria

The Constitution of India has similar provisions to that of Nigeria on Directive Principles of State Policy in Part IV thereof. In the India case of *Mangru* v. *Commissioners of Budge, Budge Municipality*,[8] it was held that the Directive Principles require to be implemented by legislation and so long as there is no law carrying out the policy laid down in a Directive neither the State nor an individual can violate any existing law or legal right under guise of following a Directive.

The scope and purpose of Chapter 11 of the Constitution on Fundamental Objectives and Directive Principles of State Policy impose an obligation on the Federal Government with particular reference to Sections 13 and 15(5) of the 1999 Constitution to eradicate corrupt practices in the country. In *Miners of Mills* v. *Union of India AIR* (1980) SC 184, Bhagwati, J. held that Directive Principles impose an obligation on the State (i.e. the government of India) to take positive

---

[4] (1920) 28 CLR 129.
[5] *Sakal Newspapers Ltd* v. *The Union of India* (1962) 3 SCR 842; PSAC v. Canada (1987) 1 SCR 424.
[6] *Sakal Newspapers Ltd.* v. *The Union of India* Ibid.
[7] *Law Society of Upper* v. *Skapinker* (1984) 1 SCR 357.
[8] (1951) 87 CLJ 369, see also Basu, D.D *Shorter Constitution of India* (12th Edition) at pp. 296-297, A.G. *Ondo State* v. *AG Federation* (2002) FWLR (Pt. 111) p. 1972 at p. 2070.

action for creating socio-economic conditions in which there shall be egalitarian social order and economic justice for all.

Chapter 11 of the Nigerian Constitution represents a charter between the government and the society.

Basu quoting a passage from Commentary on the Constitution of India differentiated Directive Principles from Fundamental Rights. According to the learned author Directives are not enforceable in the courts and do not create any justifiable rights in favour of individuals; and that they require to be implemented by legislation, and so long, as there is no law carrying out the policy laid down in a Directive, neither the State nor an individual can violate any existing law or legal right under colour of following and abiding by a Directive.

As to the non-justiciability of the Fundamental Objectives and Directive Principles of State Policy in Chapter II of the Nigerian Constitution, they cannot be enforced by legal process but would be seen as a failure of duty and responsibility of State organs if they acted in clear disregard of them, the nature of the consequences of which having to depend on the aspect of the infringement in some cases the political will of those in power to redress the situation.

In Chapter 17 of the Constitution of the Federal Republic of Nigeria, viz: Fundamental Objectives and Directives Principles of State Policy, under section 15(5) it has been provided that the State shall abolish all corrupt practices and abuse of power and under item 60 (a) of the Exclusive Legislative List which provides for:

The establishment and regulation of authorities for the Federation or any part thereof:

(a)   to promote and enforce the observance of the Fundamental Objectives and Directive Principles contained in this Constitution.

On the nature and obligations imposed on the State, the Fundamental Objectives and Directives Principles of State Policy under chapter 11 of the Constitution of Nigeria gives the Nigerian Nation a sense of direction and purpose and spells out in detail the rights of citizens, and the duties and obligations of the government that flow from these rights.[9]

Similarly in the Indian case of *Hinds and Others* v. *R.* Lord Diplock said:

> A Constitution is the organic law of a country. It sets the parameters within which the country shall be governed. It establishes the institutional structures of government and either expressly or by necessary implication

---

[9] *Miners* v. *Union of India* (AIR) 1980 SC 1847.

their inter relations and spells out the basic rights of citizens and the obligations of the executive.[10]

One of the most significant and exact provisions/innovations of contemporary Constitutions in Nigeria is the inclusion of the chapter on Fundamental Objectives and Directive Principles of State Policy, an idea which Nigeria borrowed from the India Consitution[11] while the India Constitution on the other hand drew its inspiration and menthol from the Irish Constitution.[12]

In Nigeria and India where people give priority to local interests, the objectives and principles serves as a constant reminder and guide to successive government to maintain a sense of unity. The reports of the Constitution Drafting Committee in Nigeria observed that:

> The need for such provision in Nigerian Constitution is all the greater because of the heterogeneity of the society, the increasing gap between the rich and poor, the growing cleavage between the social grouping, all of which combine to confuse march to orderly progress, only an express statement of objectives and directive principles which clearly set out the parameters of Government and informs its policies and actions can generate a spirit of cooperation, peace, unity and progress.[13]

The underlying objectives of the Directive Principles of the position or situation in India can better be understood from the speech of Dr. Ambedkar in the Constituent Assembly of India. He said:

> ...in my judgment the directive principles have a great value for they lay down that our idea is economic democracy...our object in framing this Constitution is really two fold: (1)to lay down that our idea is economic democracy and also to prescribe that every Government whatsoever is in power, shall strive to bring about economic democracy,
>
> (2) to lay down the form of political democracy[14]

---

[10] (1975) 24 WLR 326 at 330.

[11] Report of Constitutional Drafting Committee, Vol. 1 Lagos: Federal Ministry of Information Printing Division, 1976 p. v.

[12] Anad, C.L. (1966) *The Constitution of India Delhi*: Law Book Company p. 208.

[13] Report of the Constitutional Drafting Committees Vol. II Lagos: Federal Ministry of Information Printing Division, 1976.

[14] Indian Constituent Assembly Debates, Vol. viii, pp. 494-495 cited in Pandey J.N. (1982) *Constitutional Law of India*, Allahabad: Central Law Agency p. 208, see also Adebayo M.K, Kamal, L.D and Bazza, H.I Fundamental Objectives and Directive Principles of State Policy in Constitutions: The Nigeria and India

The Directive Principles of State Policy have been a great source of legal, jurisprudential and constitutional support for the judiciary in making decisions, besides guiding Governmental Bodies in formulating human development policies, thereby promoting good governance.

The concept Fundamental Objectives and Directive Principles of State Policy differs from Fundamental Human Rights in a lot of aspects though the general assertion is that the two concepts are related. By analogy, Fundamental Human Rights can be said to be certain, essential, basic, natural and inalienable rights or freedoms which the State protects through the force of law in order that human dignity, liberty may be preserved and protected.

Fundamental Human Rights are entrenched in such a way that they may not be violated by any oppressive Government; they can only be taken away by formal process of constitutional amendment. They consist of civil and political rights for example right to life; dignity of person; personal liberty; fair hearing; private and family life; freedom of thought, conscience and religion; peaceful assembly and association; freedom from discrimination and compulsory acquisition of property.[15] Fundamental Human Rights are essential for the protection of the rights and liberties of the citizens against encroachment by the Government, they are essentials for the protection of private and public rights, they are Fundamental because they are essential for the attainment by the individual of the full intellectual, moral and spiritual stature; these rights are entrenched in the Constitution as extant feature and are enforceable by the courts; the courts are bound to declare as void any law that is inconsistent with any of the Fundamental Rights.[16]

The Directive Principles are not enforceable while Fundamental Rights are enforceable. Thus the Supreme Court of India observed in *State of Mandras* v. *Champakam Dorairajan* that:

> The Directive Principles of State Policy which by Article 17 are expressly made unenforceable by courts cannot override the provision found in part III which notwithstanding other provisions, are expressly made enforceable by appropriate writs, orders or directions under Articles 32. The chapter on Fundamental Human Rights is sacrosanct and not liable to be abridge by legislature or executive acts, orders or except to the extent provided for in the appropriate Articles in part III. The directive principles of state policy have to conform and to run as subsidiary to the chapter on Fundamental

---

Experience. Islamic University in Uganda Journal of Comparative law, Faculty of Law, Islamic University in Uganda, Mbale-Uganda Vol. 1 July, 2007 pp. 163-191.

[15] Chapter IV, Sections 33-45 of the Constitution of the Federal Republic of Nigeria 1979 as well as Article 19-35 of the Indian Constitution 1950, part III.

[16] Pandey, J.N. (1982) Constitutional Law of India Allahabad: Central Law Agency p. 208.

Rights. In our opinion that is the correct approach in which the provision found in parts III and IV have to be understood...[17]

In Nigeria and India, there has been a modified approach and a change in the attitude of the courts in resolving conflicts between Fundamental Rights and Directive Principles. The courts have started giving some value to the Directive Principles from a legal point of view. For instance, the courts have come to adopt the view that while Directive Principles are non-enforceable, nevertheless, in statutory interpretation, the courts could look for a guide from the Directive Principles[18]. In *Mumbai Kamgar Sabha* v. *AbdulBhai*[19] the court held that where two judicial choices are available, the construction in conformity with the social philosophy of Directive Principles should prevail[20]. Furthermore, the courts also adopted the view that in determining the scope and ambit of Fundamental Rights, the Directive Principles should not be completely ignored and that the courts should adopt the principle of harmonious construction and attempt to give effect to both as far as possible.

Equally the courts in Nigeria have adopted a similar view. In *Archbishop Olubunmi Okogie & Ors* v. *Attorney General of Lagos State,* it was held that:

The Directive Principles of State Policy in Chapter 11 of the Constitution have to conform to and run subsidiary to the Fundamental Rights and that chapter 11 is subject to legislative powers conferred on the State.[21]

On the issue of admissibility of document in evidence, both the Nigerian and the Indian Constitution allow admission in evidence of the record of proceedings of the National Assembly as proof of compliance with the procedure for the passage of the Bill into law.

In *Attorney-General of Bendel State* v. *Attorney-General of the Federation and 22 Ors,*[22] the question is whether the Supreme Court of Nigeria is entitled to admit in evidence records of votes and proceedings in the National Assembly for the purpose of an inquiry as to the validity or constitutionality of any law passed by the National Assembly.

Sections 73(1) (c) and 112 (b) of the Nigerian Evidence Act[23] provides as follows:

---

[17] (1951) A.I.R. SC p. 522.
[18] Jain, M.P. (1978) *Indian Constitutional Law,* Bombay: N.M Tripathi Private Ltd. p. 598.
[19] (1976) A.I.R SC1455
[20] (1981) INCLR p. 218.
[21] Ibid.
[22] (1981) I ALL NLR p. 85.
[23] Cap. 62 Laws of the Federation of Nigeria.

73 (1): the court shall take judicial notice of the following facts:
(c)   The course of proceeding of Parliament and of the Federal Legislative House of Nigeria and of the Legislative House of the Regions of Nigeria.
112: The following public documents may be proved as follows:
(b)   The proceedings of the Legislative Council or of a Federal Legislative House by minutes of that body or by published ordinances or abstracts, or by copies purporting to be printed by   order of Government.

The court admitted the notes and proceedings of the National Assembly as evidence to support the fact that the Joint Committee on Finance of the National Assembly failed to comply with the provision of section 55 of the 1979 Constitution by not sending the amended Bill to the National Assembly before passing the Bill to the President. As observed by Idigbe, JSC.

It seems quite clear from the "journal" or records of votes and proceedings of the National Assembly in evidence in these proceedings a Joint Finances Committee; whether as is shown from these records or journals the Committee was referred to as the Joint Conference on Revenue Allocation or the Joint Committee on Finance is for the purpose of all these proceedings immaterial. The material facts, however, are: (a) the Revenue Allocation Bill was passed with amendments by one House and later passed with further amendments by the other House; (b) the Bill was then sent to this Committee (the Joint Finance Committee) which according to Exhibit SC6 later "passed the Bill"; Exhibit SC 6 does not state how exactly the Committee "passed the Bill", that is how the difference or amendments were resolved. What, however, is certain is that the agreed − solution of the Committee, (i.e. the end-product of its resolution) never went back to the two Houses for consideration; for if the earlier differences or amendments of the two Houses were indeed, resolved by the Committee then there was a new bill and that bill should, in pursuance of the provisions of section 54 (1) of the Constitution, be 'passes' by the two Houses. This was never done. To the extent that Exhibit SC.6 states that the Bill was 'passed by the Joint Committee on Finance' that, indeed, is, by virtue of the provisions of subsection (4) of section 58 of the 1979 Constitution "a legal fallacy". Indeed, the certificate of the Clerk of the National Assembly (Exhibit SC6) attached to the schedule to the Allocation of Revenue (Federation Account etc) Act 1981 (Exhibit SC.11) "carries its death warrant in its hand"; for it shows that the Revenue Allocation Bill was passed by the Senate on 15-1-81, by House of Representatives on 22-1-81 and "by the Joint Committee on Finance" (i.e. the Joint Finance Committee) on 29-1-81. I have already said that the Committee has no power to pass a Bill into law. It follows, therefore, that the passage into law of the Revenue Allocation Bill of 1981 was unconstitutional; and accordingly the Allocation of Revenue (Federation Account etc) Act 1981 is invalid, that is, null and void[24]

Section 57 of the Indian Evidence Act[25] provides:

A judge is entitled to use his own knowledge of general or public facts, historical, scientific or otherwise. He is entitled to take judicial notice of matters which have reached the court... He is also entitled to take judicial notice of proceedings in the Assembly not of the facts asserted in the speeches but of the fact that such speeches were made.[26]

A special Bench of High Court of Nagpur in India[27] took the view that proceedings or journals of the Legislature were admissible in evidence in a matter before it relating to the Press (Emergency Powers) Act of 1931.

In *Shagwati Charon Shulka* v. *Provincial Government S.P. and Berar*[28] the court observed that:

...Now we will be more specific, we will refer to the debates in the Central Assembly.

Whatever may be the view regarding our right to take into consideration the general political situation at the time, there can, we think be no doubt that we are entitled to take judicial notice of proceedings in the Assembly – not indeed of the truth of the facts asserted in the speeches but of the fact that the speeches were made. The official report of the Central Assembly proceedings shows that a resolution was moved on 24-19-42...[29]

In countries with a written Constitution like Nigeria and India the Court has power to examine the exercise of legislative power[30] by the National Assembly[31] and if it falls short of the provisions of the Constitution to declare such law

[24] *Attorney General of Bendel State* v. *Attorney General of the Federation and 22 others* op. cit. at p. 170.
[25] 1872
[26] Ibid
[27] Pollock, Bose and Puranick JJ
[28] (1947) A.I.R (NAGPUR) p.1.
[29] Ibid.
[30] In a proper case i.e. where S6(6(b) or S. 212 apply.
[31] Which involves the process of law making.

unconstitutional. Thus the court has the power to inquire into the validity of the exercise of legislative power. In making the inquiry the court is guided by the principles that Parliament in a written Constitution which has spelt out the limits of its powers cannot go outside those limits in the exercise of that legislative power. Such Parliament cannot go contrary to the Constitution which has set down the conditions under which it will make laws. Thus the National Assembly cannot ignore the conditions of law making that are imposed by the instrument i.e. the Constitution which itself regulates its authority or power to make law.[32]

Section 4 (8) of the Nigerian Constitution[33] gives the courts power to inquire into the exercise of legislative power and to take appropriate action if legislation has not been passed in accordance with the provisions of the Constitution. Thus any law which seeks to preclude this inquiry is contrary to the provisions of the Constitution and is therefore null and void. Section 1 subsection (3) of the Constitution specifically provides that "If any law is inconsistent with the provisions of this Constitution, the Constitution shall prevail and that other law shall to the extent of the inconsistency be void". [34]

Where the words of a statute are clear and unambiguous the position is that the court should apply them. This is the position often adopted by the Nigerian and Indian courts.

In *Attorney-General of Bendel State* v. *Attorney-General of the Federation & Ors*, the Supreme Court of Nigeria, Per Obaseki, JSC laid down some principles to guide in the interpretation of the Constitution. Among these is the principle that:

The language of the Constitution where clear and unambiguous must be given its plain evident meaning. [35]

Idigbe, JSC in *Ogbunyiya & Ors* v. *Obi Okudo* had declared that:

One of the cardinal rules of construction of written instruments is that the words of a written instrument must in general be taken in their ordinary sense, notwithstanding the fact that any such construction may not appear to carry out the purpose which it might otherwise be supposed was intended by the maker or makers of the instrument.[36]

Again, in *Ifezue* v. *Mbadugba*, Bello JSC said:

---

[32] See *Bribery Commissioner* v. *Ranasinghe* (1965) A.C. 172.
[33] 1979 Constitution of the Federal Republic of Nigeria.
[34] Ibid.
[35] (1982) 2 NCLR p. 1 at pp. 77-78.
[36] (1979) ALL NLR 105.

...where the words of any section are clear and unambiguous, they must be given their ordinary meaning unless this would lead to absurdity or be in conflict with other provisions of the Constitution and effect must be given to those provisions without any recourse to any other consideration.[37]

In *Oke* v. *Atoloye*,[38] the Supreme Court of Nigeria held that the provisions of section 4 of the Constitution (Amendment) (No. 2) Decree 1976 are clear and unambiguous and they should be given their plain literal meaning. Obaseki, JSC at pages 590-591, declared:

The provisions of section 4(1), (2), (3) and (4) of the Decree clearly provide the answer to the objection raised by the appellants. The provisions are formulated in clear, simple and unambiguous terms that any interpretation other than that provided by the plain literal meaning of the words used is unwarranted.[39]

In Braithwaite v. GDM & Ors, Ayoola, JCA observed that:

If the words are plain and unambiguous recourse to interpretative aids by use of preamble, title, context and purpose will not be necessary. [40]

The position of the Indian courts is not different from that of the Nigerian courts. In an Indian case, cited by Basu in his Commentary on the Indian Constitution[41] *Ralla Raun* v. *East Punjab*, it was declared that:

But when the words of a statute are clear and unambiguous, and they are not unfamiliar or uncommon words as may aptly be described as "terms of art", it is unnecessary to travel beyond the Act for the purpose of construing them. [42]

Differences
(a) Australia and Canada
On judicial review, one of the recurrent themes of judicial review is the way the constitutional interpretation has run counter to the original intentions of constitutional design. In Australia, where the intention was to limit central power

---

[37] (1984) 1 SCNLR 4217, (1984) 5 SC 79, 101.
[38] (1985) 2 NWLR (pt. 9) 578.
[39] Ibid. at pp. 590-591.
[40] (1998) 7 NWLR (pt. 557) 307
[41] (4th ed.) vol. 1 at p. 27.
[42] (1949) 12 FLJ 3, 11.

by means of strict enumeration, the courts have supported centralization by giving broad interpretations to implied powers contained in general clauses.

In Canada on the other hand, where the original intention was to limit sub-national powers, these have been interpreted more generously and at the expense of central power.

(b) Canada and India

On the issue of right to life, liberty and security, there appears to be a great difference in the interpretation of the Canadian and Indian Constitutions on this issue. For instance Section 7 of the Canadian Charter of Rights and Freedoms reads:

> Everyone has the right to life, liberty and security if the person and the right not to be deprived thereof except in accordance with the principles of fundamental justice. [43]

Also section 21 of the Constitution of India reads:

> No person shall be deprived of his life or personal liberty except according to procedure established by the law. [44]

Despite the near identical wordings of these provisions, in their interpretation two very different paths with respect to constitutional protection of subsistence rights have been taken. Such rights are appreciated in Canadian public discourse, but have been consistently pushed beyond the purview of Section 7 of the Supreme Court of Canada. India, by contrast, features vast socio-economic gaps; yet its Supreme Court has consistently declared claims for subsistence social rights justiciable and enforceable through constitutional litigation that draws on Section 21.[45] The extent of constitutional protection of subsistence rights in a given polity does not necessarily reflect the prevalence of such rights in that polity's public discourse.

---

[43] Canadian Charter of Rights and Freedoms, Part 1 of the Constitution Act, 1982, being Schedule B to the Canada Act 1982 (U.K) 1982, C 11 (Charter).

[44] Constitution of India Part III, S. 21, Online: Indian Ministry of Law and Justice Legis.lawmin.nic.in/coi/coiason 29 July 08 pdf.

[45] See e.g. Olga Tellis v. Bombay Municipal Corporation, A.I.R 1986 SC 180; *Unni Krishnan J.P.* v. *State of Andhra Pradesh*, A.I.R. 1993 SC 2178. Note that in 2002, a new section (21A) was added to the Constitution of India. It warrants that "the State shall provide free and compulsory education to all children of the age of six to fourteen years in such manner as the State may by law determine".

(c) India and Nigeria

The Fundamental Objectives and Directive Principles of State Policy under Chapter II of the 1999 Constitution of Nigeria which make provisions for Political objective, Economic objective, Social objective, Educational objective, Foreign Policy objectives, Environmental objective, Directive on Nigerian Culture, Obligation of Mass Media, National Ethic and duties of the citizens are not justiciable. Judicial pronouncements from some Nigerian courts of law in certain cases have shown that provisions on Fundamental objective and Directive Principles of State Policy are not justiciable in Nigerian courts of law. For instance, in *Archbishop Anthony Olubunmi Okogie and Others* v. *Attorney-General of Lagos State*, the Court of Appeal said:

> The arbiter for any breach of the objectives and Directive Principles of State Policy is the legislature itself or the electorate. [46]

Whereas in India, the Constitution of India recognizes certain basic fundamental rights for every citizen of India, such as Right to Equality, the Right to Freedom, the Right against exploitation, the Right to Freedom of Religion, Culture and Educational rights, and the Right to Constitutional remedies. Any infringement of fundamental rights can be challenged by any citizen of India in the court of law. The Constitution of India also prescribes some fundamental duties on every citizens of India.

Rationale for the Similarities and Differences

The Constitution of Nigeria just like that of Australia, Canada, India and Nigeria is unique. It is set against the background of Nigeria peculiar circumstances, with the aim of satisfying the various aspirations and peculiarities of Nigeria.

Viscount Radcliffe in *Adegbenro* v. *Akintola and Aderemi* observed thus:

> The Constitution of Western Nigeria is now contained in a written instrument in which it has been sought to formulate with precision the powers and duties of the various agencies that it hold in balance stands on its own right and while it may well be useful on occasions to draw on British practice or doctrine in interpreting a doubtful phrase whose origin can be traced or to study decisions on the Constitutions of Australia or the United State where federal issues are involved, it is in the end the wording of the Constitution itself that is to be interpreted, and supplied, and this wording

---

[46] (1981) 1NCLR 218 see also *Adewole & Ors* v. *Alhaji Jakande & Ors* (1981) 1NCLR 262. Idowu A.A. Human Rights, Democracy and Development: The Nigerian Experience, Research Journal of International Studies-Issue 8 (November, 2008). P. 27 at p. 29.

can never be overridden by the extraneous principles of other Constitutions which are not explicitly incorporated in the formulae that have been chosen by the framer of this Constitution. [47]

Udo Udoma, JSC in *Nafiu Rabiu* v. *Kano State* said:

It is not a correct approach to the proper interpretation of our Constitution to begin by looking at the meaning or interpretation of a statutory provision or Constitution of other countries...foreign Constitutions or statutes with identical provisions accepted as *in pari materia* with the relevant provisions of our Constitution will naturally carry some weight in their persuasive influence bearing in mind always that even in such cases, circumstance may vary. [48]

Thus, the decisions of courts of Australia, Canada, India and indeed of the Commonwealth countries which operate written Constitutions are not binding on the Nigerian courts, just as that of Nigeria are not binding on them, although they are of course of considerable persuasive force especially where they relate to sections of the Constitutions of those countries which are *in pari materia* with sections of the Nigerian Constitution. As Viscourt Simords observed:

It is right, however, that in the interpretation of constitutional instruments guidance should be sought from those courts whose constant duty it has been to construe similar instruments, if only because, as it appears to me, a flexibility of construction is admissible in regard to such instruments which ought to be rejected in construing ordinary statutes or inter parties documents. The courts of Northern Ireland have not hesitated to adopt this course and have found assistance in their task of construing their own Constitution from the manner in which great judges among the English-Speaking peoples overseas have dealt with kindred problems. [49]

Most Commonwealth countries applied different canons of construction in interpreting their Constitutions. Some of the canons of interpretation take the form of broad general principles only. Consequently, a common feature of most of them is that they are of little practical assistance in settling doubts about interpretation in particular cases. This is partly due to vagueness, but also because in many cases, where one canon appears to support a particular interpretation, there is another canon, often of equal status, which can be invoked in favour of an

---

[47] (1962) 1 ALL NLR 465 at p. 479.
[48] Ibid.
[49] *Belfast Corporation* v. *O.D. Cars Ltd* 1960 Appeal Cases 490 at p. 518.

interpretation which could lead to a different result. It is in this regard that the courts of Australia, Canada, India and Nigeria adopted other approaches taking into consideration the social-political situations in their countries to interpret their Constitution. It is in this respect that Fatai-Williams CJN remarked in *Awolowo* v. *Shagari* thus:

> Some of these canons of interpretation take the form of broad general principles only. Consequently, a common feature of most of them is that they are of little practical assistance in settling doubts about interpretation in particular cases. This is partly due to vagueness, but also became, in many cases, where one canon appears to support a particular interpretation, there is another canon, often of equal status, which can be invoked in favour of an interpretation which could lead to different result. [50]

Judicial prudence dictates the gradual or "go slow" approach in the interpretation of the Constitution. This is an approach accepted by the Supreme Court of Nigeria in *Adesanya* v. *The President of the Federal Republic of Nigeria and Another*[51] and by the Superior Courts in Australia, Canada and India and in other Commonwealth jurisdictions.[52]

The view that the court should look at the proceedings of the National Assembly as provided under Sections 73 and 112 of the Evidence Act in Nigeria, [53] the position of the Supreme Court of Nigeria adopted in *Attorney-General of Bendel State* v. *Attorney-General of the Federation* [54] is indeed radical and runs contrary to the rule applicable in Australia, Canada, India and in most Commonwealth countries. Discussing the rule Nwabueze, B.O. said:

> The rationale for the rule is that the signing of an enrolled bill by the presiding officials is an official attestation by the legislative Houses of such a bill having been duly passed by them. It is a declaration by them, through their presiding officers, to the head of State that the bill has received, in due form, the sanction of the legislative branch. And when, upon the strength of that declaration, the bill is approved and signed by the head of State, his signature together with those of the presiding officials is a solemn assurance to the court and to the nation that all necessary formalities have been observed. The respect due to co-equal and independent departments

---

[50] (1979) 6-9 at p. 64.
[51] (1981) 5 SC 112, see also *Attorney-General of Benue State* v. *Attorney-General of the Federation and 22 Ors* (1981) 1 ALLNLR p. 85 at p. 235.
[52] *Euclid* v. *Amber Reality Co.* (1926) 272 US 365, 47 S. ct 114 at 121; The State of Wyoming on the relation of fire Fighters Local, etc 420 Pacific Reporter 2nd Series (1966) 254 at pp. 256-257
[53] Cap. 62 Laws of the Federation of Nigeria.
[54] (1981) 1 ALL NLR p. 85.

requires the court to accept and act upon that assurance. To go behind the assurance would involve the subordination of the legislative and the executive branches to the court. Further, public policy requires that enrolled act should not be put in question after the public has given faith in its validity and regulated its relations and dealings accordingly. Great uncertainty and instability in statute law would result if an enrolled and duly authenticated act were to be subjected to impeachment on the basis of some evidence of lack of due passage.[55]

What Nigeria has benefited from other Commonwealth Jurisdictions

On the issue of interpretation of the Nigerian Constitution it is proper to look into the relevant provisions of the Constitution to be able to ascertain the meaning intended by the legislature.

Nnamani JSC in *Attorney-General of Bendel State* v. *Attorney-General of the Federation and 22 Ors* observed thus:

The other preliminary matter I would wish to touch is the enormous volume of legal authorities cited to us in this suit-authorities from the United States, England, India and Australia. These authorities have no more persuasive authority. While I do reiterate the view I had previously expressed that they are helpful while interpreting the provisions of our Constitution, it must be emphasized that in determining the meaning of those provisions it is to our own Constitution that we must principally turn. Those authorities can in fact only be helpful if they relate to provisions in the Constitutions of the countries in which they were made similar to provisions in our own Constitution. It is a fact that in relation to many of the more complex of the provisions of our Constitution that had to be construed in the course of this suit, no similar provisions were available in the Constitution of U.S.A or Australia. If I recollect correctly, it was only in respect of India that a provision – Article 131 – was found to be similar to section 212 of our Constitution. As regards the Constitution of the United Kingdom, no parallels can be drawn between it and our Constitution. There is no written Constitution and the supremacy of the British Parliament ensures that no court there would challenge the validity of a dully enrolled Act of Parliament. The provisions for dealing with money Bills under these Constitutions are different from the provisions of sections 55(2) and 55(3) or 55(4) of our Constitution. [56]

---

[55] Judicialism in Commonwealth Africa: the role of the courts in Government London: Hurst, 1977 the at pp. 259-260.
[56] (1981) 1 ALLNLR p. 85 at pp. 235-236.

Where the intention of the legislature is to be looked for, it can only be found in the words used and not in any speculative opinion of the court. It is not for the court to determine what the legislature meant to say but what is actually said. Nor is the court to read something into such provisions on the grounds of[57] expediency or justice,[58] or political exigency,[59] motives of the framers or possibility of abuse of power.[60] In *Vacher v. London Society of Compositors*, Lord Macnaghten observed that:

> Some people may think the policy of the Act unwise and even dangerous to the community. Some may think it at variance with principles which have long been held sacred. But a judicial tribunal has nothing to do with the policy of any Act which it may be called upon to interpret. That may be a matter of private judgment. The duty of the court, and its only duty, is to expound the language of the Act in accordance with the settled rules of construction. [61]

Per Vissent Radcliffe in *Adegbenro v. Akintola* opined that "it is the wording of the Constitution itself that is to be interpreted and applied."[62]

The Directive Principles of State Policy under the Indian Constitution have been a great source of legal jurisprudential and constitutional support for the judiciary in Nigeria. The Constitution of India on the Directive Principles of State Policy has positive impact on the constitutional development in Nigeria. Most decisions of the courts in Nigeria in the recent times followed similar examples from the Indian experience. It also guided the government of Nigeria in formulating human development policies, thereby promoting good governance in the country. Thus, one of the most important innovations of the contemporary Constitutions in Nigeria is the inclusion of the chapter on fundamental objectives and Directive Principles of State Policy, an idea which Nigeria borrowed from the India Constitution.

---

[57] *Vacher & Sons v. London Society of Compositors* (1913) AC 107, 118.

[58] *U.S. v. Brunett,* 53 F 2d. 219.

[59] *Amalgamated Society of Engineers v. Adelande Steamship Company* (1920) CLR 129, 149.

[60] *Bank of Toronto v. Lambe* (1887) 12 App Cas 575-586.

[61] (1913) AC 107.

[62] *Adegbenro v. Akintola* (1963) AC 614.

Chapter Six

Conclusion

If the legislature creates rules to fit every situation, it would cause such a proliferation of rules which would eventually lead to a comparable impairment of function.[1]

The choice of deciding which canons of interpretation to apply in any set of circumstances is a discretionary affair of the court. Professing a reliance on a set of legal canons of constitutional interpretation is not convincing.[2] The courts often adopted theories or approaches in constitutional interpretation. The courts in Australia,[3] Canada,[4] India[5] and Nigeria[6] adopted these methods in addition to the canons of interpretation.

The theories of constitutional interpretation in Australia, Canada, India and Nigeria though vary due to the socio-political differences in these countries, nevertheless they have one thing in common, that is, that the Constitution should be given liberal interpretation except where by so doing, would result to absurdity.

It has also been observed that the theories of interpretation adopted by the courts in Australia, Canada, India and Nigeria suffer a major set back as the

---

[1] Wassertrom, R.A. *The Judicial Decision* Stanford University Press 1961 p. 106.
[2] *Obafemi Awolowo* v. *Alhaji Sheu Shagari* (1978) 6/9 SC 51 at 92/95; The three common rules of statutory interpretation which dominate the historical perspective are the Literal Rule, Golden Rule and Mischief Rule. They have been useful aids in the interpretation of statutes in common law countries. In recent times, the court also adopted other rules of interpretation of statute such as the beneficial construction, constructing previous legislation, *ur res magis valeat quam pereat rule, ejusdam genaris* rule, internal aids and presumptions. The rules of statutory interpretation mentioned above are not strange to the Nigeria Jurisdiction, itself having its origin in the common law.
[3] The judicial approach to constitutional interpretation started from Coordinate Federalism to Centralizing Legalism, rapid Centralisation, Political Legalism, Human Right Protection and to Legal Realism or Judicial Activism. The traditional theoretical approaches to constitutional interpretation are usually described as Literalism, Legalism, Textualism, Originalism and Moderate Originalism.
[4] The theories of interpretation of the Constitution in Canada include, Originalism, or Frozen Right Theory, The Living Tree Doctrine, Progressive Interpretation, the Dynamic Interpretation, and Deconstruction and Critical Legal Studies. The approaches to constitutional interpretation in Canada include, Original Intent Approach, Textual and Practical Approach and Practical or Progressive Approach.
[5] The Doctrines (theories) of Interpretation in India include, the Basic Features Doctrine, Doctrine of Pith and Substance, Doctrine of Colourable Legislation, Doctrine of Severability, Doctrine of Eclipse and Judicial Activism.
[6] The Principles of constitutional interpretation are textual, historical, functional, doctrinal, prudential, equitable and natural.

canons of interpretation thereby prompting the courts of these countries to consider in appropriate cases, other factors like the prevailing socio-political situation in their countries.

Judicial interpretation of the Constitution is one of the primary functions of the courts in most modern democracies. Such interpretation is aimed at discovering the latent intention of the Parliament. As has been already stated, owing to the fact that Nigerian laws are largely expressed in English Language, there is usually the need for the courts to discover the intents of the legislators whenever it is desirable to do so.[7]

Therefore, the role of judges should be that of legal engineers who must engage in the task of constructing Constitutions armed with a sound knowledge of the basic philosophies of their respective societies.[8]

There is the need for the courts in Australia, Canada, India and Nigeria to assume a supportive and constructive role in order to complement the legislature in their law making function. The legislature may not have had the benefit of forming an intention, one way or the other, or may have fallen into a legislative quandary through inadvertence. In such cases of genuine lapses, the courts should not run away from the fundamental duty of reconstructing the real purpose of the Constitution in order to fashion out a clear, workable law better suited to the interest of the society. The Constitutions of Australia, Canada, India and Nigeria may never achieve their declared objectives without the active cooperation of the judges who, aware of the social milieu act of government policies, are well placed to identify the gaps therein and furnish appropriate remedies. Judges should not fetter their judicial powers by denying this role, thereby leaving the aggrieved parties without remedy or depriving the law of its full effect.[9]

The legislature in Australia, Canada, India and Nigeria expended much time and resources, human and material, in the course of enacting a Constitution. The legislature would have considered all apparent loopholes and sought to resolve any uncertainty in order to ensure that the law, when finally passed, is clear and certain and that it is, as much as possible, devoid of all ambiguities. But ambiguities are almost always unavoidable. Each Constitution emerges with its own combinations of words, words which are endowed with as much legal

---

[7] Susu, B.A., "Judicial Discretion Statutory Interpretation and Constitutional Issues" Justice, A Journal of Contemporary Legal Problems (1991) JUS, Vol. 2 No. 7 p. 71 at pp. 75 – 76.

[8] Olagbaiye, T. *"Justice and Judicial Interpretation of Statute"*, in Omotola, J.A. Issues in Nigerian Law. The Caxton Press (West African) Ltd., Ibadan, 1991 p. 17.

[9] Nimmo v. Alexandar (1968) A.C. 107, per Wilberforce, L. J., at 130, *Kammins* v. *Zenith Investment Ltd.* (1971) A.C. 830, per Diplock L.J., at 81, Asein, J. O., "Rules of Statutory Interpretation" Introduction to Nigerian Legal System (2nd ed) Ababa Press Ltd. Lagos, 2005.

authority as the general spirit of the enactment.[10] Despite extreme precautions, some words are prone to distortions, and are occasionally given mangled interpretations by the executive in the course of implementation and by the judiciary when called upon to adjudicate between disputants. According to Denning, M.R.,[11] *'The draftsman ... conceived certainty but has brought forth obscurity; sometimes even absurdity'* unless these absurdities are corrected by subsequent legislation, they remain binding as law. The proper construction to be given to the provisions of a Constitution is invariably the burden of the courts, a duty that is discharged through Constitutional interpretation. This is the process *'by which the courts seek to ascertain the meaning of the legislation through the medium of the authoritative forms in which it is expressed.'*[12]

The problem is usually that of language, not only as a means of communication, but as the chief medium of thought. The ambiguity in language may either result from the change in the meaning of the words used, or from the inherent ambivalence in the words *per se*. Some words are necessarily contextual and relative. For instance, a law may simply provide that *'the Governor may be impeached for good cause.* What will amount to good cause in this statement would depend on the subjective values of those that are entrusted with the power of impeachment. Similarly, value-laden words like *'reasonable time'*, *'fairness'*, *'just'*, are incapable of precise objective definitions.

The current trend today in Australia, Canada, India and Nigeria in construing Constitutional provisions requires Judges to ascertain the legislative intent of the law makers, a task somewhat akin to pinpointing the intent of a testator or of disputing parties to a contract. It is the modern view that proper judicial construction of Constitutional provisions requires recognition and implementation of the underlying legislative purpose.[13]

Thus where liberal interpretation of a word or words used in an enactment will result in an absurdity or injustice, it will be the duty of the court to consider the enactment as a whole with a view to ascertain whether the language of the enactment is capable of any other fair interpretation, or whether it may not be desirable to put a secondary meaning on such language, or even to adopt a construction which is not quite strictly grammatical.[14] The principles of justice require that where something is not expressly provided for in an enactment, the

---

[10] Fitzgerald, *Salmond on Jurisprudent* (12th ed.) London Sweet and Maxwell. 1979 p. 132.
[11] Denning, M. R., *The Disciple of Law,* London, Butterworths, 1979 p. 9.
[12] Fitzgerald, *op. cit.*
[13] *Train* v. *Colorado Public Interest Research Group Inc.* 426 V51, 9-10 (1976).
[14] Craeis *On Statute Law*, 7th Edition.

court, in interpreting such enactment, will take into consideration the spirit and meaning of the enactment as a whole and construe it accordingly. [15]

The rules of Constitutional interpretation, or the seeming absence of any coherent system of such rules, are a matter of serious concern to the various categories of legislative audience to which a Constitution may be directed. Apart from the more obvious categories of specialist advisers such as lawyers and accountants, many sections of the public such as employees, traders, officials, social workers, motorists and tax payers, require in the conditions of modern society at least a working knowledge of the main principles of constitutional law affecting them, and in some cases a detailed knowledge of particular provisions.

It is true that such persons may have access to a wide range of explanatory material and be able to take expert advice, but the value of such comment or advice will in large measure depend on the degree of assurance with which it can be expressed; this in turn depends on the extent to which the interpretative process of the courts can be predicted.

The main purpose of an examination of the interpretation of Constitution should be to make some contributions, through analysis and constructive criticism to the existing law and practice, to this educational process, rather than to formulate proposals for legislative intervention.

The duty to interpret laws, imposed on Australia, Canada, India and Nigerian judges, does not presuppose a blind-black-letter interpretation of the Constitution while wearing a predetermined judicial garb that is not alive to the society in which the judge lives. Therefore, there is a clarion call on the judges in these countries to wake up and adopt an interpretation approach, that is, proactive, that will bring to light the purpose or policy goals for which the Constitution is enacted.

Therefore, Australia, Canada, India and Nigerian courts should adopt the present position in England that "the courts in (England) now adopt a purposive approach which seeks to give effect to the true purpose of the legislation."[16]

The phrase "purposive approach" could mean different things to different people indeed, some view purposive approach as a method of construction that will not be used to seek the purpose or the intention of the legislature outside the purview of the provisions of words used.[17] Others may see the purposive approach as a model used by the courts to fish out the intent or purpose of the Constitution being construed. Hence, judges may be at liberty to read in words not used in the legislation to interpret it: so as to clearly reflect in their decisions the intentions of

---

[15] Bathlam Hospital (1875), LR 19.

[16] See *Pepper* v. *Hart* (1993) AC 593 at 617.

[17] Natalie, L. A Purposive Approach to the Interpretation of Tax Statutes? (1999) 20 rat. L. R. 124 at 128.

the legislature.[18] In doing this, judges are suppose to be mindful of not only the words used, but also the entire text and context in which they are used.[19]

The proactive model tries to find out the very purpose of the legislation being construed. That is, the purpose for the enactment of the legislation in question is very important to understanding the true meaning of the legislation under examination. The purposive approach suggested is similar to the mischief rule but not the same. The mischief rule seeks to unravel the purpose behind the enactment of a legislation being examined. But it lays emphasis on finding the very mischief that the enactment in question tends to solve. Therefore, the mischief rule examines the purpose of the legislation just as the purposive approach does. However, it could be argued that the purposive approach recommended is wider in scope than the mischief. While the mischief rule focuses on the "mischief" or the social problem (purpose of the legislation) that the Constitution is enacted to address, the purposive approach considers in wider term the purpose(s) for which the Constitution is made.[20]

The proactive approach concentrates on directing or guiding the judge (s) to examine the policy object behind the Constitution being construed. The court will be able to achieve this objective if, before interpreting the Constitution in question, ask itself "what is the policy object behind the enactment of this Constitution." The determination of this question will be possible by looking at the actual words used, the context in which the words were used, the state policy goals behind the Constitution and the meaning to be ascribed. The words or passage being construed should reinforce or support the policy goals of the government.

The reason for above suggestion is that every Constitution is an embodiment of policy goals of government: for legislation are not enacted in a vacuum or just for the mere purpose of having a law. Indeed, the importance of Constitution in social, political and economic planning can never be over-emphasized. Based on this knowledge that virtually every provision of Constitution is enacted for a particular policy object, the courts are enjoined to use its tool of construction in identifying the very policy object of the Constitution in question. Doing this will be a great construction by the court, through interpretation, in furthering and strengthening the policy object of the government. This is essentially needed at this time of Nigeria's economic life that economic growth, alleviation of poverty and generally the raising of the living standard of Nigerians are seriously needed.

---

[18] ibid.

[19] In fact it is this later understanding of the purposive approach, which of course seeks to bring out the purpose of the legislation.

[20] Natalie, L. op. cit., at p. 129.

Hence, any decision that fails to consider the policy object behind the Constitution has failed to advance the interest of the people and government.

It is the duty of the court to dig in and discover the policy goal underlying the Constitution. For even if there is a hole in the provisions of the Constitution, courts have been found to fill-gaps and should not shy away from their duties based on the feeble reason that rule of law and separation of powers may not be maintained. Rule of law is not all about procedural fairness, it is also about substantive fairness and interpretation of the law is a clear province of the law courts.

The policy goals of the present Nigerian government are clearly stipulated in the National Economic and Empowerment Strategy (NEEDS) policy documents. Thus, to assist the court in using the proactive approach of construction, it is advisable that the policy blue print of government regarding the overall economy must be examined. In the Nigerian case, the NEEDS documents, budget speeches, the entire legislation being reviewed must be considered. This will also assist the court in resolving any conflicting policy goals. It is also advocated that legislation should state, even briefly, the policy goals it intends to achieve. Alternatively, it could link up its policy goals to the overall policy objects of the government for instance NEEDs. The Nigerian Constitution reflects the yearning of the people and should be supported by the court-another democratic institution – through the instrumentality of interpretation.

Justice is attained when a procedural fairness is accompanied by a substantive fairness. Thus, the theory of rule of law recognizes the role of judges in furthering the goal of justice and fairness through interpretation of matters that come before them. Therefore, judges should not be confined or restricted only to the contents of the laws being reviewed but should actually move out of the strict content of the law to ensure that the policy object of the law is not defeated. The theory of the rule of law views the independence of judges not as a blanket approval of total indifference and apathy of judges to prevailing social, political and economic condition in the society but an independence which allows judges to ensure that substantive justice supports the purpose of the legislation is done. Thus, the independence stands for the moral autonomy of the judges to take decisions without interference from anybody.

Furthermore, the proactive approach helps the judge to know that he/she will search for the policy object behind the enactment of the legislation.[21]

---

[21] In criticizing the strict model of construction, David G. Duff in his article "Interpreting the Incomes Tax Act – Part 2: Towards a Pragmatic Approach (1999) 47 Canadian Tax Journal 741 at 747 writes that: in weighing these competing values, strict construction tended to ignore the social purposes of taxation while emphasizing the extent to which taxation interferes with individual liberty, they need for certainty in the application of tax statutes, and the relative ease with which Parliament can amend a tax statute to correct any deficiency. With respect to the purposes of taxation, strict construction was based on a largely

Therefore, this policy objects will obviously, help the judge in arriving at an expected answer that will help further the interest of justice and object of the Constitution.

Nigeria is a democracy, her citizens expects the dividends of democracy to affect everybody in the country. Of course, dividend of democracy stands, generally, for a better life for the citizenry. Therefore, the state owes it a duty to her citizens and resident to provide security, amenities and other public utilities that no individual is expected to provide for him/her alone. Equally, the State owes it a duty to uplift the living conditions of its residents and citizens. And for the State to provide these necessities and social amenities to her citizens it needs funds to structure the economy so as to achieve certain desired political, economic and social goals. These goals will never be attained without the judges using canons of interpretation that will reinforce the policy object behind such enactment.

The proactive approach to interpretation of Constitution will confer more certainty to the purpose of legislation, based on the fact that no word has a single and definite meaning without drawing from the values, bias, perception, prejudice and training of the interpreter (judge). In fact, it is far better that a policy goal or object is set to direct the court on what to consider when interpreting Constitutions. This will assist the court reinforcing and upholding the policy goal of the Constitution in question. The interpretational model needed is the one that will not only seek the purpose of the legislation but also specifically ask for the policy object behind the Constitution being construed. Once this policy object is determined, interpretation becomes much easier for the judge and also helps the judge in giving a true interpretation of the meaning of words used. The proactive approach does not confer additional duty on the judges, rather judges are still within their judicial enclave. Only that they are urged to look beyond the literal meaning of the words being construed to make sure that the policy object of the enactment is not defeated. Judges are still performing their adjudicative duties only that they are becoming more responsive to practical problems facing the society. Therefore, the proactive approach, which reinforce the policy object behind a Constitution, is what Nigerian needs to help us to revive our economy. The proactive approach does not conferred legislative duties on the judges, except the duties already conferred by the law. Consequently, proactive approach is the most suitable model of interpretation Nigerian courts should follow at this time of the country's economic struggles. It is hoped that courts in Australia, Canada and India would do the same.

---

despotic conception of the State, according to which, as John Willis observed, "first Kings and then legislatures taxed the masses in order to benefit a few court favourites. Private property in contrast was viewed as an essential bulkwark of individual liberty.

Recommendations

Judges, in construing a Constitution, should always bear in mind the ever occurring shifts in the meanings of words. It should be remembered as Denning M.R. puts it that *'it is not within human powers to foresee the manifold sets of facts which may arise, and even if it were, it is not possible to provide for them in terms free from all ambiguity.'*[22]

The primary duty of the court is to arrive at the intention of the legislature based on the letters of the Constitution which are merely the external manifestations of the former.[23] This privilege does not authorise the courts to rewrite Constitutions. So, as a general rule, the court cannot, under the guise of reformulating the intention of the lawmaker, tamper with the Constitution or impose its own conceived version of what that intention should be. It should not concern itself with the alteration of words in a Constitution, merely to make it read the way it thinks 'proper'. This tendency was disapproved of by Bairamiah, JSC. in *Okumagba* v. *Egbe*[24] when he remarked that *'the office of a Judge is to state the law, not to give law,*[25] i.e. the function of the judge is *jus dicere NOT jus dare.*

It must however be noted that the court could make corrections in a statute where the mistake, on the face of it, if uncorrected will depart from the obvious intention of the legislature or where it would, otherwise, render the provision meaningless. For example, the statute may contain an obvious logical defect that is semantic, syntactic or simply due to the absence of a more accurate expression[26] or may contain a clerical slip.[27]

The Judge in performing its legislative function should consider the prevailing social value and context. This does not mean upholding decisions contrary to the laws. All that is acknowledged is that the judiciary must be *'bound up with the existence and identity'* of the government of which it is a part.

The court in the exercise of its interpretive function should not allow personal factor to alter its sense of value judgment. The personal factor which often affects the exercise of discretion by the Judge is therefore an inevitable element of the judicial process.[28]

The court should detect the intention of the legislature by looking at the policy, scope and object of the Constitution, if the words are ambiguous. The

---

[22] *Seaford Court Estate Ltd,* v. *Asher* (1949) 2 K. B. 481.
[23] *Martin Scbroder and Co.* v. *Major and Co (Nig.) Ltd* (1989) 2 NWLR p. 1 at 12, *Ifezue* v. *Mbadagbe* (1984) 1 SCNLR p. 427, *Onasile* v. *Sami* (1962) 1 ALL NLR p. 272.
[24] (1965) 1 ALL NLR p. 62.
[25] See also *Atolagbe* v. *Awuni* (1997) 9 NWLR p. 536.
[26] Fitzgerald, *op. cit.,* P. 132.
[27] Ibid. p. 137
[28] Susu, *op. cit..* pp. 71 – 82.

canon adopted should be in accordance with the policy and object of the Constitution that is being interpreted. The object or policy of the legislation often affords the answer to problems arising from ambiguities or doubts. A consideration of the object of a Constitution enables one to understand the meaning of the words introduced into the enactment[29]. A look at the types of problem the legislature held in mind when the Act was passed can help to understand the meaning of complicated legislation.[30]

In *Newman Manufacturing Co. v. Marrable*,[31] Section 9(1) of the English Finance Act 1928 imposed an import duty on imported '*button finished or unfinished*'. Button blanks nearly spherical in shape made of trocas shell and pierced with one hole were imported. The court held that in constructing the meaning of '*unfinished*' it should consider the object of the Financial Act, which was to project the English button trade. The court further held that the bulk of the work on button had been done abroad, and that the button blanks were '*unfinished buttons*' within the meaning of the Act.

Thus, a consideration of the object of a Constitution can be a useful tool for understanding the meaning of words in a Constitution and discovering intention of the legislature.[32]

The Judge in his interpretative function can adjust the stated law to the applicable socio-political content sometimes placing the judiciary and the judicial process in the fore front of the nation's socio–political development. This is what Reynolds[33] was referring to when he spoke of the remolding process of judicial decision making '*even occasionally discarding a finished piece or making a completely new one*'. Obviously, one must view this not as a personal and individual disregard of the value base of stated law. Rather, it is a question of re-interpreting or re-applying already accepted basic norms within a new or changing socio-political context. As Professor Corbin[34] explains '*it is the function of our courts, to keep the doctrines up to date with the mores by continuous restatement and by giving them a continually new context. This is judicial legislation.*'

The deduction of societal norms upon which specific laws are based should be left to the legislature which should be able to lift such norms from the existing socio-political context. Thus the statutory–interpretation function of a Judge has

---

[29] *RDC* v. *Sutton District Water Co.* (1908) 99 L. T. 168 at 170.
[30] Denning M. R. in *Escoigre Properties Ltd* v. *IRC* (1958) A. C. J p. 49 566.
[31] (1931) 2 K. B. 297.
[32] ibid. p. 31.
[33] Reynolds, W. H., *Judicial Process*, West Publishing 1980 p. 193.
[34] Corbin, Arthur L. 29 Yale L. Journal 771.

been described by Lord Simmonds[35] as '*a naked usurpation of the legislative function under the thin guise of interpretation.*'

It is apparent that stated law, and accepted precedents of interpretation might not quite serve the purpose of the Constitution or the statutory intent when the context becomes more complex. It is then the duty of the courts to fashion out a new interpretation, to reactivate the intent and original spirit of the provision.[36]

It is important to recognize that in a Constitution such as the Nigerian Constitution which is relatively young, to take care of the vagaries and other hidden problems in an unsophisticated society as ours, though vibrant in its intendment and orientation because it is still developing, construction of the provisions must be equally vibrant to be in accentuation with the growth of a dynamic society. In other words, beneficial interpretation which would give meaning and life to the society should always be adopted in order to enthrone peace, justice and egalitarianism in the society.[37] While it should not empirically speaking be within the ambits of the courts to cause to insert or arrogate to itself the messianic power to give a different meaning to the words of the Constitution as to more or less complete with the legislature, I believe it is the duty of the court to breathe life into a provision which is woolly or cloudy, and in which a conservative learning interpretation may do incalculable harm.

Hall, D[38]and Darf, M[39] have written on the various modes and attitudinal bents courts should resort to in the interpretation of the words of the Constitution. There is the liberal approach sometimes described as the modernist approach, and the originalism approach. These concepts could be deceitful and liable to render constructions strictly based on them a mere forage into academic dialectics of interpretation. An autochthonous Constitution like ours which seeks to give a framework of a law or stipulation that binds us should as much as possible reflect positive tendencies to liberalise the mind from the cocoon of antiquated and fossilized   ideas or philosophy which might militate against judicial progressivism that would situate the Constitution in a vibrate clime.[40]

Where a judge is faced with construction, interpretation and application of a constitutional provision to the facts ascertained by him in a case, he must;

a.   read the Constitution to ascertain whether and how its meaning relates to the case in controversy.

---

[35] *Major and St. Mellons Rural District Council* v. *Newport Corp* (1952) A. C. 189 p. 191, H. L., (1950) 2 ALL E. R. 1226.

[36] Cardozo, B., *Selected Writings*, Matthew Bender, 1947 p. 158.

[37] *F.R.N.* v. *Osahon* (2006) ALL FWLR p. 1975 at p. 2018

[38] Hall, D. *Constitutional Law: Cases and Commentary.*

[39] Darf, M & Tribe, L. *Reading the Constitution.*

[40] *FRN* v. *Osahon* (2005) ALL FWLR p. 1975 at pp. 2020 – 2021.

b. if the language, i.e. the words or meaning ascertained from that language resolves the controversy, the inquiry terminates there;

c. but if the language or meaning does not resolve the controversy, then the judge must adjust and apply appropriate judicial rule to decide and resolve the case or the issue in controversy.[41]

The duty of the court is to ascertain the law and apply it to the fact, when it is clear and unambiguous, but not to amend or reconstruct it. In case of statutory construction the court's authority is limited. Where the statutory language and legislative intent are clear and plain, the judicial inquiry terminates there. Under our jurisprudence, the presumption is that ill-considered or unwise legislation will be corrected through democratic process. A court is not permitted to distort a statute's meaning in order to make it conform with the judge's own views of sound social policy.[42]

For the courts in Australia, Canada, India and Nigeria to perform the above task in line with the various rules of constitutional interpretation discussed above, it is recommended as follows:

(1) the rules of interpretation currently adopted by the courts are conflicting and if each judge is not to introduce into the exercise his own nuances and predilections, there must be a unified modus for carrying out the exercise. It would therefore be very useful, if the legislature can indicate in an enactment what principle must be used in its interpretation;[43]

(2) to enable the court to effectively discover the intention of the parliament, the courts must be allowed to look at all relevant parliamentary documents and must be given opportunity to derive relevant information from all credible sources including parliamentary debates and bills;[44]

(3) an attempt to discover the intention of the legislature requires a proper understanding of legal principles. Thus, judges must be skilled in the art of interpretation and construction of legal documents. Judges must be well informed of the general intention of the legislature as expressed in enactments. This could only be achieved through regular in-service training for judicial officials by the government and its agencies,[45] bearing in mind the famous

---

[41] *Adewumi.v. Attorney- General, Ekiti State* (2002) FWLR (pt.92) p.1835 at pp. 1864-   1865.

[42] *Tva* v. *Hill* 43 U.S. 153 (1979)

[43] Olagbaiye, *op. cit.,* p. 26.

[44] Pearce, D. C., *Statutory Interpretation in Australia.* Butterworths, 1974 pp. 1 – 4, 'Denning M. R. referred to the Minister's second reading speech on a bill relating to power of local authorities to licenses amendment arcades.

[45] Olagbaiye *op. cit.* p. 26.

words in the Justinian Institutes – '*ignorantia judicis est calamitas innocientis*' (The ignorance of the judge is the calamity of the innocent).[46]

---

[46] D.A. Ijalaye, Justice As Administered by the Nigerian Courts, Justice Idigbe Memorial Lecture Series Five University of Benin, 6th February 1992 at p. 66.

Bibliography

Adebayo, M.K. Kamal, et al (2007) "Fundamental Objectives and Directive Principles of State Policy in Constitution". The Nigerian and Indian Experience. *"Islamic University in Uganda Journal of Comparative Law"*.

Aguda, T.A. (1983) *The Judiciary and Democracy – The Nigerian Experience.* New Horn Press Ltd., Ibadan.

Anthony, M. (1986) "The Role of a Constitutional Court in a Federation: A comparism of the Australian and US Experience *FED L* 13.

Asein, J.O. (1997) *Introduction to Nigerian Legal System.* Ibadan: Sam Bookman Publishers,.

Asein, J.O. (2005) *Rules of Statutory Interpretation* Introduction to Nigerian Legal System (2nd ed.) Ababa Press Ltd. Lagos.

Badaiki, A.D. (1996) *Interpretation of Statute.* Tiken Publishers, Lagos.

Bakare, Sir John (1983). *The Guardian*, Monday, August 24,.

Bennion, FAR (1992) Statutory Interpretation: A Code (2nd ed.) London: Butterworth.

Brest, P. (1980) "The Misconceived Quest for the Original Understanding" *Boston Uni L. Rev.*

Bruce, A. (2000) "The New Separation of Powers" *Harv. L. Rev.*

Cardozo (1947) *Selected Writings.* Matthew Bender.

Charles, B.N. (1940) "The Ambiguity of Unambiguous Statutes". 24 Minesola Law Review.

Collins, J.S. (1987) "Judicial Review and the American Constitution" *FED.L REV.*

Corry, J.A. (1954) "The Use of Legislative History in the interpretation of statutes" *Can Bar Rev.*

Craven G. (1992). "The Crisis of Constitutional Literalism in Australia" in HP Lee and G. Winterton (eds) *Australia Constitutional Perspectives.*

Craven, G. (1990) "Original Intent and the Australian Constitution coming soon to a court Near You? *Public Law Review.*

Curties, C.P. (1950) "A Better Theory of Legal Interpretation". 3 *Land Law Review.*

Curtis, CP. (1949). "A Better Theory of Legal Interpretation" *The Record of the Association of the Bar of the City of New York 321.*

D' Neil (1987) "Constitutional Human Rights in Australia" *FEDL REV.*

David, A.P. (1989) "Taking Rights Cynically: A Review of Critical Legal Studies". *Cambridge Law Journal.*

Dawson, F.G. & Ivan, L.H. (1971) *International Law, National Tribunals and the Rights of Aliens.* Syracuse University Press..

Denning, M.R. (1979) *The Disciplines of Law.* London: Butterworths.

Driedger (1994) *The Constriction of Constitution* (3rd ed.) Toronto: Butterworths.

Dworkin, R.M. (1967) "The Model of Rules". 35 *University of Chicago L. Rev.*

Edgar, S.G.G. (1971) *Craies on Statute Law.* London.

Eisentein, J. (1973) *Politics and the Legal Process,* Herpen & Rew.

Erin, D. (2001) *United States Supreme Court,* Tony Blackshield et al eds.

Eskridge, William N. Jr. (1989) "Spinning Legislative Supremacy". 78 *Geo L.J.* 319.

Evans, (1988) *Statutory Interpretation: Problems of Communication* Auckland: Oxford University Press, 60.

Evershed, M.R. (1956). "The Impact of Statutes on the Law of England" *Maccabeam Lecture in Jurisprudence, Proceedings of the British Academy.*

Felix Frank Furter, (1947) "Some Reflections on the Reading of Statutes", 47 *Columbian Law Review.*

Fitzgerald, (1979) *Salmon on Jurisprudence* (12th ed.) London, Sweet and Maxwell.

Frankfurther, J. "Some Reflections on the Reading of Statutes" *The Record of the Association of the Bar of the City of New York.*

Frederick, J. de Sloovere (1940) "Extrinsic Aids in the Interpretation of Statutes". 88 *UPAL Rev.*

Gerim-Lajoie (1951)"Du pouvoir d'amendment Constitutionel on Canada". *CAN.B.REV.*

Gilbert, C. (1986) *Australian and Canadian Federalism* Melbourne University Press.

Glanville, W. (1981). "The Meaning of Literal Interpretation" 11, *Butterworth Publication*, Thursday November 12, Vol. 131, No. 6027.

Glanville, W. "Language and the Law". (1945) 61 *LQR* 71 (1946) 62 LQR 381.

Glanville, W. *The Meaning and Literal Interpretation* 11, Butterworth Publication, 1981.

Goldsworthy (1997) "Originalism in Constitutional Interpretation" *FED L. Rev.*

Idowu, A.A. (2008) "Human Rights democracy and Development: The Nigerian Experience, *Research Journal of Interpretation Studies.*

Ijalaye, D.A. (1992). "Justice As Administered by the Nigerian Courts" Justice *Idigbe Memorial Lecture Series, Five University of Benin.*

Jack N.R. (1996) *Original Meanings: Politics and Ideas in the making of the Constitution* New York: Knopf.

Jackson, J. (1948) "The Meaning of Statutes" What the Congress says or what the Court says" *AB A Journal.*

Jain, M.P. (1978) *Indian Constitutional Law* Bombay N.M. Tripathi Private Ltd.

Jerome Frank, (1947) "Words and Music: Some Remarks on Statutory Interpretation". 47. *Columbian Law Review.*

Jones, Harry, W. (1937) "The Plain Meaning Rule and Extrinsic Aids in the Interpretation of Federal Statutes". 25 *WASH ULQ.*

Kin, Y. "Statutory Interpretation, General Principles and Recent Trends *CRS Report for Congress.*

Kirby, M. (1999). "Constitutional Interpretation and Original Intent. A Form of Ancestor Worship?" *Sir Anthony Mason Lecture.*

Livingston "(1951) The Amending Power of the Canadian Parliament L.REV.

Llewellyn, K. (1950) "Remarks on the Theory of Appelate Decision and the Rules or Canons and how students are construed" *Vanderbitt Law Review.*

Longan, P.J. (1976) *Maxwell on Interpretation of Statutes* (12th ed.) Bombay, Tripathi.

Lwellyn, K.N. (1934) "The Constitution as an Institution". 34 *Columbian Law Review.*

Mason, A. (1993). "In Virtue B. High Court is Planning New Rules," *Australian Lawyer.*

Max Radin, (1930) "Statutory Interpretation". 43 *Harvard Law Review.*

Miller, G.C. (1993) "The Case of the Spuluncean Explorers: Contemporary Proceedings". 61, *George Washington Law Review.*

Morgan, H. (1992) *The Australian Constitution: A Living Document* The Samuel Griffith Society.

Murphy, L & Nagel, T. (2002) *The Myth of Ownership: Taxes and Justice* New York: Oxford University Press.

Natalie, L. (1999) "A Purposive Approach to Interpretation of Tax Statutes? *Start LR.*

Natalie, L.A. (1999). "Purposive Approach to the Interpretation of Tax Statutes" *RA LR.*

Niki T. (1996) *Source of Law* Lagos: MIJ Professional Publishers Ltd.

Niki, T. (1996) *Sources of Nigeria Law*, Lagos: MIJ Professional Publishers Ltd.

Oba, A.A. "Judicial Attitude to Notice of Revocation under the Land Use Act, Revisited". *Journal of Commercial Private and Property Law*, 1999, Vol. 2.

Oba, A.A. (2004) "Statutes as their own Interpreters: Internal Aids to Interpretation of Statutes in Nigeria. *UDUS Law Journal*, Vol. 1.

Obilade, A.O. (1979) *The Nigerian Legal System.* Sweet & Maxwell, London,.

Obilade, A.O. (1990) *The Nigerian Legal System.* Spectrum Law Publishing, Ibadan,.

Okonkwo and Narsh, (1980) *Nigerian Criminal* Law. London. Sweet & Maxwell.

Olagbaiye, T. (1991) "Justice and Judicial Interpretation of Statutes in Omotola, J.A., On Issues in Nigerian Law. The Caxton Press (West Africa) Ltd. Ibadan.

Omotola, J.A. (1991) *Issues in Nigerian Law.* The Carton Press (West Africa) Ltd., Ibadan.

Pandey, J.N. (1982) *Constitutional Law of India* Allahabad: Central Law Agency.

Papadatos, P. (1963) *The Eichman Trail*, Praeger.

Patapan, H. (1997) "The Dead Hand of the Founders? Original intent and the Constitutional Protection Rights and Freedoms in Australia" *Fed L. Rev.*

Patrick, A.K. (2008). "In Celebration of the Constitution" *Presented at the Banco Court in Brisbane.*

Pearce, D.C. (1974) *Statutory Interpretation in Australia.* Butterworths.

Radin, M. (1942) "A Short way with Statutes". 56 *Harvard Law Review.*

Rex, J. (1972) "Legal Principles and Limits of Law". 81 *Yale L. Journal.*

Roscow, P. (1907) "Spurious Interpretation", 7 *Colombian Law Review.*

Rosson, J. (1997) "Originalist Sin". *New Republic,* 5 May.

Sagay, I.E. (1995) "Customary Law and Freedom of Testament Power" *Journal of African Law,* Vol. 39, No. 2.

Sarathi, (1986) *Interpretation of Statutes* (3rd ed.) Eastman Book Company,.

Shapiro, D.L. (1992) "Continuity and Change in Statutory Interpretation *NYUL Rev.*

Solan L. (1993). When Judges Use the Dictionary, 68 *Am speech* 9, 50.

Stephen, G. (1987) "Foundations of Australia Federalism and the Role of Judicial Review" *FED L. REV.*

Stevens, R. (2005) *The English Judges: Their Role in the Changing Constitution.* Oxford: Hart.

Susu, B.A. (1991) "Judicial Discretion, Statutory Interpretation and Constitutional Issues". Justice, *A Journal of Contemporary Legal Problems.* Vol. 2, No. 7.

Wesserstron, R.A. (1961) *The Judicial Decision.* Stanford University Press.

Winckel, A. (1999) *The Contextual Role of a Preamble in Statutory Interpretation,* Melbourne.

Zines, L. (1908) *The High Court and the Constitution of Australia* Butterworths.